PELICAN BOOKS

CITIES AND THE WEALTH OF NATIONS

Jane Jacobs was born in Scranton, Pennsylvania, in 1916, and now lives in Toronto, Canada. She has also written *The Death and Life of Great American Cities*, *The Economy of Cities* and *The Question of Separatism: Quebec and the Struggle over Sovereignty*.

CITIES AND THE WEALTH OF NATIONS

Jane Jacobs

PENGUIN BOOKS

Penguin Books Ltd, Harmondsworth, Middlesex, England
Viking Penguin Inc., 40 West 23rd Street, New York, New York 10010, U.S.A.
Penguin Books Australia Ltd, Ringwood, Victoria, Australia
Penguin Books Canada Limited, 2801 John Street, Markham, Ontario, Canada L3R 1B4
Penguin Books (N.Z.) Ltd, 182–190 Wairau Road, Auckland 10, New Zealand

First published in the U.S.A. by Random House and simultaneously in Canada by
Random House of Canada 1984
First published in Great Britain by Viking 1985
Published in Pelican Books 1986

The acknowledgements on p. v constitute an extension of this copyright page

Made and printed in Great Britain by
Hazell Watson & Viney Limited,
Member of the BPCC Group,
Aylesbury, Bucks

*This book is for
Jason Epstein,
who has waited so long for it
with good humor and good counsel*

CONTENTS

1   Fool's Paradise   3

2   Back to Reality   29

3   Cities' Own Regions   45

4   Supply Regions   59

5   Regions Workers Abandon   72

6   Technology and Clearances   79

7   Transplant Regions   93

8   Capital for Regions Without Cities   105

9   Bypassed Places   124

10   Why Backward Cities Need One Another   135

11   Faulty Feedback to Cities   156

12   Transactions of Decline   182

13   The Predicament   204

14   Drift   221

    Acknowledgments   233

    Notes   234

    Index   245

CITIES AND THE WEALTH OF NATIONS

ONE

Fool's Paradise

For a little while in the middle of this century it seemed that the wild, intractable, dismal science of economics had yielded up something we all want: instructions for getting or keeping prosperity. Economists and the rulers they advise had thought up so many ideas for ridding national and international economies of chanciness and disaster, and the ideas had such an air of rationality, predictability and informed statistical analysis, that governments took to supposing they need only muster up commitment, expertise and money to make economic life do their bidding.

Under this delusion, Mao Tse-tung decreed that the economy of China was to take a Great Leap Forward. Khrushchev, visiting the United Nations, banged his shoe on the table and foretold a Soviet economy that by 1975 would overtake America's and thereafter proceed to "bury" the West. In the United States, Presidents Kennedy and Johnson and their advisers not only assumed, as most Americans did, that the country's high productivity and economic supremacy were assured far into the future; they also assumed that the fiscal measures they were using to fine-tune the economy were going to eliminate even its jiggles: no more depressions, and soon no more recessions. The British were constructing, or thought they were, a prospering and advancing welfare state with work and a decent, continually improving living standard for all, somewhat on the Scandinavian model. The

3

European Economic Community, modeling itself on the continentally integrated U.S. economy, was working well for its original member states. Six or seven South American countries were taking the first steps to adopt it as a model for their continent. Poor countries on the fringes of Europe were anticipating great prosperity when it came their turn to join the European community and share in supplying its huge, integrated and safely wealthy markets. The Bretton Woods agreements of 1944, pegging the values of Canadian and most Western European currencies firmly to the rock of the U.S. dollar, and Soviet money-management techniques which equally firmly pegged Soviet-bloc currencies to the ruble, were taken to demonstrate that fluctuating currency values among national trading partners—so painful for debtor nations, so unsettling to the calculations of multinational corporations and tourist industries—were vestiges of a less sophisticated past. People and rulers in backward countries, including those that had just won independence from colonial rule or were still struggling to do so, expected professionally drawn up development schemes to engineer prosperity and progress for them too. Their expectations were fully shared in countries financing development schemes with loans or gifts. Thus the very phrases "backward countries" and "poorest countries" dropped from the vocabularies of economists, civil servants, bankers and editors and were replaced by "developing countries" and "less developed developing countries," or DCs and LDDCs, as the confident shorthand had it.

Recipes for accomplishing all this—creating prosperity where it didn't exist and maintaining it where it did—differed under the influence of differing ideologies, but less than one might suppose. For example, when the American and Soviet governments competed for allegiance of a poor country by offering economic aid, the competition didn't take the form of different conceptions of aid. Rather, the two powers competed to supply much the same dams, roads, fertilizer plants and irrigation systems. The economic programs Poland's government adopted were largely financed by West German and American bankers. The bankers disapproved of Communist state ownership and probably of many other Polish arrangements as well; all the same, Polish conceptions of how an economy expands and develops, what it needs for the purpose, and how it earns the wherewithal to carry and repay development financing were perfectly familiar conceptions to the capitalist bankers: conventional, logical.

In theory everything was so logical. In reality so little worked out the way it was supposed to.

Now we live in a distraught time of failed development schemes. The results range from outright disasters, as in Poland, Iran, Uruguay, Argentina, Brazil, Mexico, Turkey and most of Africa, to the mere disappointments, as in Ireland, Canada, southern Italy, Yugoslavia, Cuba and India, to mention a few examples in both categories. China, after the swift, catastrophic failure of the Great Leap, has thrashed about, trying first this strategy to overcome its poverty and backwardness, then that, each new departure hailed as revolutionary and each petering out in confusion and recriminations.

The Soviet Union, far from demonstrating the superiority of its planning and performance, continues unable so much as to feed itself, nor in other respects does it produce amply and diversely for its own people and producers. Indeed, as an economy, the Soviet Union is eerily beginning to resemble a "colonial" country, for it depends increasingly upon exporting natural resources to more highly developed countries and on importing sophisticated manufactured goods, including even the machinery needed to exploit its natural resources for export. To arrive at economic colonialism was hardly the aim of all those Five Year Plans, yet that is how things are working out.

Britain first tried to reverse its decline and decay by depending primarily on what are called demand-side measures, to no avail. Then it joined the European Economic Community, to no avail. Then it switched to what are called supply-side measures, again to no avail. No matter what Britain has tried, it has continued in the grip of unrelenting decline, much like any other faded, fabled empire of the distant past before people had economic theories and instructions and statistics to guide them.

In the United States, the unthinkable has happened. The country's manufacturing economy has gradually but steadily been eroding, and much of what remains has been slipping into technological backwardness relative to industry in Japan and the more vigorous parts of Europe. Great American industries that once led the world flounder and founder. Productivity rates diminish. Military production has become increasingly indispensable to keep skilled people at work and to prevent whole regions of the country that rely heavily upon military work from collapsing economically.

To be sure, while economic disappointments and debacles have been in the making, so have stunning economic successes—most notably in Japan and, among formerly backward places, in the group of small economies known jointly as the Pacific Rim: Hong Kong, Singapore, Taiwan and Korea. But success has turned out to be as puzzling as failure because any measures, policies or combinations of them that are conventionally singled out as responsible for these successes can only too readily be matched by equivalent measures and policies followed only by failures somewhere else. Caught in these intellectual impasses, economists have been falling back on cultural platitudes: the Japanese are intelligent, like to work hard and skillfully use consensus; the Chinese (outside China) are prodigiously successful traders, and the members of families help one another acquire capital; the British have abandoned the work ethic; and so on. For enlightenment of this quality we don't need economics or economists. Perceptive tourists do quite as well.

Macro-economics—large-scale economics—is the branch of learning entrusted with the theory and practice of understanding and fostering national and international economies. It is a shambles. Its undoing was the good fortune of having been believed in and acted upon in a big way. We think of the experiments of particle physicists and space explorers as being extraordinarily expensive, and so they are. But the costs are as nothing compared with the incomprehensibly huge resources that banks, industries, governments and international institutions like the World Bank, the International Monetary Fund and the United Nations have poured into tests of macro-economic theory. Never has a science, or supposed science, been so generously indulged. And never have ex-

periments left in their wakes more wreckage, unpleasant surprises,
blasted hopes and confusion, to the point that the question seriously arises whether the wreckage is reparable; if it is, certainly
not with more of the same.

Failures can help set us straight if we attend to what they tell
us about realities. But observation of realities has never, to put it
mildly, been one of the strengths of economic development theory. Consider, for example, the curious case of the actual results
of Marshall Plan aid, and the unwarranted expectations that development experts drew from it.

As we all know, if an economy is devastated by famines, epi-
demics, earthquakes, tidal waves, floods or fires, unharmed economies can help put people and their enterprises back on their feet.
Just so, Marshall Plan aid from America after World War II
helped put Europeans and their enterprises back on their feet
after the ruin wrought by bombing, tanks and artillery. The
devastation was enormous, and the scope and scale of aid were
comparably enormous. Economic recovery would have taken
longer and imposed greater postwar privation without the loco-
motives, fleets of trucks, electric generators, cement factories, rolling mills, fertilizers, tractors, machine tools, radiology equipment,
medicines, textbooks, telephone switchboards, refrigeration machinery, earthmovers, pipes, pumps, cables, cutting edges and
much more sent from unharmed America. The Miracle of the Marshall Plan, as the results were sometimes called, was that the equipment helped to heal and restore, and helped so well that when it
was combined with Europeans' own production, it brought the
continent out of the ashes and death of war more speedily and
successfully than anticipated.

But here we must pause for a moment and take notice that the
healing of organisms—including the organisms known as economies—is not at all the same as the metamorphosis of organisms,
the conversion of them into something different. The distinction
has usually been well understood by everyone. For example, back
at the time when San Francisco recovered from its devastating
earthquake and fire of 1906 and then proceeded to prosper prodigiously, nobody was addled enough to suggest that the Red

Cross should therefore go into the business of rushing aid indiscriminately to economically declining or stagnant cities on the ground that this would make them prosper like San Francisco.

The Marshall Plan did not, of course, metamorphose stagnant or declining European economies into developing, expanding, self-generating economies. Some of the aided economies, such as those of the Netherlands, West Germany, parts of France and parts of Italy, did proceed to expand and develop—as San Francisco did after its disaster. But others did nothing of the kind. Britain received Marshall Plan equipment, as West Germany did, but this bounty did not make Britain's economy behave like West Germany's. Southern Italy received Marshall Plan aid, just as northern Italy did, but the sequels were strikingly different. Northern Italy, already the most prosperous and economically creative part of the country, proceeded to prosper, develop and expand further. Southern Italy, which had previously been persistently backward, poor and economically passive, stayed so. Insofar as Marshall Plan aid (or the much larger aid given later from the north of Italy) changed southern Italy, the changes did not transcend the gifts themselves, for southern Italy's economy did not take to expanding and developing on its own account or under its own steam; people continued having to leave it in great numbers to find work and income in the very different kinds of economies prevailing in northern Italy and farther afield.

There the realities were, for all to see; and yet the Marshall Plan was seized upon as a demonstration that aid could metamorphose stagnant economies into developing, self-generating economies. Promising exactly that, national and international aid and development agencies proliferated amazingly, often enough describing their purposes in a catchy way as Marshall Plans for the Third World, Little Marshall Plans, or programs to Do What the Marshall Plan Did.

The consequences of those groundless promises are appalling: angry, disillusioned populations in countries that have remained stagnant and poor after hopes were raised so high; cynicism about the worth of aiding others—and worse, about the worth of people who have gotten aid—on the part of taxpayers who funded such aid; vast, unpayable debts assumed by backward countries under the illusion that their "development" would justify and carry the costs; debt-carrying charges that eat into poor countries' export earnings, to the extent that some desperately poor societies have been working, in effect, virtually for nothing except for the honor of having been promoted for a brief decade or two from "backward" to "developing"; and an international banking community staving off collapse with moratoriums on inherently unrepayable loans, further loans to pay interest on unrepayable loans, and other frantic forms of holding things together as long as possible with baling wire.

In the meantime, many already advanced countries—among them the United States—have become victims of an insidious phenomenon called stagflation, a combination of rising unemployment and inflated prices. In theory it shouldn't even exist, but it does, and nobody knows how to combat it without intensifying unemployment on the one hand, or inflation on the other. The puzzle of stagflation has done more than destroy expectations of smoothly running, manageable economic life in already well developed economies. It has destroyed the very intellectual foundations upon which all schools of macro-economic theory rest. The reality of stagflation has done nothing less than make nonsense of some two centuries and more of elaborate theoretical thought.

Rising prices are no hardship when jobs multiply rapidly, incomes outrun prices, and people are becoming generally better off. This cheerful face of inflation has interested economists for centuries and there is a long tradition of attempts to explain it. Richard Cantillon, a French economist born in Ireland in 1680, had this to say in about 1730:

> If the increase of actual money grows from mines of gold or silver in the State, the owners of these mines, the adventurers, the smelters, refiners, and all the other workers will increase their expenses in proportion to their gains. They will consume in their households more meat, wine or beer than before, will accustom themselves to wear better clothes, finer linen, to have better furnished houses and choicer commodities . . . [The] demands for meat, wine, wool, etc., being more intense than usual, will not fail to raise their prices. These high

prices will determine the farmers to employ more land to produce them in another year; these same farmers will profit by this rise of prices and will increase the expenditure of their families like the others.

Because of all this, he said,

I consider in general that an increase of actual money causes in a State a corresponding increase of consumption which gradually brings about increased prices.*

Antiquated as this sounds in part, the reasoning is anything but quaint. Cantillon had asked himself four great questions economists have been asking themselves ever since and are asking still: Why does economic activity increase? Why do prices rise? Is there a connection? If so, how does the connection work?

Cantillon's answers to himself propounded what we now call a demand-side theory of economic expansion, meaning that demand for goods and services leads the way in an expanding and prospering economy, while supply to fill the demand follows in its wake. Still further, he was proposing that an influx of money propelled the increased demand. In a somewhat primitive way, Cantillon was the first Keynesian economist, almost exactly two centuries before his time.

The reverse of Cantillon's questions are these: Why does economic activity decrease? Why do prices fall? Is there a connection? If so, how does the connection work? Most economists who have asked themselves Cantillon's questions have posed the reverse questions too. Some, like Marx, have begun with the second set; but over the centuries, either set of these questions has implied the other because of the fact that normally (later we shall see what "normally" means) price levels and unemployment rates seem to work like a seesaw, prices sitting on one end of the board, unemployment rates on the other. During times of economic expansion such as Cantillon was concerned with, prices tend to rise and unemployment to fall. During periods of recession or depression, prices tend to fall and unemployment to rise. Prices up, unemployment down; prices down, unemployment up.

* For source acknowledgments, see Notes under chapter headings following the text.

Stagflation doesn't obey those rules, for it combines both rising prices and rising unemployment, making the seesaw image absurd. To describe stagflation we should have to imagine the board broken on its fulcrum and the two ends rising simultaneously in defiance of the principles of mechanics and the law of gravity. Once stagflation creeps into an economy it seems to operate in spite of shorter-term seesaw movements. For example, in the United States stagflation first began showing up statistically in 1967 and 1968. Thereafter stagflation has gradually intensified through good times and bad, taking the bloom off good times and making bad times worse. Roughly speaking, during each period of prosperity and expansion, unemployment levels have failed to drop as low as during the previous expansion. Thus the nation's rock-bottom unemployment level, its permanent, irreducible unemployment level, has kept inching higher. And during each recession, unemployment has tended to be more severe than during the one before. In sum, since the late 1960s the nation has persistently been developing an ever higher percentage of workers for whom the economy has no work. At the same time, the inflation rate was behaving no less strangely. During each recession, prices have continued rising instead of dropping or at least remaining the same. The rate of rise has merely slowed. During each recovery, the rate of inflation started surging upward sooner than it had after previous recessions, and has tended to accelerate more rapidly too.

Thus, behind the short-term jiggles of the economy, unemployment and prices were persistently rising together. In only a few of these years was the inflation rate 10 percent or higher, but since inflation compounds itself, prices rose by almost 200 percent between 1967 and 1983 and continued to rise even in 1983 when unemployment reached an alarming rate of more than 10 percent, much higher if those who had become discouraged from looking for work were taken into account.

High unemployment and bankruptcy rates in 1982 reminded older Americans of the Great Depression of the 1930s. But during the Great Depression, as unemployment rose, prices fell. At that time the familiar seesaw was operating. In the 1980s something different was happening, something unprecedented in the country's national economy before 1967. The United States is not the only victim of stagflation. Britain has been stagflated even longer. A few years after stagflation emerged in the United States it appeared in Canada, and it has also crept into many of continental Europe's economies. But the whole world is not stagflated, at least not yet; while the United States was stagflating, rising prices in Switzerland and Japan, for example, were still wearing the cheerful face that interested Cantillon.

Where stagflation has taken hold, remedies have led only to still worse unemployment as a sacrifice to the fight against inflation, or to still worse inflation as a sacrifice to the fight against unemployment. Behind this terrible dilemma is a terrible theoretical void, for rummage as we may through volumes of economic theory, we will find nothing there that acknowledges the fact of stagflation, much less tells us how to deal with it or what it means.

Cantillon's line of thought was not pursued by Adam Smith, who published forty-five years after Cantillon had proposed his demand-side theory of expansion. Smith was a supply-side economist. That is, he attributed economic expansion to expanding production and trade, with expanding demand as a by-product and consequence. However, unlike later supply-side economists, Smith did not draw a connection between rising prices and falling unemployment or vice versa, nor did he think of money as a factor in depressing or stimulating production.

Smith attributed general price rises solely to rulers' propensities for adulterating coinage with base metal, particularly when they wanted to finance foreign wars; or to sheer increases in the amounts of gold and silver available for circulation. He thus espoused what we now think of as the government printing-press explanation of inflation. He thought of these "nominal" price changes as being superficial compared with "real" prices of goods and services. True prices, as well as real wealth, he traced to labor. Wealth, considered from every angle and in all its permutations including capital, comes from the toil and trouble, the sheer work that goes into producing it, he said. Thus labor, being the cost of everything, is the real price, "the real measure of the exchangeable value of commodities."

To be sure, said Smith, the money value of labor does fluctuate, depending on the demand for labor by producers and merchants. Where labor is in high demand—unemployment low—wages rise in spite of employers' attempts to combine to keep them down. And conversely, where labor is surplus—unemployment high—wages fall. But Smith was at pains to argue that this does not account for general price rises. He identified those as nationwide, while changes in wage rates are local, he said, owing to their cause. He cited as an example the high wages in England, the low wages in Scotland, although the two places were in the same nation, the United Kingdom, and subject alike to general price rises. In sum, Smith not only offered no explanation for a working connection between general price and unemployment levels, but denied there was a connection.

Nevertheless, one need only discount Smith's insistence that wage rates are local and we have the wage theory of inflation. For if it is true that all costs derive from labor costs, and if it is also true, as it most certainly is, that wages tend to rise when unemployment falls, then the following chain of reasoning seems theoretically plausible: first, a high demand for labor; then wages rise; thus all costs rise; therefore all prices rise. This also seems, at least theoretically, to be a plausible explanation for the countermovements of the seesaw: low demand for labor; wages fall; costs fall; therefore prices fall.

The wage theory has an attractive simplicity and probably for that reason has been perennially popular. But it is too simple. It leaves too much unexplained. Most important, it does not throw any light upon why demand for labor should fluctuate in any case. This is the central problem, which all serious theorists of a price-unemployment relationship, from Cantillon on, have tried to address. The missing piece is crucial. If demand for labor is the force that makes the seesaw move, we are left with a force coming out of nowhere unless the rise and fall of demand for labor can be accounted for, too.

In analogy to the wage theory, or sometimes in association with it, are various other cost-push theories of inflation: costs rise; prices rise; therefore wages must rise; therefore costs rise further;

therefore prices rise further; therefore wages rise still further; etc. While this seems plausibly to explain why inflation can spiral, it suffers from the same fatal simplicity as the unadorned wage theory itself.

John Stuart Mill, in 1844, proposed that the crucial force moving the seesaw, including demand for labor, is expansion or contraction of credit advanced by lenders to producers. Mill was a supply-side economist. His ideas about credit complemented the thoughts of David Ricardo in England and Jean Baptiste Say in France, two of the most influential economists of the early nineteenth century. Ricardo and Say argued not only that production takes the lead in economic expansion but also that there is no practical limit to a nation's capacity to use capital productively. Mill propounded the existence of a gratuitous limit. He pointed out that if the working capital available to producers contracts, then production itself must contract, thus reducing demand for labor and, it follows, reducing consumption and demand generally, along with prices. Expansion of credit for producers would have the reverse effects. Mill, like Cantillon and unlike Adam Smith, was stressing a stimulative effect of increased money (in the form of credit), but being a supply-side economist, he reasoned out a path or avenue of stimulation different from Cantillon's.

Karl Marx, whose writings on economics overlapped those of Mill, was infuriated by Ricardo and Say, and by Mill, too, insofar as ideas about credit were concerned. What charlatans! What miserable creatures; what humbug they were spreading! Marx was a demand-side economist. Demand, which he identified as need on the part of a populace, is inherently unlimited, he said, and gratuitous limits on *that* are what limit economic activity. Ricardo and Say had it all backwards with their talk about no inherent limit to uses for capital; Mill, too. It isn't producers who need money to keep economic life expanding, said Marx, but the populace. Lack of money in consumers' and would-be consumers' hands, not in producers' hands, constricts and undermines economic life.

Marx reasoned that since profits come out of the sale price of goods and services, the wage earners who produce the goods and services can't afford, in the aggregate, to buy all they produce.

This inexorably leads to overproduction, he said, followed by collapse of both prices and employment. He thought the built-in discrepancy between wages and prices, by creating a demand gap, led to periodic cyclic crises of unemployment and price collapse, and must also lead before long to a final insurmountable crisis of capitalism, to be followed by socialism, which would eliminate the demand gap by eliminating private profits.

Marx's case was a complicated one to argue because, as he himself well understood, profits do not evaporate out of economic life. In part they are used for buying consumers' goods and services, especially luxuries, he noted. In part they are used for buying capital goods, such as tools, shipping, drained or cleared lands, whatever. These uses of profits all represent demand as surely as the avails of wages do. So how could a fatal demand gap arise?

The trouble, as Marx analyzed it, was largely one of proportion: the proportion of sale prices taken as profits compared to the proportion devoted to wages. He argued that capital inexorably becomes concentrated in fewer hands as time passes, and that monopolization of capital permits capitalists to take ever larger shares of income for themselves, leaving ever smaller shares for wage earners. Capitalist working forces were therefore, he thought, doomed to become increasingly exploited and impoverished. The exorbitant profits would not be used productively, as Ricardo and Say would have one believe; in fact, Marx said, they could not be used productively in view of the impoverishment of customers, the workers.

For many reasons—formation of new enterprises counteracting consolidation of older enterprises, political action, the hard but successful struggles of trade unions, the upward pressures on wages in good times, which Adam Smith had noted—the drama of an increasingly impoverished working force did not unfold in the advanced, capitalist economies of Europe and America as Marx had anticipated. Nevertheless, leaving aside his analysis of how a gap might come about and why, the thought of a gap lends itself to an elegant theoretical explanation for the price-unemployment seesaw.

If it is true that a gap in demand pushes prices down and unemployment up, which is a reasonable-sounding assumption, then the opposite must also be true (as Cantillon had already reasoned). Amplified demand must lower unemployment and push up prices. Furthermore, if unproductively used capital could create a demand gap, the idled funds need not belong to arrant profiteers, as Marx reasoned they must. They could be savings accumulated by workers who weren't being impoverished, or could be savings of both workers and owners.

With these modifications of Marxist thought, we are arriving at the Keynesian theory of the seesaw. John Maynard Keynes, the most influential economist of this century, reasoned that economies undergo periods when investment becomes flaccid, even uneconomic, and yet savings accumulate nevertheless. People defer spending in favor of saving, and the savings don't pull their weight in supporting demand for capital goods or for anything else. The gap in demand leads to falling production of capital equipment, to unemployment, to falling demand for consumers' goods as unemployment increases, and so to further unemployment, to falling prices, to falling and vanishing profits, to bankruptcies, defaults, foreclosures. Savings themselves evaporate in the course of such a debacle and thus the very wherewithal for reversing and retrieving the situation is lost out of the system.

In formulating his theory, Keynes was trying to arrive at an explanation for the Great Depression of the 1930s, with the object of understanding how to combat it and prevent or minimize similar catastrophes in the future. He reasoned that a national government could step into the breach by increasing its own expenditures above and beyond the yield received from taxes. Thus he prescribed deficit financing, not for the purpose of meeting the government's own needs (which would simply have been inflationary according to the Adam Smith or the printing-press theories of inflation), but rather to meet the economy's needs. A government, in short, could deliberately undertake to correct a demand gap incapable of correcting itself. Keynes reasoned that in good times a government could return to balanced budgets. Of course Keynes well understood that more demand requires that more capital be put to work to satisfy growing demand. As a demand-side economist, however, he thought of demand leading the way, with supply following in its wake, which is one reason governments adopting Keynesian deficit financing have tended to favor spending programs and income-transfer schemes that get money into hands of consumers.

Keynes's followers, some of whom in due course became advisers to presidents and prime ministers, and many of whom became government employees throughout the Western world, aimed to use Keynesian fiscal tools responsibly and with precision as far as this could be done within the exigencies of politics. The object was to keep unemployment levels low, yet avoid excess demand—too much money chasing too few goods—which would cause inflationary price rises; the object, in sum, was to keep the seesaw in balance.

The strategy seemed to them so clear, constructive and correct that Keynesians thought of the problem as being mainly how to refine tactics: tax manipulations, interest-rate manipulations, size and nature of public spending programs, construction of national budgets, choices of how to finance the budgets, and proper timing of whatever interventions were chosen. The Keynesians thus concentrated on creating a science of fiscal intervention—a real science, like chemistry or physics, in which one can count on precise, quantifiable interventions yielding predictable, quantifiable results.

By 1960 it seemed to Keynesians that they had in their hands instruments to serve both as intervention guides and as tables of predictable results. These instruments were known as Phillips curves in recognition of their inventor, the late A. W. H. Phillips, a New Zealand electrical engineer who had become a student, and subsequently a professor, at the London School of Economics.

As an economics student in the years just after World War II, Phillips learned to construct economic models, as all serious economics students did then, and still do. The models are exercises on paper—or nowadays on computer printouts—which purport to demonstrate mathematically how a given economy will behave if various of its factors change, or do not change. Studying Keynes's major work, *The General Theory of Employment, Interest and Money*, Phillips constructed a mathematical model of a Keynesian economy which struck him as looking wonderfully like a description of a hydraulic system. So he proceeded to build a physical model out of pipes, pumps and valves. Sure enough, when pressure over here was increased, whole successions of valves opened beautifully over there. Phillips' toy enjoyed some success as a teaching device in British, American and Australian universities (the Ford Motor Co. also acquired it) but Phillips handed the manufacturing over to a British plastics firm and returned to mathematical analyses.

Britain is a splendid mine of data, and among the treasures from the archives which researchers were digging up and putting together in the latter 1940s and 1950s was a table of changes in British price levels for the years 1858–1914, and another of production levels for the same years. Comparing the two in 1954, Phillips found that production had moved upward at times of rising prices and downward at times of falling prices: the familiar seesaw. But Phillips took the relationship a step further. He quantified the seesaw movements by analyzing—in percentages of price rise or fall and production rise or fall—precisely where each end of the seesaw stood each year, and compared the rates of percentage change. He learned that over and over again a given rate of change at one end of the board corresponded to a given rate of change at the other. A few years later he made similar comparisons, this time between unemployment rates in Britain's unionized labor force during the first half of this century, and union wage rates during the same period. In 1958 he distilled his findings into a graph (which actually looked more like a sloping line than a curve). What the graph or curve seemed to show was that any given rate of wage increase was precisely associated with a given rate of unemployment.

Phillips himself disclaimed that his curve supplied a theory of inflation, and at least at the time he made the curve, he thought of his discovery as merely a refinement of what everybody already knew anyway. But economists trying to make a science out of managing the messy, mysterious, deplorably unpredictable behavior of the real world fell upon the curve with unbounded professional faith and joy. Specific inflation rates corresponded, it seemed, precisely with specific unemployment rates. This could logically be taken to mean that if a government wanted a given change in its national unemployment rate, most likely a reduction, the new rate desired could be gotten by arranging for a predetermined inflation rate, which in turn could be achieved by fiscal intervention; that is, by fiddling with tax and interest rates and spending programs. Conversely, if a government wanted a given inflation rate, most likely a reduction, that too could be achieved by fiscal manipulation, and the cost in jobs would be predictable, therefore could be judged as acceptable or not, and planned for.

In short order, economists far and wide were making and refining their own national Phillips curves, and in schools of economics throughout the Western World, students were being taught how to construct and use them. The first curve based on U.S. data was worked out in 1960, one of its two co-authors being Paul A. Samuelson, the leading American economics textbook author, and subsequently a Nobel laureate in economics. In America an unemployment rate between 3 and 4 percent was deemed to represent full employment on grounds that the slack represents people changing jobs or just entering the labor market for the first time. In Switzerland a rate of 1 percent or less is deemed full employment; differing national mores or expectations of this sort were supposed to be taken into account through the construction of Phillips curves specific to specific countries.

In America the object was to keep the unemployment level at or below a rate of 4 percent. Historically, it seemed that this was associated with an inflation rate of less than 3 percent annually. So that was the balance sought for the seesaw. In 1964, the unemployment rate moved up too high at 5.2 percent. No need to worry; the inflation rate could be taken as being too low, at 1.3 percent. The seesaw need only be brought into better balance through measures that could be counted on to raise the rate of inflation a bit. This was the sort of fine-tuning which had led Presidents Kennedy and Johnson to imagine that the country was entering a new era in which the business cycle was being demystified or at any rate was no longer to be feared.

But by 1967, inflation wasn't quite trading off against sufficient drops in unemployment, and from then on it became increasingly clear that it really wasn't trading off at all. At first the emerging misbehavior of the economy, and of the Phillips curves, was discounted as a temporary aberration, and every few years a new and different circumstantial reason for the misfits was seized upon: insufficient taxation for supporting the Vietnam war and then, later, rising oil prices were favorite explanations. But as early as 1971 a few Keynesians began to suspect that their faith in the curves was misplaced; by 1975, when unemployment in the United States stood at 8.5 percent and the inflation rate at 9.1 percent, most Keynesians, including Samuelson, had to concede the curves were red herrings, though they didn't know why.

Abandoning the curves went hard with Keynesian enonomists because the loss they were suffering was greater than mere loss of faith in a technique or instrument. What was being lost was confidence in Keynesian economics itself. If its prescriptions were not achieving what theory said they should, the theory itself must be suspected of underlying error, or else the economists who had been trying to put it into practice must be suspected of not having understood the theory.

As Keynesianism was succumbing to stagflation, bafflement and dispute over what Keynes had meant anyhow, monetarists came to the fore. Monetarists are supply-side economists. Their serious theoretical grounding rests largely on the Great Depression theory of the late Irving Fisher, a professor of economics at Yale University, although monetarists became known colloquially as the Chicago School because Fisher's ideas were much refined and further developed at the University of Chicago under the leadership of Milton Friedman, who, like Samuelson, is a Nobel laureate in economics.

Fisher's basic idea was the same as that advanced by John Stuart Mill almost a century earlier, which had subsequently been taken up by American folk and populist economic theorists and by third-party political movements such as the post–Civil War Greenback Labor Party and the Depression-era Social Credit movements. Fisher argued that the cause of the Depression was drastic contraction of credit, owing to panic on the part of bankers who feared—with only too much reason—for the solvency of their banks. He attributed both the fear and its consequences to the fact that banks, quite legally, are permitted to lend multiples of their own capital: multiples of the reserves they hold in cash and other assets ultimately backed by government obligations. He reasoned that the way to overcome the Depression was to expand credit to producers, and that the way to prevent similar debacles in future was to stabilize the volume of bank credit, prevent it from fluctuating wildly. To achieve this, he proposed that a government should take full responsibility for issuing all the money its nation's economy requires, instead of relying upon banks to create most of the money by lending beyond their reserves.

Banks, Fisher thought, should be required to hold full reserves against loans, in government-backed obligations. On the one hand, this would make it impossible for bankers to inflate credit above and beyond the government-mandated volume of money; on the other hand, the security conferred upon banks by their 100 per-cent reserves would make it unnecessary for them to contract credit fearfully, and they would have no reason to do so capriciously because not to lend up to their full reserves would only lose them income. If demand for loans was low, lower interest rates would work as an automatic correction; if high, rising interest rates would be the response. Interest rates, cost of money, would thus fluctuate according to the law of supply and demand, but volume of credit would not.

Fisher proposed further that a government should assume responsibility for gradually and steadily increasing the volume of a nation's money at a preordained annual rate calculated to sustain steadily expanding production, but not more, in order to keep prices stable and avoid inflation. Fisher had persuasive statistical data to back up his arguments; in both good times and bad, the gross national product in the United States amounted to about three times the nation's volume of currency plus demand deposits —checking accounts—in banks. Since demand deposits trace back directly and indirectly into bank loans, Fisher said the figures proved that volume of loans determines the volume of economic activity, including rates of employment. Unlike Keynes's prescription, Fisher's were not adopted in America or elsewhere; nevertheless, under Friedman's leadership, monetarism remained alive as an intellectual force.

For many technical reasons it is difficult to define what "money" is, and this has become increasingly a problem since Fisher's time. To modern monetarists, as to Fisher, money means currency and checks actively used in commercial transactions; but statistically separating this M-1, as it is now called, from savings deposits and other forms of money has become an arcane specialty. It is a specialty of greatest importance to monetarists because the core of their theory continues to be the advisability of a steady, gradual national increase in volume of money. "When money and output grow at the same pace, demand and supply remain in balance and prices on average are stable," as one monetarist summed up the belief in 1981. To monetarists, therefore, sporadic, remedial injections of money into an economy as prescribed by Keynesians are anathema.

After stagflation had discredited Keynesianism, the governments of Britain, the United States, Chile and a number of other countries turned to the monetarists for counsel. They were prepared. Since stagflation is a two-headed monster, their proposed remedies were two-pronged. To attack inflation, they prescribed tight money —high interest rates—and cuts in government spending, particularly spending to support demand as opposed to spending for support of production. To attack unemployment, which they traced to insufficient investment in produciton, they advocated reducing tax rates, the purpose being to release funds for private investment and also to increase incentives for investing by lowering the tax bite on its rewards. Since the lower tax rates were supposed to stimulate production and employment, they were supposed to yield more government revenue than higher rates; another curve, the Laffer curve, suggested that this result could be depended on.

Alas. When these prescriptions were tried in practice, the high interest rates made borrowing uneconomic for producers and bankrupted, or helped bankrupt, many. And at a time when production in reality was contracting and unemployment was soaring, lowered tax rates could not produce the desired yields and could serve only to magnify government deficits. In sum, measures contrived to fight inflation were proving ruinous to producers and their work forces, while measures contrived to help producers were enlarging government deficits. In short order, the two-headed monster had undercut the remedies of monetarists as decisively as it undercut the prescriptions of Keynesians.

One might suppose that at this point the rulers of Marxist economies would have reason to gloat over the failure of capitalist theory. They could ill afford gloating, however. Stagnation was victimizing them, too. It was veiled by policies of overmanning enterprises with workers who were actually surplus, and by price subsidies which periodically had to give under the pressures of inflation. Furthermore, many Marxist economies had become heavily dependent on American, Japanese and West European sources for capital which they weren't generating themselves and which, as time passed, it was becoming increasingly evident they were in no position to repay.

Small wonder the theories I have touched upon have yielded no germane responses to stagflation. Far from explaining what it is or what can be done about it, from start to finish they have explained, instead, that stagflation cannot exist! Going all the way back to Cantillon, that has been the message. The rising prices of which Cantillon spoke were indissolubly linked with the increased activity (reduced unemployment) of which he *also* spoke. Break that link and his entire chain of reasoning disintegrates to nothing. It is the same with the wage theory; break the link between rising prices *and* low unemployment rates and nothing is left. So it is with Mill's ideas on the effects of credit, and with the ideas of the later monetarists, too; credit to producers, whether expanding or contracting, does not permit stagflation, because it powers a seesaw. Break the seesaw and nothing is left of the reasoning. Marx, who supposed he had so little in common with the supply-side economists of his time, had this in common: his theory outlawed stagflation too. Overproduction, after all, mandates *both* unemployment and falling prices, a point Marx himself made over and over and over and over. Remove the twin consequences of overproduction from Marx's reasoning and his logic

23

collapses. But leave them in and stagflation cannot be. Nor does stagflation enter Keynesian analysis; it is impossible, as the Phillips curves so seductively demonstrated. We comb through economic theory in vain when we search there for enlightenment on stagflation.

The late Arthur M. Okun, who was an expert on Phillips curves and who had served as chief economic adviser to President Lyndon Johnson, was one of the first Keynesians to become suspicious of his science. After stagflation had emerged he suggested half seriously and half facetiously that unemployment and inflation rates ought to be merged into one single stagflation figure, "the economic discomfort index." His analogy was to the Weather Bureau's summertime discomfort index, a figure that merges the humidity rate and the temperature into one figure to help people understand why they are so uncomfortable on muggy days. Okun was making two points. Stagflation is economically uncomfortable, he said, no matter how you slice it analytically. That is, inflation at 10 percent, say, and unemployment at 6 percent are not really improved by converting them to inflation at 5 percent and unemployment at 11 percent; either way, the merged rates yield an uncomfortable 16. Actually, he thought, the unemployment component contributes more heavily to the discomfort than the inflation component, but his point was that an improvement of the one rate at the expense of the other is illusory. His second point was political. No matter how the economic discomfort index is sliced analytically, a high stagflation figure plunges a democratic government into serious trouble with its voters. Economists found Okun's wry analogy amusing but didn't take his proposed index seriously. Mixing apples and oranges may serve to make a political point, but keeping them separate is supposed to be more enlightening for purposes of analysis.

However, suppose we carry Okun's analogy a little further. The reason the Weather Bureau produces a discomfort index, instead of confining itself only to separately reported factors, is that it wants to depict a condition. Just so, we can think of stagflation as a coherent condition in its own right: a condition of high prices and too little work.

The moment we think of it so, we instantly realize that this condition is not abnormal or unprecedented. Rather, it is the normal and ordinary condition to be found in poor and backward economies the world over. The condition is abnormal only in economies that are developing and expanding or have been doing so in the recent past, which of course are exactly the economies which have harbored, among so much else, economic scholars and thinkers from Cantillon right down to Milton Friedman and Arthur Okun.

We often fail to think of prices in poor, backward, long-stagnated economies as being wildly inflated because, to us, those prices seem low. When I visited Portugal in 1974, the prices in the fish-market stalls of Lisbon, the costs of tiles in building-supply stores, the bus fares, the restaurant meals (except in tourist restaurants) all seemed to me bargains. But to the Portuguese the prices were very high. Household comforts and luxuries that people of modest means in the United States and Canada were taking for granted at the time were out of the reach of all but the exceptionally well off in Portugal. Jobs, not just good jobs but any jobs, were also hard to come by for a large proportion of the Portuguese population and this was not an abnormal or cyclic situation. It was the normal situation. That is why many Portuguese had migrated from their country for decades, for generations. In sum, a condition of high prices and of high unemployment and underemployment was normal there. To a Portuguese of modest means who somehow could raise the fare for a visit to Madras, prices there would seem bargains; but they aren't bargains to Indians. The condition of high prices and scant work is a still more extreme condition in India than in Portugal, but normal.

When Adam Smith drew attention to the surplus of labor in Scotland and yet noted that Scotland was subject to high prices, he was observing in effect that stagflation was normal in Scotland. Actually, stagflation is not as unprecedented or abnormal as we may suppose in the United States. One need only look at economic life in the poor county seats that string through Appalachia, or at life in any other poor and backward pockets of the country, to realize that high prices and scant work have long been normal in such places. In poor Canadian economies, like that of New Brunswick, prices are permanently and wildly high relative to people's means, and unemployment is permanently high too. Only recently have these twin afflictions begun victimizing the country taken as a statistical whole. *That* is what is abnormal in Canada, as it is in the United States.

In Britain, prices seem disastrously high to the British, high for those who are working as well as for those on the dole. But visitors from currently more highly developed economies across the English Channel find Britain a holiday and shopping bargain, much as I found Portugal to be. Or to look at the same phenomenon from another angle, an English writer and translator living in the Netherlands complains that when he writes an article for a London newspaper on a complicated Dutch political situation it earns him only the equivalent of 95 florins, whereas a more easily tossed off article in Dutch "for a paper in Holland with far less than half the London paper's circulation figure brings in 225 florins." If Adam Smith were alive, he could draw much the same comparison between England and Holland that he once drew between England and Scotland, only now England would have become, as it were, the Scotland of the comparison. In the recent past one could observe that few households in poor pockets of the United States could afford a house costing the median price in the country taken as a statistical whole; but in the country taken as a statistical whole, a household with an income close to the median could afford a median-priced house, which is why the United States, by and large, was a nation of home owners. However, by 1981, the median house price required an income that only 10 percent of all households could claim. A condition formerly normal only in poor parts of the country had become normal for the nation.

There is a distinction between being terminally ill and being dead, as there is between just-emerging stagflation and long-established, seemingly permanent stagflation. A really moribund economy has already reached such a severe and fixed condition of high prices and high unemployment that the process of getting there is over and done with. An economy in which prices and unemployment are newly in process of rising in concert is not yet moribund; but it inevitably will be, given no reversal of its condition. I cannot see any way of understanding stagflation except as a normal consequence of economic stagnation, just as backwardness and low productivity are other normal consequences of stagnation. If I am correct, the emergence of stagflation in formerly developing and expanding economies is appalling in its implications and portents. It is not just a problem of inflation to be gotten under control along with a problem of unemployment to be dealt with by mastering inflation, or vice versa. It is a condition in its own right, the condition of sliding into profound economic decline.

Recently, some monetarists have tried to account for the disappointing results of their remedies by postulating a "high natural unemployment rate." Their reasoning goes that if an economy develops a high natural rate, and if the rate is then pushed below that natural level, unemployment can still remain high and yet be accompanied by inflation as a consequence of the unemployment being "unnaturally" reduced. This tortuous attempt to claim that the seesaw still works may merely represent the high natural aspirations of theorists to save their theories, but it is also a way of saying that something has gone wrong which the theories hadn't taken into account. Keynes gloomily commented, as he observed the economic decline of Britain, that possibly an economy could develop structural flaws lying beyond help from his remedies: another way of saying that things can go wrong which his theory couldn't account for.

To speak of structural flaws or of permanently high rates of unemployment merely brings us back by a different route to the mysteries of the differing effects of Marshall Plan aid in differing economies and the failure of so many elaborately rationalized and well-funded development schemes. We do not understand how to catalyze development in backward economies, and we do not understand how to prevent developed economies from sliding into backwardness themselves: two sides of the same mystery.

One thing we do know by now because events have rubbed our faces in it: it would be rash to suppose that macro-economics, as it stands today, has useful guidance for us. Several centuries of hard, ingenious thought about supply and demand chasing each other around, tails in their mouths, have told us almost nothing about the rise and decline of wealth. We must find more realistic and fruitful lines of observation and thought than we have tried to use so far. Choosing among the existing schools of thought is bootless. We are on our own.

TWO

Back to Reality

When a technological enterprise like the design of a machine or a building runs into trouble, the appropriate response can be "Back to the drawing board," meaning the thing is basically sound in conception but needs to be worked out more carefully. This has also been the response of economists and governments as their economic expectations have crumbled. They have gone over and over and over what they think they already know, trying to use their tools with greater sophistication, shuffling the same old conceptions into new combinations and permutations to run through the computers or the legislatures. However, in the face of so many nasty surprises, arising in so many different circumstances and under so many differing regimes, we must be suspicious that some basic assumption or other is in error, most likely an assumption so much taken for granted that it escapes identification and skepticism.

Macro-economic theory does contain such an assumption. It is the idea that national economies are useful and salient entities for understanding how economic life works and what its structure may be: that national economies and not some other entity provide the fundamental data for macro-economic analysis. The assumption is about four centuries old, coming down to us from the early mercantilist economists who happened to be preoccupied with the rivalries of European powers for trade and treasure during the period when Portuguese, Spanish, French, English and

Dutch were exploring and conquering the New World and the lands and seas that lay along the trade routes around Africa to the Indies and beyond. These early mercantilists assumed that the national rivalries unfolding before them were the very keys to understanding what wealth itself is and how it arises, how it is maintained, how lost. According to the theory they propounded, wealth consists of gold, and gold is amassed as a nation manages to sell more goods than it buys (hence the designation "mercantilist" for this thinking), in the process piling up national treasure. Of course if wealth is defined in this way, national economies automatically become the salient units of economic life; that idea is merely a tautology, the repetition of another idea, in this case the idea of national treasure. Cantillon's thinking was an early attempt to transcend the simplistic equation of wealth with gold, but we can see the connection to mercantilist thought in the passage I quoted earlier, "If the increase of actual money grows from mines of gold or silver in the State . . ."

In due course Adam Smith, in his great work of 1776, *An Inquiry into the Nature and Causes of the Wealth of Nations*, redefined wealth as production (supply) for purposes of consumption (demand) and sought its sources not in mines of gold or silver but in capital and labor, and in domestic trade as well as in foreign or imperial trade. Smith questioned and discarded many ideas previously accepted, and in each of the subjects he considered, whether he was discarding, accepting, or breaking new ground, he painstakingly pilots us through his observations and reasoning.

But Smith failed to question everything that came to him ready-made. For example, he accepted without comment the mercantilist tautology that nations are the salient entities for understanding the structure of economic life. As far as one can tell from his writings, he gave that point no thought but took it so much for granted that he used it as his point of departure. This is explicit not only in the title of his work, but in its first sentence:

The annual labor of every nation is the fund which originally supplies it with all the necessaries and conveniences of life which it annually consumes, and which consist always either in the immediate produce of that labor or in what is purchased with that produce from other nations.

In short, Smith began with what we have come to know as the gross national product and proceeded on from there.

In the two centuries since Smith published, most of what he wrote has been questioned and much has been amplified, elaborated and modified. But the one thing not questioned has been the same idea Smith himself failed to question: the old mercantilist tautology that nations are the salient entities for understanding the structure of economic life. Ever since, that same notion has continued to be taken for granted. How strange; surely no other body of scholars or scientists in the modern world has remained as credulous as economists, for so long a time, about the merit of their subject matter's most formative and venerable assumption.

To be sure, Marx based his economic analysis upon class structure rather than nations, and anticipated that when class was set to rights, the State would wither away. But in practice, Marxist economics has been assimilated into the prevailing assumption. Nobody places more faith in the nation as the suitable entity for analyzing economic life and its prospects than the rulers of Communist and socialist countries, nor more faith in the State as the salient instrument for shaping economies. Anarchists, of course, deny the validity of the State; but that is no help as far as economic analysis is concerned because anarchists (like pure or abstract Marxist theoreticians) have been preoccupied with their conceptions of how economic life ought to work and dismiss how it actually does work, which is in ways they reject out of hand, as it were.

Nations are political and military entities, and so are blocs of nations. But it doesn't necessarily follow from this that they are also the basic, salient entities of economic life or that they are particularly useful for probing the mysteries of economic structure, the reasons for rise and decline of wealth. Indeed, the failure of national governments and blocs of nations to force economic

31

life to do their bidding suggests some sort of essential irrelevance. It also affronts common sense, if nothing else, to think of units as disparate as, say, Singapore and the United States, or Ecuador and the Soviet Union, or the Netherlands and Canada, as economic common denominators. All they really have in common is the political fact of sovereignty.

Once we remove the blinders of the mercantilist tautology and try looking at the real economic world in its own right rather than as a dependent artifact of politics, we can't avoid seeing that most nations are composed of collections or grab bags of very different economies, rich regions and poor ones within the same nation.

We can't avoid seeing, too, that among all the various types of economies, cities are unique in their abilities to shape and reshape the economies of other settlements, including those far removed from them geographically. To take a simple and small example, consider the twists and turns to be found in the economy of a single hamlet, in this case a little cluster of stone houses perched high in the Cevennes Mountains in south-central France, one of the poorest parts of that country. The hamlet, Bardou, found its way into my Toronto morning paper because it is so charming, having become a kind of Shangri-la for writers, musicians, artists and craftsmen fleeing the cities of Europe, the United States and Canada in search of beauty and a cheap, quiet place in which to work.

Bardou has a long past about which something is known. Some two thousand years ago, when Gaul became a province of Rome, the site was linked into the imperial economy by roads terminating in a collection of iron mines nearby. The iron found there was not shaped at the site into swords, lances, chisels, hinges, plows, wheel rims, cauldrons or the many other items for which iron was useful at the time, and where it went for manufacturing is now unknown. A logical guess would be forges in Nîmes, an extremely ancient city which had already become a metropolis of this part of Gaul in pre-Roman times; or it might have been carried to Lugdunum, now Lyons, which has traditionally been a center of metalworking and was the hub of the Roman road system in Gaul. Wherever the market was, the iron was in sufficient demand to justify mine roads so well engineered and solidly built that they still serve admirably as hikers' trails, though they have gone largely untended and unrepaired for some fifteen centuries or more. Both the mines and roads were abandoned when economic life in this part of Gaul disintegrated, probably in the fourth century.

The area then reverted to wilderness, unpopulated as far as has been discovered, until the sixteenth century when squatters—probably landless peasants pushed up from the valley and slopes below—built themselves the stone houses of the present-day hamlet. They scratched out little garden plots among the rocks, gathered chestnuts and no doubt caught game in the surrounding forests, and on their poor and rocky soil pursued as well as they could the subsistence arts they had inherited from economies of the distant past more creative than their own. Lifetime after lifetime, nothing changed in this subsistence economy. We may infer that life was not only hard but also boring and mean because tradition has it that people were accustomed to stealing one another's garden produce by shifting boundary markers in the night, then interminably quarreled over the thefts. Such were the excitements for about three and a half centuries.

Then abruptly in the 1870s a radical change began. Word somehow penetrated that a more desirable life was to be found far away. Perhaps the information percolated back from army recruits who were stationed in Paris or passed through there in the aftermath of the Franco-Prussian War; perhaps word came from migrants who had left villages on the mountains' lower slopes. Paris had been drawing in rural French migrants for untold generations; the word was very late in reaching Bardou but once a few venturesome souls from the hamlet left, a slow and almost total exodus followed. By 1900, half the population had departed. During the following forty years everybody left except for three families.

In 1966, when two hikers, a German and an American, happened by on the old Roman roads, the ruins sheltered only one aged man. The hikers bought the hamlet from him and from such descendants of former inhabitants as they and their lawyers could trace, and when legal title had been established, the new owners moved in and invited kindred spirits to join them and help pay expenses. In this incarnation, Bardou has a rotating core of year-round residents who live on their savings or by selling their works to publishers and other city customers. Holiday renters and campers are welcomed, along with the income they bring. Residents and vacationers alike live chiefly on imported food of course, and they import nearly all their other necessities, but they make a virtue of getting along without such amenities and conveniences as electricity, telephones and hot water. A piped cold-water system was financed when a motion picture company rented the hamlet briefly to make location shots and paid well for the privilege.

Bardou's history is unique but only in the sense that every place, like every person and every snowflake, is unique. Otherwise, the same kinds of changes and events to be found in Bardou's story are duplicated in principle in many other places, and on much larger scale. Bardou is an example, in microcosm, of what I am going to call passive economies, meaning economies that do not create economic change themselves but instead respond to forces unloosed in distant cities. Time and again, like a toy on a string, Bardou has been jerked by some *external* economic energy or other. In ancient times the site was exploited for its iron, then abandoned. In modern times it was depopulated when distant city jobs attracted its people, then repopulated by city people. The jerks were not gentle. But when cities and city people let Bardou alone, had no uses for it, the place either had no economy whatever, as when it was a wilderness, or else a subsistence economy that remained unchanging.

We could beat our brains out trying to explain Bardou's economic history in terms of its own attributes, right down to compiling statistics on the probable average yield of chestnuts, the tools used there, the amount and quality of iron taken out and that remaining, the man-hours required to build a house, the nature of the soil, the annual rainfall, and so on—and none of this would enlighten us at all as to why and how Bardou's economy took the twists and turns it actually did. On that subject, the local clues stand mute, for the clues that in reality explain Bardou's twists and turns are to be found in distant city markets, jobs, city work transplanted, city technology (the new water system, the old roads), city capital. To understand both the changes that occurred in Bardou and why there were periods when nothing changed, we must look to clues that do not define Bardou in any way *except as they have acted upon Bardou.*

At first thought it may seem like hairsplitting to differentiate between jerks administered to Bardou by various cities, and jerks administered by something we can choose to call, instead, by such names as the Roman Empire, France, the European Economic Community or the international economy. But it is not hairsplitting. In the first place, the reality—and we must always pay close attention to reality or we shall be lost in fogs of our own making —is that those jerks to Bardou were administered from particular cities, and in this case always distant cities. All around Bardou lies something called "the French national economy" but that has not been what put Bardou through its economic twists and turns. Why be fuzzy about these things if we can be specific? Rome, perhaps Nîmes or Lyons, Paris, and the various cities from which its current population of artists, writers and vacationers (and the motion picture company) have come—these cities are the salient economic entities that have shaped and reshaped Bardou.

Distinctions between city economies and the potpourris we call national economies are important not only for getting a grip on realities; they are of the essence where practical attempts to reshape economic life are concerned. For example, failures to make such distinctions are directly responsible for many wildly expensive economic debacles in backward countries, debacles which have resulted from the failure to observe that the all-important function of import-replacing or import-substitution is in real life specifically a city function, rather than something a "national economy" can be made to do. I shall be writing a good deal in this book about how cities grow and become economically versatile by replacing goods that they once imported with goods that they make themselves, for blindness to this common, ordinary reality is the source of much confusion in how we think of economics in general, as well as the source of much nonsense, waste and lost opportunity for development.

People have long observed that poor regions or nations typically import more than they can afford or else are terribly deprived because they fail to produce wide ranges of things for themselves. A poignant description of the shortcoming was contained in a speech made in 1889 by a Southerner to a gathering of industrialists and bankers in Boston, and then repeated to a similar gathering in New York. Henry Grady, an essayist and the editor of the leading newspaper in Atlanta, Georgia, told of a funeral he said he had attended a few years previously in Pickens County, some eighty miles north of Atlanta.

> The grave was dug through solid marble, but the marble headstone came from Vermont. It was in a pine wilderness but the pine coffin came from Cincinnati. An iron mountain over-shadowed it but the coffin nails and the screws and the shovel came from Pittsburgh. With hard wood and metal abounding, the corpse was hauled on a wagon from South Bend, Indiana. A hickory grove grew near by, but the pick and shovel handles came from New York. The cotton shirt on the dead man came from Cincinnati, the coat and breeches from Chicago, the shoes from Boston; the folded hands were encased in white gloves from New York, and round the poor neck, which had worn all its living days the bondage of lost opportunity, was twisted a cheap cravat from Philadelphia. That country, so rich in undeveloped resources, furnished nothing for the funeral except the corpse and the hole in the ground and would probably have imported both of those if it could have done so. And as the poor fellow was lowered to his rest, on coffin bands from Lowell, he carried nothing into the next world as a reminder of his home in this, save the halted blood in his veins, the chilled marrow in his bones, and the echo of the dull clods that fell on his coffin lid.

Of the fourteen items in Grady's litany, eleven came from big cities of his time: the coffin and shirt from Cincinnati, the nails, screws and shovel from Pittsburgh, the tool handles and white gloves from New York, the coat and breeches from Chicago, the shoes from Boston, the cravat from Philadelphia; while another, the wagon from South Bend, came from a small city. Only the marble from rural Vermont and the coffin bands from Lowell—a textile town whose work had been received as a transplant from the Boston economy—did not come from cities.

What Grady might have asked himself was why none of Pickens County's imports came from his own city, Atlanta. But he didn't because it didn't occur to him that cities were germane to the problem concerning him: the problem of poor economies that do not produce amply and diversely for their own people. Thinking instead in terms of large, amorphous regional economies only, he himself apparently didn't hear what he was saying. His object in making the speech was to obtain for the southern United States transplanted industries from the northern United States to achieve something he called the New South. He was a forerunner of the hosts of "development" officials who today work so hard to attract industries into moribund economies which for seemingly mysterious reasons are too passive to generate industries of their own, and who therefore scramble and compete for the insufficient supplies of such enterprises cast up from an insufficient supply of active and creative city economies.

The items Grady mentioned, although this did not occur to him either, were themselves products of import-replacing. None of those items had been invented in the cities that sent them to Pickens County. Most were old and familiar in Western culture before cities in America had so much as formed. But enterprises in some of the first colonial American cities, especially Boston and Philadelphia, had taken to making such things (and many others) for consumers and for other producers in their own cities instead of interminably importing them from London or other English cities, and had then taken to exporting the items not only to their own environs and to each other, but also to still younger cities farther west as they formed. In turn, as cities like Chicago, Pittsburgh and Cincinnati grew, and in the process laid a foundation for versatility at producing, they also replaced with their own production wide ranges of the imports they were receiving from eastern cities—and in their turns exported some of those same items as well. That is the trail by which a shirt from Cincinnati and a shovel from Pittsburgh reached Pickens County.

Doubtless the imported items for the funeral passed through Atlanta, for Atlanta was the transportation hub of the South; and Atlanta itself consumed far greater volumes of city-made imported goods, and many more kinds of them, than Pickens County did. But Atlanta, for reasons I shall discuss later in this book, was not an import-replacing city, nor were any other cities in the South at the time. That is why Pickens County's city-made imports came from such distances.

Behind the items Grady was thinking about, behind the finished goods, were many, many other items to which he gave no thought as far as one can tell: things like carpenters' planes and T squares, lathes, punches, knives, dye vats, brass-smelting cauldrons, ladles, printing presses, bookkeeping ledgers, button stampers, lights so that work could continue on dark days, tongs, sewing machines, telegraph keys, freight-car axles . . .

Cities that replace imports significantly replace not only finished goods but, concurrently, many, many items of producers' goods and services. They do it in swiftly emerging, logical chains. For example, first comes the local processing of fruit preserves that were formerly imported, then the production of jars or wrappings formerly imported for which there was no local market of producers until the first step had been taken. Or first comes the assembly of formerly imported pumps for which, once the assembly step has been taken, parts are imported; then the making of parts for which metal is imported; then possibly even the smelting of metal for these and other import-replacements. The process pays for itself as it goes along. When Tokyo went into the bicycle business, first came repair work cannibalizing imported bicycles, then manufacture of some of the parts most in demand for repair work, then manufacture of still more parts, finally assembly of whole, Tokyo-made bicycles. And almost as soon as Tokyo began exporting bicycles to other Japanese cities, there arose in some of those customer cities much the same process of replacing bicycles imported from Tokyo, rather than from abroad, as had happened with many items sent from city to city in the United States.

A city's current production of goods for export—the work that pays for the imports—helps feed the city import-replacing process. For example, an enterprise that electroplates tableware for export can also be capable of electroplating metal chair and table legs, and thus can play a part in replacing with local production furniture which formerly had been imported. Or better yet, workers can break away from the parent plant and set up a second plant based upon this initial work, but this time they will be working not for a tableware company but in a furniture-replacing enterprise. I say "better yet" because now there are two establishments, not one, to help feed or carry out the import-replacing process.

Import-replacing is now, as it was in Grady's time and always has been, a *city* process for good practical reasons. In the first place, the replacement of former imports is impossible to achieve economically, skillfully and flexibly—meaning in ways suitable to the time and place—except in a settlement that is already versatile enough at production to possess the necessary foundation for the new and added production work. Cities can build up that kind of versatility, often very rapidly, in part as a result of their already existing export work (if it is reasonably diversified), in part as a result of their previous simpler achievements in import-replacing, and in part through the complex symbiotic relationships formed among their various producers. In the second place, city markets—whether of consumers or producers—are at once diverse and concentrated. These two qualities of the local market make production of many kinds of goods and services economically feasible that would not be feasible in rural places, company towns or little market towns, and most especially so at the time production of former imports is just starting up and getting a first foothold in its markets.

Economic life develops by grace of innovating; it expands by grace of import-replacing. These two master economic processes are closely related, both being functions of city economies. Furthermore, successful import-replacing often entails adaptations in design, materials or methods of production, and these require innovating and improvising, especially of producers' goods and services.

Describing in 1982 an extraordinary proliferation of "innumerable small firms" during the previous decade in a great cluster of small industrial cities between Bologna and Venice in northeastern Italy, Charles F. Sabel, a social scientist at the Massachusetts Institute of Technology, illustrates the kinds of improvisations and innovations that occur as an everyday matter. A small shop producing tractor transmissions for a large manufacturer modifies the design of the transmission to suit the need of a small manufacturer of high-quality seeders. In another little shop "a conventional automatic packing machine is redesigned to fit the available space in a particular assembly line. A machine that injects one type of plastic into molds is modified to inject another, cheaper plastic. A membrane pump used in automobiles is modified to suit agricultural machinery. A standard loom or cloth-cutting machine is adjusted to work efficiently with particularly fine threads."

Sabel was amazed at the small size of these innovative and highly successful firms, most of which "employ from 5 to 50 workers, a few as many as 100, and a very few 250 or more," in the aggregate "specializing in virtually every phase of the production of textiles, automatic machines, machine tools, automobiles, buses and agricultural equipment," and was impressed by the sophistication and quality of the work being done in production of ceramics, shoes, plastic furniture, motorcycles, woodcutting machinery, metal-cutting machinery, ceramics machinery. He reports the ease with which new enterprises have formed through breakaway of workers from older enterprises, and the amazing economies of scale that are obtained not, as has been conventionally assumed, within the framework of huge organizations but rather through large symbiotic collections of little enterprises.

"The innovative capacity of this type of firm," Sabel goes on, "depends on its flexible use of technology; its close relations with other, similarly innovative firms in the same and adjacent sectors; and above all on the close collaboration of workers with different kinds of expertise. These firms practice boldly and spontaneously the fusion of conception and execution, abstract and practical knowledge, that only a few exceptional giant firms . . . have so far been able to achieve on a grand scale."

It all suggests, he says, "radically new ways of organizing industrial society" in line with the first signs (such as the reindustrialization debate in the United States) "of an epochal redefinition of markets, technologies and industrial hierarchies."

The strengths and wonders that Sabel observed in these tight-packed bunches of symbiotic enterprises, and that suggest to him epochal changes, have always been the strengths and wonders of creative cities, for there is nothing new in this way "of organizing industrial society." The realities Sabel observed—the huge collections of little firms, the symbiosis, the ease of breakaways, the flexibility, the economies, efficiencies and adaptiveness—are precisely the realities that, among other things, have always made successful and significant import-replacing a process realizable only in cities and their nearby hinterlands.

For obvious reasons, most city replacements of former imports consist of city-made goods and services, but not all. Some of the most momentous instances of city import-replacing involve former rural goods. A few examples from the past are replacements of natural ice with the city-originated work of manufacturing mechanical refrigeration equipment; replacements of cotton, flax, silk and furs with artificial, city-devised fibers; replacements of ivory and tortoise shell with plastics. No doubt in such cities as continue to be creative at replacing imports in the future, there will be many other such instances, like city-devised replacements for fossil fuels which already have a head start in Japanese cities, where hundreds of thousands of dwellings are now successfully using solar heaters. But for the most part, city import-replacing is not all that economically glamorous. The replacements are usually small initially, frequently involve items that in themselves are frivolous, and in many cases are absolutely imitative—but nevertheless, in the aggregate, they add up to momentous economic forces, the very force that the MIT scholar found "epochal."

Any settlement that becomes good at import-replacing *becomes* a city. And any city that repeatedly experiences, from time to time, explosive episodes of import-replacing keeps its economy up-to-date and helps keep itself capable of casting forth streams of innovative export work. Why "explosive" and why "episodes"? In real life, whenever import-replacing occurs significantly at all, it occurs in explosive episodes because it works as a chain reaction. The process feeds itself, and once well under way, does not die down in a given city until all the imports that are economically feasible to replace at that time and in that place have been replaced. In an earlier book, *The Economy of Cities*, I described in some detail how and why these chain reactions operate, and why they are triggered off. To summarize briefly, once replacements start, they stimulate more replacements. When such an episode is over, a city must build up new funds of potentially replaceable imports, mostly the products of other cities, if it is to experience another chain reaction. The process vastly enlarges city economies as well as diversifying them, and causes cities to grow in spurts, not evenly and gradually. The growth is by no means all net growth, however. Much import-replacing, especially in already large cities, merely compensates for losses of older work. Cities are forever losing older work; some because former customer cities take to replacing imports themselves and even become competitive producers of the items they formerly imported; some because well-established enterprises, after having first developed in the symbiotic city nest, transplant their operations to distant places like Pickens County; some because old work and many old enterprises, too, grow obsolete.

Whenever a city replaces imports with its own production, other settlements, mostly other cities, lose sales accordingly. However, these other settlements—either the same ones which have lost export sales or different ones—gain an equivalent value of *new* export work. This is because an import-replacing city does not, upon replacing former imports, import less than it otherwise would, but shifts to other purchases in lieu of what it no longer needs from outside. Economic life as a whole has expanded to the extent that the import-replacing city has everything it formerly had, *plus* its complement of new and different imports. Indeed, as far as I can see, city import-replacing is in this way at the root of all economic expansion.

It is important, if we are to understand the rise and decline of wealth, for us not to be fuzzy about an abstraction like "expansion" but to be concrete and specific about how expansion occurs and of what it consists. The expansion that derives from city import-replacing consists specifically of these five forms of growth: abruptly enlarged city markets for new and different imports consisting largely of rural goods and of innovations being produced in other cities; abruptly increased numbers and kinds of jobs in the import-replacing city; increased transplants of city work into non-urban locations as older enterprises are crowded out; new uses for technology, particularly to increase rural production and productivity; and growth of city capital.

These five great forces exert far-reaching effects outside of import-replacing cities as well as within them, ultimately rippling out even to the remotest places, like Bardou.

Henry Grady, almost a century ago, saw that the great deficiency of poverty-stricken and backward economies is that they do not produce amply and diversely for themselves, depending to a ridiculous degree on imports instead. But he made no connection between this fact and the fact that cities grow by replacing imports. The development experts of this century, for all their statistics and sophisticated, plausible-sounding schemes, have advanced not one whit beyond Henry Grady's intellectual limits. Where Grady thought in terms of regional economies, they think in terms of national economies and suffer many misconceptions.

For example, thinking in terms of national economies, they naturally think of import-replacing or import substitution as a process involving only foreign imports, blinded to the fact that replacements of domestic imports are quite as important to the expansion and development of economic life, and often more so. A city economy which does not or cannot replace domestic imports with its own production is feeble at best, and helpless at worst, when it comes to replacing foreign imports. So little is this acknowledged, although the realities are there for all to see, that we do not even have a word meaning "both the domestic and foreign purchases alike" of a city or of any other settlement. Too bad, because in the workings of a city's economy it makes no inherent difference which of its imports or how many originate within its own country and which in others, and the same is true of the destinations of its exports. Whatever the source of its imports, the consequence of replacing many kinds is improved versatility at producing and the process releases the same five great forces of economic expansion. Indeed, as we shall see later while examining why backward cities need one another, in some cases replacements of domestic imports are the only practical means of building the kind of versatility that can lead to feasible replacements of foreign imports as well.

Another unfortunate consequence of preoccupation with national economies is that development experts, like Grady in his day, do not think of import-replacing as the city process it is.

Thinking of it instead as a national process, they often advocate that already completely developed factories (producing foreign imports of course) be set down arbitrarily any place—in little towns, in the countryside, usually wherever jobs are badly needed. All this, although it goes under the name of import-replacing or import substitution, is remote from the realities of where and how the feat of replacing imports is successfully pulled off in the real world; so remote from the realities that such schemes can, and indeed have, bankrupted countries instead of helping them to prosper. Such are the practical penalties—that fall indirectly upon us all—when well-intentioned and learned people commit such a mild little sin as taking for granted old and unexamined assumptions like the mercantilist tautology that nations are salient entities for understanding the structure of economic life.

In the chapter that follows I am going to describe how the five great forces unleashed by import-replacing cities—markets, jobs, transplants, technology, capital—transform cities' own immediate hinterlands, their own regions. Then I shall describe the entirely different ways in which those same forces of cities shape regions lacking cities of their own. Later I will discuss how clusters or teams of import-replacing cities spring into being, and also why clusters or teams of formerly creative cities stagnate, with disastrous effects upon their nations. None of this can we comprehend at all by dwelling on theories about abstracted supply and demand chasing themselves around in the amorphous blurs known as national economies.

44

THREE

Cities'
Own Regions

In the hinterlands of some cities—beginning just beyond their suburbs—rural, industrial and commercial work places are all mixed up together. Such city regions are unique, being the richest, densest and most intricate of all types of economies except for cities themselves.

City regions are not defined by natural boundaries, because they are wholly the artifacts of the cities at their nuclei; the boundaries move outward—or halt—only as city economic energy dictates. The largest and densest city region in the world today is Tokyo's. As it grew over the years it vaulted over mountains so rugged that building rail lines and roads across them required spectacular feats of late-nineteenth-century engineering. The city region of Toronto, where I live, is bounded in some directions by the Great Lakes, but in other directions it simply peters out and halts on gently rolling land presenting no change in natural landscape. Boston's city region extends into the southern part of New Hampshire, a circumstance that exasperates municipal and state officials in New Hampshire who would like to see, instead, a nice even smear of economic activity over the whole state. To that end they contrive special inducements to lure Boston enterprises and people into the north, where work is badly needed, and impose special obstacles to discourage them in the south, which is already prosperous; but to little avail. For the time being, southern New Hampshire and southern Maine are as far north as Boston reaches in its capacity to reshape its own hinterland radically.

By no means do all cities generate city regions. For example, Glasgow has never done so, even though in the latter nineteenth century and the first decade of this century Glasgow was at the forefront of industry and technology, its engineers and engineered products renowned throughout the world, finding export markets far and wide. Fifty miles to its east lies Edinburgh, cultural and commercial capital of Scotland: Edinburgh has had its export triumphs too but has never generated a city region either. Not even the combined economies of the two cities have created a dense, rich mixture of city and rural activities within spaces that lie between them. Marseilles is the most important French seaport and in addition has built up considerable industry alongside its shipping work. But Marseilles has no city region to speak of, even though it is the metropolis of all of southern France. Naples in the sixteenth century was the largest city in Christendom. It enjoyed a vast export trade in dyed and woven silks, linens, laces, ribbons, braids and sweetmeats. At the time, smaller contemporaries like Milan, Paris, London, Antwerp and Amsterdam were shaping and extending true city regions, but not Naples. Rome has an amazingly small and feeble city region, considering the city's own size. Copenhagen has generated a city region, but not Dublin, Belfast, Cardiff, Liverpool, Lisbon, Madrid, Zagreb, Moscow. São Paulo has one, but not Rio de Janeiro, Buenos Aires or Montevideo. Neither Havana nor Santiago de Cuba generated one, whether before or during Castro's regime. San Juan never generated one, whether under Spanish or subsequent American rule.

In central Japan so many cities have generated city regions that they merge and overlap; but Sapporo, the chief city of Hokkaido, the large northernmost island of Japan, has not generated a city region. Atlanta, Grady's city, metropolis of the U.S. Southeast, has no city region to speak of and neither does Seattle, metropolis of the Northwest; but Los Angeles and San Francisco have both generated city regions at the western edge of the continent, and Boston and New York have both done so in the Northeast.

All the rapidly developing Pacific Rim economies contain cities that have recently and rapidly generated remarkably dense and intricate city regions: most notably Singapore, Seoul, Taipei and Hong Kong. But Manila in the Philippines has not. Hong Kong's city region has now spilled over into the adjacent province of Guangdong (Kwantung) in China, but the city of Canton itself, ancient nucleus of that province, hasn't been generating a city region of its own. Yet Shanghai has; so has the cluster of cities in Hubei province, Hankow, Hanyang and Wuhan, now sometimes jointly called Wuhan, on the lower Yangtze River. One could go on and on, pondering these incongruities.

Obviously, cities good at working up export activities or drawing visitors or serving as cultural, political or religious capitals do not necessarily generate city regions. Something more than exporting or administration is required. That something more is the capacity of the city to replace wide ranges of its imports exuberantly and repeatedly. Cities that generate city regions of any significance possess that capacity, or have possessed it in the past. The very mechanics of city import-replacing automatically decree the formation of city regions.

As mentioned in the previous chapter, city import-replacing of any significance occurs explosively and unleashes five great economic forces of expansion: city markets for new and different imports; abruptly increased city jobs; technology for increasing rural production and productivity; transplanted city work; city-generated capital. All these mighty forces surge up simultaneously in an import-replacing city, but only in the city's immediate hinterland does the full panoply come to bear simultaneously, with each of the forces exerted to a degree roughly proportional to that of the others. As we shall see later, when these forces are exerted beyond a city's own hinterland, as they also always are, they are no longer twined together.

To see what happens when all the forces are brought to bear upon the city's own hinterland or region, let us look at one Japanese hamlet which formerly was outside the Tokyo city region, and notice how it changed when the expanding Tokyo city region finally reached it in the late 1950s and incorporated it into a city regional economy. The example is extreme precisely because the Tokyo economy is so powerful, but the changes wrought here are the same in their nature as those which are wrought in all city regions everywhere.

The hamlet's experience has been described by Ronald P. Dore, a British authority on contemporary Japan and a specialist in agricultural land policies and agricultural economics. I am drawing my information from his splendid book, *Shinohata: A Portrait of a Japanese Village*, but I shall interpret the information in terms of the five great city forces for economic expansion. Dore derived his knowledge of the hamlet from a series of visits he made there over a period of twenty years, beginning in 1955 when the hamlet's traditional rural economy was still intact. So candid were the people, then and later, in disclosing to Dore their incomes, failures and successes, as well as many other matters of intimate personal and community concerns, that to protect their privacy Dore gave the place a fictitious name. But Shinohata is a real hamlet, engulfed by a real city region. It consists of forty-nine households and their lands, located about a hundred miles northwest of Tokyo (by rail and road, not as the crow flies), well beyond those rugged mountains which Tokyo's expanding city region vaulted years ago. It lies at the head of a valley up against another mountain.

In the dim and distant past, Shinohata may have been a settlement living wholly by subsistence agriculture and subsistence crafts without any city trading ties, but for as long as memory now runs, merchants from Edo, as Tokyo was formerly known, arrived from time to time; to them the people of the hamlet sold a few cash crops and in return bought a few kinds of goods such as tea and paper and earned the wherewithal to pay such taxes as were demanded in cash. The two chief cash crops in that traditional economy were rice and silk cocoons, the latter becoming increasingly important as time passed. The hamlet people also sold the merchants a little timber, small quantities of forest mushrooms gathered in season, and charcoal of their own manufacture. To get the last three products, as well as firewood for themselves, they diligently combed and recombed the forested mountain. In hard years they combed it in desperation. Forest roots, berries and herbs are still called collectively "famine food" in Shinohata.

Between 1900 and 1955, improved methods and tools increased rice yields considerably. Time saved on rice growing went into the fussy and demanding work of cocoon production, important work during the earlier part of the century when silk was still the country's chief international export. But as far as Shinohata was concerned, the returns were small. Although some families were able to earn a few untraditional goods such as bicycles, the hamlet stayed poor and life was an endless round of drudgery and anxiety, or so it seems in retrospect to those who endured it, and they ought to know.

The fates that befall traditional rural settlements tend to be drab and dispiriting when only one or another of the great city forces impinges upon them. Changing markets might well have meant worse poverty for Shinohata if the changes only meant declining demand for its traditional cash crops, as indeed markets for silk cocoons have declined. The pull of distant city jobs might simply have depopulated it, as Bardou was depopulated. A heavy influx of city technology to save farm labor, taken only by itself, might have left most of its people idle. A single transplanted city factory might have made Shinohata a company town. Or it might have come mainly to live on outside money, either earnings sent back home by sons, daughters or husbands who had left, or welfare subsidies of some sort.

In the event, however, Shinohata's fate after 1955 was radically different from any of these and from its own past as well. The moment Tokyo's expanding city region reached out to embrace Shinohata, all five forces of expansion came to bear on it, each force interplaying with the others, but let us look at them in the order previously mentioned: markets, city jobs, technology, transplants and capital.

Tokyo's expanding solvent markets for new and different imports opened up, in its own city region, practical possibilities for crop diversification. Beginning in the late 1950s, people in Shinohata found they could make good money for things never in demand from them before: table peaches, grapes, tomatoes, ornamental shrubs and trees for city gardens, and oak mushrooms, a delicacy commanding a very high price in the city, while experiments with hops, tobacco and canning peaches were failures, soon dropped. Diversification had a side effect on local diets. Shinohatans now also grow eggplant, chestnuts, Irish potatoes, radishes, carrots, strawberries, squash, lettuce and cabbage, not as significant cash crops but for their own use and gifts to one another, a polite form of barter familiar to neighborly gardeners everywhere. Since horses are now no longer necessary, some households have taken to raising beef cattle instead, and cattle manure has taken the place of horse manure for fertilizer. Only twenty of the forty-nine households were still nurturing silk cocoons in 1975, and even in these households dependence on them had much decreased. But forty-eight of the forty-nine households were still farming seriously, and of these almost all continued to grow rice. Indeed, rice yield actually increased stupendously, alongside the new cash crops.

While those changes were occurring, the multiplying city jobs in Tokyo were exerting their pull on Shinohata. Before 1956 almost nobody migrated to Tokyo; among the rare exceptions had been two sons of the schoolmaster in the previous generation, one of whom became an astronomer, the other a physician. But from 1956 on, so many young people were attracted by work and life in Tokyo that by 1975 all the children in fourteen of the households had left, while in many of the others some among the children had left. In the meantime, one outside family arrived and added a fiftieth house to the hamlet: a Tokyo professor and his wife chose it as a place for a weekend and holiday retreat. Dore surmises others like them will follow.

With people leaving the farms, and yet with demand for farm produce growing, something had to give. What gave were the old methods of doing things. Labor-saving devices were an imperative. Shinohata had experienced the classic impasse which occurs in city regions and it responded in the classic way—a way that explains why, historically, rural labor-saving devices have almost invariably first been developed in city regions and only later extended to other types of regions. In Shinohata, as labor-saving devices were rapidly acquired, both for work in the fields and work inside the houses, the productivity of individuals working the land soared. For example, by 1975 the hours necessary for rice growing were just about half what they had been in 1955, a much more rapid change than had come about in the previous half-century.

The example of soaring rural production and productivity that most astonishes me in Dore's descriptions concerns oak mushrooms. In the mid-1960s three farmers began experimenting with a new method of production. They bought logs from contractors, drilled holes in them, and inserted plugs of sawdust containing mushroom spores. They then left the stacked logs for a year and a half. After this maturing period the logs were soaked; in a few days the mushrooms sprouted, and after they were harvested, the logs were dried out and the cycle repeated. By 1975 these farmers each had forty to fifty thousand logs and were making daily shipments of mushrooms to Tokyo all year around, using heated greenhouses in the winter. "Great piles of logs are moved in metal frames from truck to dousing tank and back again by electric overhead lifters running on steel girders," Dore reports. By 1975 imitators, at smaller scale, were emerging in nearby hamlets as well. Mushrooms in huge quantities are among many, many items Tokyo can now afford to import, in place of former imports it produces for itself.

Owing to labor-saving equipment, some Shinohata farmers became able to run their operations part-time, combining agriculture with wage-earning jobs in Shinohata or its vicinity (about which more in a moment), but more commonly some members of a family farmed while others brought in wages and helped out part-time in the busiest seasons. In many families the older members took primary responsibility for the land while the young people took the jobs. Seven elderly women who were living alone in 1975 were successfully running farms by themselves, a feat impossible for either man or woman before the hamlet began drawing extensively on labor-saving equipment. In some cases purchase of equipment for farming parents was financed by their children who had taken jobs in Tokyo.

At the same time all these changes were occurring, transplanted Tokyo industries were arriving. Dore calls the most impressive of the transplants, which was also the first to arrive, only The Factory in the interests of maintaining Shinohata's anonymity, but he describes it as a huge, efficient, capital-intensive processing plant producing an unspecified food product. The enterprise features in its advertising The Factory's pure natural environment, an image enhanced by a bird sanctuary slightly setting the plant apart from the hamlet. The Factory's main economic effect upon Shinohata has not been owing to the work it provides but rather to the good price it paid for the factory and sanctuary land, most of which had been held in common by the whole hamlet. Proceeds from the sale were divided among all the households and financed much renovation, kitchen modernization and new construction which otherwise could not have been afforded so soon. One man who profited more than the others because the purchase included a good piece of his own land made a gift to the community of a water-filtration plant. One is reminded of the water system in Bardou, financed by the windfall from the motion picture company.

The reason The Factory is little depended on for employment is that its work force is small in any case, and in addition so many other new enterprises arrived soon after. Shinohata itself has four more: a factory that buys waste from The Factory and recycles it into animal feed; a structural-steel fabricating yard; a building-materials supply yard; and an electrical shop where centrifugal separators used in medical and chemical analyses are repaired. This last enterprise was started by a Shinohata man who first worked for a time in the Tokyo factory where the equipment is manufactured. Wanting to return to Shinohata, he persuaded his employer to give him the district repair franchise.

These transplants of city work convey scant idea, however, of the wide range of nonagricultural livelihoods that have opened up because Shinohata is now intricately connected economically with other settlements in the valley and beyond, in a fashion foreign to the old economy but typical of settlements incorporated into city regions. For example, in one family the wife works in an underwear factory transplanted into a nearby hamlet; her husband has a job in a dye works. In another household the husband works for a Factory subcontractor, his wife sells life insurance, while one son has become an apprentice cook at a big Tokyo airport hotel. Another man has an office job in Sano, the bustling prefectural administrative center and market town twenty-five miles down the valley. Another drives a truck for an electric company in the next prefecture; another works for a lumber firm; another has become a guard, appointed by the receivers, for a small factory which he himself started but which went bankrupt. One man has become an agricultural extension agent specializing in potatoes, while another works for a nearby agricultural experiment station. Several men are among the thirty-five employees of the township agricultural cooperative, the township being an administrative unit embracing a group of hamlets with 1,300 households, about 5,000 people. The granary division of a collection of township cooperatives has started a factory of its own, specifically to provide part-time and off-season jobs for young farmers. One Shinohata man who first found work at a commercial trout pond in a nearby village left that when his wife got a construction job earning "a man's wage." This enables her to support her husband, who does a bit of farming but whose chief preoccupation is nature study, an interest he could formerly have indulged only at the price of extreme poverty.

In its nooks and crannies, this new economy affords niches for people who, like the man studying nature, would either have been frustrated or very poor in the old Shinohata. For example, the hamlet itself together with the local Shinto shrine and several owners of tree plantations who are too busy with other things to attend to their timber, jointly employ a worker whose function was unknown in the past: a forester, hired to look after the mountain. He is the last remaining member of a family that had never been successful. In fact, its members had been the local ne'er-do-wells, but he is a success as the forester. A man Dore calls "the eloquent scoundrel" of the hamlet lives by what he picks up as a go-between and mediator. Actually, the need for his services has declined because, with affluence, conflicts among neighbors have dwindled, partly because people have so many other concerns more interesting to them than squabbling and partly because it has become easy to be generous with one another. Even though the mediator's work has dwindled, his income hasn't because his clients find it easy to be generous to him too. One young woman does nothing except watch over and play with her toddler. The other young women have no wish to emulate her, says Dore, but she is envied by the older women, who remember their own unrelieved drudging outdoors and in, at the time they were young mothers. The forest, no longer combed day in and day out, is in effect almost the private preserve of the forester and has grown wilder. Bears and boars have returned to it; a new niche in the new economy has opened for them, too.

By 1975 the hamlet was deriving less than half its total income from agriculture, but that was not because income from farming had declined; on the contrary, it had increased.

While all these changes were occurring, the fifth great city force, capital, was working its changes too. Politics in the township, says Dore, is mainly about roads, bridges, schools and irrigation channels "and the gentle art of getting central government subsidies for these things." In the aggregate, public expenditures have been financed 15 percent by the township itself and 40 percent by the prefectural and national treasuries in the form of routinized grants for generalized public purposes; the other 45 percent has come in the form of special grants for specific purposes. The most important other infusions of city-derived capital have been the land price paid by The Factory, as previously mentioned, and the subsidy which the government builds into the price of rice, a subsidy ultimately paid by city consumers.

Among the special grants from which Shinohata has benefited, the most important was the consequence of a typhoon and flood in 1959. Back in 1814, the government's official gazeteer called the river that tumbles down the mountain and through the valley "the great curse of the district. It brings down so much sand and rock that it fills up all its channels and the bed is constantly rising. The dikes have to be constantly raised. In some places the water level can rise to six or ten feet above the level of the surrounding fields and inevitably, some times, it breaks through, pouring sand and rocks onto the rice fields which it takes years to remove." That disaster happened, on the average, about once each generation in Shinohata and was one reason the old hamlet sometimes had desperate recourse to famine food.

When the disaster recurred in 1959, a recovery grant paid for equipment and labor to rehabilitate the fields quickly and was followed by funds for huge improved concrete dikes and for clearing the riverbed of boulders. This was followed by gravel excavation, with two objectives. The excavations have lowered the riverbed itself, and have provided gravel mix for concrete— much of it bought by builders in Tokyo, yet another manifestation of the city's market for goods of its own region. When Dore revisited Shinohata in 1975, a stream of trucks was still hauling gravel from the river and the work showed no sign of abating. In retrospect, people in Shinohata speak of the 1959 typhoon as one of the greatest strokes of luck to befall the hamlet because of the improvements it instigated, which Shinohata could not possibly have afforded to undertake on its own.

It is tempting to attribute Shinohata's economic transformations to the industriousness, intelligence and resourcefulness of its people. But people in the transformed Shinohata are the first to admit that their forebears worked harder than they do. As for resourcefulness, it takes more of that to make straw rain capes, as the people of old Shinohata did, than to go to a store and buy rain gear as Shinohatans do today. Considering how little they had to work with, the people of old Shinohata were unbelievably resourceful. Their present-day descendants are the "same" people— some of them literally the same individuals, in fact. What has changed is not their attributes as human beings, but rather the fact that city markets, jobs, technology, transplants and capital all came to bear upon Shinohata simultaneously, massively and in reasonable proportion to one another. The transformations are inexplicable in other terms.

The region of my city, Toronto, is much smaller, much less vigorous economically, and much less dense than Tokyo's city region, as well as somewhat less flexible in the way families combine farming with other work. Nevertheless, the towns and villages that lie within the Toronto region display analogous agglomerations and mixtures of rural and industrial work places. Between 1950 and 1971, a period during which Toronto massively replaced former imports (although, unlike Tokyo, largely in the uncreative form of welcoming branch plants to produce things formerly imported), almost two thousand manufacturing enterprises are recorded as having transplanted themselves out of the city. A very few left for far distant places. Many others moved only into Toronto suburbs. But many migrated beyond the suburbs, yet remained within the city's immediate hinterland —far enough out to gain advantages of cheap space but still close enough to remain in reasonably easy touch with their suppliers of producers' goods and services and their city and city regional markets. Branch plants, arriving from outside, acted on the same considerations.

Just as in Shinohata, young people from rural settlements in what has become the Toronto city region (which is nicknamed the Golden Horseshoe) have moved into the city job market; it is no big thing to do that. There they have joined city immigrants from very distant places as well.

Every Saturday morning in downtown Toronto one can go to a huge and splendid farmers' market. It used to be held outdoors from the backs of the farmers' trucks, but by the late 1960s its size and popularity justified a new all-weather market building. Of course, busy and big though it is, this market accounts for only a tiny percentage of the city's purchases of food and other rural goods, and even only a tiny percentage of the fraction of those purchases the city buys from its own region. But in the market one finds symbolized the same peculiarity to be seen in modern Shinohata's output: the diversity of rural goods a city buys from its own region, as compared with the sparse assortment of cash crops destined for markets other than a regional city or cities. For example, apples are among the rural cash crops of the Toronto city region, finding markets both within the region and outside it. Not many different kinds of apples are grown for markets outside the region: McIntosh, Delicious, Golden Delicious, Spies, Cortlands, Russets, Spartans; that is about it. These are of course available and popular in Toronto, too. But in the farmers' market one also finds, in season, apples that seldom leave the region: Wealthies, Baxters, Snows, Lobo, Melbas, Humes, Wolf Rivers, Ida Reds, Pola Reds, Tydeman Reds, Blenheim Orange, Orange Pippins, Empires, St. Lawrence, Cravens, Lady, Dutchess, Delaware, Transparents, Gravensteins, Sweets, Tolmans, Mutsu (a Japanese variety recently adopted). The same phenomenon can be seen in the farmers' markets of lesser cities within Toronto's region, at Hamilton, Kitchener and Waterloo. Without these city markets, right in the region itself, there simply would be no solvent markets for this diversity of apples.

The man from whom I buy marigold seedlings in the market invited me to see where they are grown. It turned out to be in a hamlet smaller than Shinohata, nothing more than what is called a-wide-place-in-the-road. His big efficient greenhouses are impressive, but they are not the only notable things in this subhamlet about thirty miles distant from Toronto. It contains several small potteries, whose wares are sold largely through outlets in Toronto, and a rather expensive restaurant, favored by customers both from the city and from other settlements in the region. This subhamlet is the kind of thing one finds in city regions, reflecting in its microscopic way diversified agglomerations of work to be found throughout the region.

City regions, like cities themselves, pack a lot of economic life into surprisingly small geographic compass. Copenhagen and its city region, for example, occupy only a small portion of Denmark's territory, yet subtract them and there goes the chief part of Denmark's total economy, almost all its economic diversity, and more than half its population. When regional populations are especially heavily concentrated, we find the concentrations are owing to city regions. The exceptionally heavily populated southeastern part of England, for example, is not only owing to the population of London and its suburbs, but also to the London city region.

Most readers of this book likely live either in cities and their suburbs or in city regions. Although the economies of city regions are incomparably more complex than those of any other types of economies except cities themselves, city regions are easy for most of us to comprehend intellectually because—in spite of their many imperfections and problems—they inherently make a kind of sense we tend to assume an economy making sense ought to embody: city regions produce amply and diversely for their own people and producers as well as for others. As we shall see, they are the only kinds of regional economies that do.

When a city at the nucleus of a city region stagnates and declines, it does so because it no longer experiences from time to time significant episodes of import-replacing. Gradually the stag-nated city's economy becomes both thinner and out-of-date. It fails to compensate, with new and different export work, for losses of its older exports, and so grows poorer as a market for its own region, for other cities, and for regions lacking cities as well. Its practical problems and those of its region pile up unsolved. Idle-ness grows. The region of an economically declining city does not revert to its former, largely rural condition. For a long time it retains its characteristic of being a mixed and intricate econ-omy, but the region's economic life slowly grows thinner and backward, too. The regional fabric develops holes and tatters as it were. Young people who leave settlements within the region for city jobs tend to bypass the region's own city or cities and go, instead, to distant cities if work there is open to them. For a long time, transplants of city work continue to leak out into the region, but that is no longer because they are being crowded out of the city by younger enterprises. Rather, they flee unsolved city prob-lems, leaving emptiness behind. Eventually the transplants cease flowing, their source having dried up.

City regions have many of the characteristics of import-replacing cities themselves, but they are not cities. For better or for worse, they are the creatures of their nuclear cities and they remain so.

FOUR

Supply Regions

Upon its own hinterland, as we have seen, all the forces of a city are brought to bear together and in roughly reasonable balance with one another. Not so when those same forces reach into distant regions, as they always do. It is as if the net of complete economic ties with which a city binds its own hinterland unravels at the borders of a city region. The various strands—markets, jobs, technology, transplants and capital—separate from the mesh and take off by themselves, each in its own idiosyncratic directions. In this fashion, cities shape stunted and bizarre economies in distant regions.

The most important among such economic grotesques are supply regions. They are disproportionately shaped by the markets of distant cities. Supply regions are often poor, and thus the stultification of their economies is often attributed to their poverty, but a rich supply region is as stunted and stultified as a poor one. The shortcomings of these regions go deeper than poverty. Indeed, sooner or later the shortcomings compel poverty.

Uruguay, as an example, was an unusually rich supply region for several generations. Uruguay made a big success of animal husbandry. It supplied meat, wool and leather to distant markets, mostly those of cities and city regions in Europe, and it produced little else but wool, meat and leather. Yet it lacked for nothing because whatever Uruguay did not produce, it could afford to import.

This was no country of downtrodden peasants dominated by big landlords. Most of the population had immigrated from Europe in the latter half of the nineteenth century, and to spur immigration the government had encouraged homesteading. The countryside was settled by self-reliant farmers and ranchers who worked hard and efficiently on their own fertile holdings, using little hired labor because wages in Uruguay were very high. Beginning in 1911, the country was able to start building what became probably the world's most generous and fully rounded welfare state. It outdid Scandinavia. There were no extremes of poverty or wealth; education was universal and accessible right through university levels. Montevideo, the capital city, prospered as an administrative, educational, cultural and distributing and shipping center. Jobs in the city were easy to come by, well paid, and easy to do because usually there wasn't all that much work entailed. Those who hadn't gone in for advanced professional education could find work in the overstaffed offices of the government or in the modern and well-equipped meat-packing and refrigerating plants and tanneries, in construction work or service jobs, or in the work of receiving, wholesaling and retailing the ample and varied imports that poured into the country from afar.

Uruguayans euphorically took to calling their country "the Switzerland of South America," a comparison suggested by the nation's small size, its beautiful mountains, its stability, and its commitment to democracy. Of course, national self-flattery should not be taken literally, but this example is interesting, for it is as far off the mark, economically, as it is possible for a comparison to be. One need only reflect how limited an economy Switzerland would have if the Swiss had simply concentrated on raising and processing animals for distant markets and dividing up the take, neglecting to develop their economic life further.

During the 1940s and early 1950s, Uruguay's already prosperous economy boomed phenomenally and imports kept pouring in. Mostly they consisted of consumers' goods because the country had so little use for producers' goods or raw materials. Nevertheless, the imports did include such goods as refrigerating units for the meat-packing plants, cranes for loading and unloading ships, sheep shears, knives, turbines, structural steel, file cabinets, elevators, x-ray machines, restaurant stoves, paper, telephone switchboards and the thousand and one other things necessary to keep the advanced communication and transportation systems operating, along with the hospitals, schools, government offices, theaters and concert halls, ranches, farms and packing plants.

Then, about 1953, things began to go wrong for Uruguay. Meat and wool production had revived in war-damaged and war-distorted economies and was now expanding to the point that countries like France were becoming preoccupied with protecting their own meat and wool producers from competition, while ranchers in Australia and New Zealand, among others, were seeking to enlarge their own markets and were succeeding (at the time) in doing so. In the meantime, moreover, manufactured substitutes for wool and leather had been invented and developed in Europe and America, and their production and sales had begun expanding.

Uruguay's distant markets for meat, wool and leather rapidly dwindled in volume, while prices declined too. This meant, of course, that Uruguay could no longer earn the ample imports it once did. It must either go without things on which it had come to depend or else try to obtain these things in a different way. The two possibilities for doing the latter were to develop alternate kinds of export work or to produce more kinds of goods in Uruguay itself for domestic use—replace wide ranges of imports with local production instead of importing almost everything. Since the country was producing nothing, even at a small scale, that could quickly and feasibly be expanded into alternate exports wanted or needed in distant solvent markets, the government decided to embark on a program of what it called import substitution.

This consisted of a crash industrialization program, based on building ambitious, complete factories producing such items as steel, textiles, shoes, electrical equipment. The result was a fiasco. When the factories could get into production at all, what they produced cost so much more than equivalent imports that people and other enterprises in Uruguay simply couldn't afford to buy the goods. In the meantime, to build and equip the factories and to feed them with materials and parts had required so many imports, and such expensive ones, that to finance the program the government first exhausted its reserves, then had to buy the necessary imports on credit, then became unable to pay interest on the loans. The country was bankrupt.

Unaware that feasible import-replacing is a city process, the government economists and planners had located the factories in whatever sections of the country needed work most badly. This would have ensured failure of the scheme in any case, but as it happened, in Uruguay it did not much matter where the locations were. Even had the factories all been clustered in or close to Montevideo, the scheme could not have worked because Montevideo itself lacked the ranges of skills, the symbiotic nests of producers' goods and services, and the practice at improvising and adapting necessary to make import-replacing a practical economic endeavor. Montevideo, never having replaced a wide range of its imports in the past or produced anything else much, had no foundation for the kind of versatile production that was now desperately needed.

The welfare benefits and transfer payments which had spread the country's wealth—meaning its import-purchasing power—could no longer be supported. Trying to support them anyhow, the government resorted to the printing press. Inflation raged. As prices and unemployment rose together and as poverty spread and intensified, the country became socially chaotic and politically distraught. Violent civil strife broke out. Half a million citizens, about a sixth of the population, fled the country. Over the rest, ultimately, a brutal military dictatorship restored a kind of peace and order—the peace and order of an economic graveyard. By 1980 the average purchasing power of consumers was only half of what it had been in 1968 at the time of the crash industrialization attempt, and in 1968 it had already fallen far below what it had been in 1950. Today Uruguay is painfully, drably and chancily attempting to build a new supply economy based on low wages, tourism and bargain leather and woolen goods exports—bargains because wages of workers producing them are now pitifully low. Even these pathetic export earnings are little help as far as living standards are concerned; a third of the earnings are eaten by interest payments on the renegotiated long-term debts and much of the rest goes for imported fuel.

Today Uruguay has what is called a Third World economy, but even when it was prospering, Uruguay had a Third World economy insofar as that term conveys backwardness, lack of development. Uruguay had merely been rich, and the difference between a rich backward economy and a poor backward economy is not all that great. Rich or poor, supply regions are inherently overspecialized and wildly unbalanced economies, hence unresilient and fragile, helpless when they lose their fragments of distant markets. The disasters that befell Uruguay are the nightmares that trouble the rulers of currently rich oil supply regions, and with good reason.

It may be tempting to lay Uruguay's economic troubles to incompetence, fecklessness, lack of foresight, self-indulgence and the like. But actually, Uruguayans ran their supply economy competently and responsibly, as well as humanely. What they did do, they did well. What they did not do was create a productive city for themselves—a city replacing wide ranges of its imports from time to time in the normal course of growth, and thus automatically generating a complex and many-sided city region producing amply and diversely for its own people and producers as well as for others. As to why neither Montevideo nor any other settlements in Uruguay developed in such a fashion, for the time being we had best suspend judgment. Later in this book I will discuss what Montevideo and cities like it are up against.

For the moment, the point I want to pursue is the inherently crippled economic situation of supply regions that remain supply regions, that do not create import-replacing cities. The reason such regions are specialized and narrow is that, in the first place, their production for others so overwhelmingly outweighs production for themselves. That unbalance is exaggerated even further because of two peculiarities of the distant city markets on which supply regions depend, peculiarities which we can see at work on Uruguay. First, the distant markets were highly selective about what they wanted from Uruguay. Second, although the distant markets were composed of the markets of different cities and city regions, they were so much in agreement as to what they wanted from Uruguay that in effect they acted as one. This concerted selectivity is an enormously powerful force. When it comes to bear upon a region as a single force, unmediated by other city forces, it is irresistible as a shaper of narrow economic specialization.

These two traits of city markets drawing supplies from distant regions are deep-seated. They long predate modern transportation, communication and industries, as well as modern mass markets. In late medieval times, for instance, Sardinia was exporting cheese to all the cities of Europe: nothing *but* cheese. Obviously its distant city markets were both selective and concerted in what they wanted from Sardinia. In Renaissance times, various rural supply regions of Poland were supplying wheat, rye and forest products to cities throughout western and northern Europe, yet nothing else of moment. The Canary Islands at the same time were supplying cane sugar to all the European cities, but nothing else. They were the prototype for the later one-crop sugar islands of the West Indies. Further back in time, the Etruscan cities of what is now northern Italy, and then after them, republican Rome, evidently wanted nothing of Elba but iron, and wanted it concertedly. One is reminded of ancient Bardou, from which the markets wanted iron, nothing but iron, and wanted it powerfully enough to justify those splendid roads to the mountain mines. I mention these few examples not because they are either freakish or extreme, but rather because they are so typical historically of trade between supply regions and distant cities.

It is the same today. Zambia supplies copper to distant markets, yet almost nothing but copper. New Zealand supplies cheese, butter, meat and wool, little else—and is suffering from dwindling markets. To take two examples from Canada, New Brunswick supplies fish, pulp, paper and timber, almost nothing else; Saskatchewan supplies wheat, potash and (in one nook) oil, little else. Wales and the mountainous area of eastern United States called Appalachia have supplied coal, not a great deal else, although recently the powerful market of Hong Kong has begun buying ginseng from Appalachia, about $30 million worth a year, a lot of money to the poor American mountaineers who do the arduous work of finding the forest roots and digging them up with mattocks. But ginseng is the only thing Hong Kong wants from Appalachia. The whole world buys oil from Saudi Arabia and

Kuwait, and almost nothing but oil. There is nothing the world's cities and city regions want so concertedly from south and central Scotland as barley in the form of Scotch whiskey.

Sometimes the concertedness of many distant markets, acting to form a huge joint market, is cloaked behind the political or commercial power of a single city; but a multiple, concerted market is there just the same. Hong Kong doesn't consume all that ginseng. Although the rye, wheat and forest products of old Poland were distributed to dozens of cities in Renaissance times, the sales appeared to be made to Amsterdam. That was because prices were set there and many of the deliveries arranged there, which in turn was because Amsterdam merchants had built up the trade and had kept their hold on it as further markets opened up. Lisbon merchants handled all the trade in Canary Islands sugar, but that didn't mean the citizens of Lisbon consumed it all or even that the confectioners of Lisbon manufactured all the sweetmeats and bonbons of Europe. When France possessed Vietnam, much of the trade was controlled from Paris, but just the same, the zinc, tin and cinnamon showed up at docks from Baltimore to Hamburg. The fact that people in old Shinohata sold their cocoons to Tokyo—at the time when Shinohata still had merely a supply economy—should not blind us to the fact that it was the concerted markets of Milan, Lyons, New York and many other places that caused Shinohata and other settlements like it to specialize so heavily on cocoon production. Trade in bananas, the chief crop nowadays of the Canary Islands, is controlled by the Spanish government. "We have to sell all our bananas to Madrid" is the way a farmer there puts it; nevertheless, the bananas are shipped to all the wholesale city produce markets in western Europe, exactly the same markets that get Canary Islands vegetables and flowers, which do not happen to be channeled through a central control and pricing point.

The narrow specialization of supply regions is sometimes obscured statistically by lumping the various specializations into lists of national exports which can be impressive in their diversity. Canada's list, for example, is a long and varied one; but of the various different supply regions within Canada, some of them geographically enormous, each actually supplies only a few specialized items—the consolidated list of wheat, hydroelectric power, rapeseed, potash, coal, gas, nickel, gold, silver, zinc, cobalt, fish, timber, furs, apples, cherries, paper and so on, notwithstanding. In Canada, the newest supply regions are the most prosperous. The old ones, in the Atlantic Provinces, have become poor over the course of time and they too would have obvious Third World economies if they were not heavily, continually and ever-increasingly subsidized from richer parts of the country, such as Toronto and its city region.

As time passes, formerly prosperous supply regions succumb to many hazards. Depletion of resources is common. Overfishing, "too many fishermen, not enough fish," as they say in Nova Scotia, has, along with timber depletion, played a part in impoverishment of some eastern Canadian supply regions. Sicily lost its position as Europe's pre-eminent supplier of wheat, a disaster from which it has never really recovered, in part owing to depletion of its overexploited soil; competition from the Americas was an additional reason.

New substitutes for old products are a hazard, one which contributed to Uruguay's decline. The least change in the way things are done can work havoc in supply regions. When American manufacturers began bagging cement in paper reinforced with artificial instead of natural fibers, and fertilizer in plastics, Tanzania suffered drastically from loss of markets for sisal, Bangladesh from loss of markets for jute, and the Philippines from loss of markets for hemp. The emergence of new products in place of old ones is absolutely necessary to economic life; otherwise the planet would long since have been ruined from excessive, monotonous exploitation of the same few resources. Still, substitutions are hard on supply regions that have lost markets for sealskins, zinc, tin, linen, coal, copper . . .

Economic competition is a hazard. Kent County, New Brunswick, in eastern Canada, can stand as illustration. In 1910 it was one of Canada's most prosperous rural counties, but competition from agricultural supply regions in the west reduced its acreage under cultivation by almost two-thirds; its 3,400 viable farms of the past have declined to 700, which are struggling and poor.

Political arrangements—with economic competition behind

them—are a hazard. Beginning in the 1970s, New Zealand has lost distant markets at a rate almost as drastic as Uruguay's losses starting twenty years earlier. In 1980, New Zealand's dwindling exports were buying only two-thirds the imports they commanded in 1973, and farm income, on which virtually all New Zealand's economy ultimately rests, had declined 40 percent. Although New Zealand is one of the world's least densely populated countries, people had begun emigrating at such a rate that net population was declining year after year. New Zealand glories in the slogan "The world's most efficient farm." It probably is, just as Uruguay was probably the world's most efficient ranch.

New political arrangements helped do in both Uruguay and New Zealand, and behind those arrangements are the plights of western Europe's old agricultural supply regions, especially those of France. Although France would seem to have plenty of cities, it does not have plenty of import-replacing cities. In all present-day France there is now really only one significant city region, that of Paris. Most of rural France thus consists of economically stunted supply regions. To protect them and other European agricultural supply regions, the countries of the European Economic Community jointly discriminate in their favor, so as to overcome competition from outside. If the EEC did not do so, it would simply have to subsidize rural Europe even more heavily than it does. Agricultural subsidies, as it is, account for three quarters of the EEC budget. Uruguay was an early victim of EEC tariffs and marketing agreements to aid Europe's own supply regions and their people. New Zealand's turn as victim came somewhat later because its chief European markets were in Britain, and Britain did not join the EEC until 1973. Political arrangements having such effects tell us that too many supply regions are jostling for the solvent markets of too few vigorous cities and city regions.

In the United States, the largest agricultural export—indeed the largest export item of any kind—is now soybeans and soybean products, largely destined for the powerful markets of Japanese cities and city regions. In the mid-1970s, noting that consumption of American vegetable oils was dropping owing to U.S. imports of palm oil, the National Soybean Processors' Association began calling for quotas on palm-oil imports from Malaysia and Africa, and an end to American loans to Third World countries if the loans were helping them undertake palm-oil production. Reporting on this situation, the *Wall Street Journal* commented: "But if soybean processors are worried about the threat of foreign palm oil, they should take a look at what . . . Third World nations are thinking of diversifying into next: soybeans themselves . . ."

Poor countries, the *Journal* report continued, depending as they do on "three or fewer raw materials for the bulk of the export earnings they need to pay for vital imports" do well to add production of vegetable oils to their repertoires but "this reasoning isn't appreciated in the United States." On the contrary, the reasoning is well appreciated in the United States. This was exactly the reasoning of American farmers themselves in cotton, corn or wheat supply regions when they added soybeans to their repertoires. Ordinarily we do not think about the similarities of supply regions in rich and poor nations, but occasionally, as in this instance, the underlying similarities of their economies rise startlingly into the open.

Added to all the other hazards to which the narrow and fragile economies of supply regions are subject is something that might be described as "comparative poverty." Over the course of time, as distant cities' economies and products develop, imports available to supply regions tend to grow more complex, various and expensive. Agricultural or raw-material exports of supply regions that were ample for buying steel penpoints, harness hardware and decorative balustrades do not stretch so far when they must earn typewriters, trucks and elevators. This type of comparative poverty has insidiously crept into the workings of all the older supply regions in Canada, the United States and Europe.

Supply regions are often said to have colonial economies. The term embodies this piece of truth: imperial powers have typically shaped conquered territories into supply regions. Often enough, they have also deliberately forestalled conquered territories from engaging in production for their own people and producers, in the interests of keeping the conquered people as captive markets for manufactured goods produced by cities of the imperial powers themselves. Although it is by no means one of the more gruesome examples, the economic reshaping of Indochina by the French, as described by Frances Fitzgerald in *Fire in the Lake*, can stand as illustration:

France had first to transform what was essentially a subsistence economy serving the Vietnamese peasants and landlords into an economy that produced surpluses for the international market. Given the particular geography of the country, the French enterprises consisted of the creation of large plantations and the development of mines to extract the rich deposits of coal, zinc and tin . . . To encourage and support the establishment of French colonists and entrepreneurs, the French administration built roads, canals, railroads and market cities linking the Vietnamese interior with the shipping routes. These public works benefited the French almost exclusively at the time, but the French officials financed them largely by an increase of taxes on the Vietnamese peasantry.

The taxes, she continues, were levied according to the practice prevailing in metropolitan France, in money instead of in kind. French government monopolies were also established over trade in matches, alcohol and opium, and the prices of these commodities were raised to six times their previous levels. The combination of the price rises and the taxes greatly increased the number of impoverished people available for hire on the plantations and in the mines.

When Canadian workers in supply regions grumble, as they occasionally do, that they are locked into dead-end "colonial" economies, they do not mean they are being bled like the Vietnamese to finance public works essential to getting out the nickel, the newsprint, the wheat, the logs, the frozen fish fillets and the fish fertilizer. Taxes from urban Canada, and to a lesser extent profits of the resource industries themselves are drawn on for these purposes. Nor do the grumbles mean that the workers wish the mills would close down or distant markets evaporate; on the contrary—that's just what the complaining workers most dread when they think of the shortcomings of economic "colonialism."

The trouble with loosely calling all supply regions "colonial" economies is that the term is too optimistic. By reverse implication it suggests that if alien domination of some sort is thrown off, a stunted, narrow economy will no longer remain stunted and narrow, will proceed to become better rounded and capable of producing amply and diversely on its own behalf as well as for others. To be sure, there are often good reasons for throwing off alien domination or influence: reasons that are politically, socially, culturally and emotionally important and sometimes economically important as well. Yet, as should be clear by now, the stultification of supply regions and the fragility of their economies are not so simply or easily corrected as the epithet "colonial" suggests. When Fidel Castro disposed of American influence in Cuba he did not throw off Cuba's servitude to sugar.

Many a supply region, far from being forced into its role, simply slides into it for sheer default of alternatives. "Saved Alberta Town, Japanese Firms Say," a Canadian newspaper headline happily shouts. The news item goes on to tell that a group of ten Japanese companies has agreed to import coking coal from the mining town of Grand Cache, and that the contract will give the town at least two more years of life. "Without buyers of its coal," the article explains, "Grand Cache with a population of some 4,000 would have no way but to collapse." Alberta is energy-rich in much the way Uruguay was cattle- and sheep-rich.

Supply economies have their intellectual enthusiasts on the grounds that their specialties represent division of labor at regional or international scale, that division of labor is efficient, and therefore that supply economies form and persist because the arrangement is efficient. Adam Smith, for one, believed this. The thought has two major flaws.

In the first place, the reasoning is teleological. It assumes that a result—in this case efficiency—is its own cause. One might as well say that rain is beneficial to plants and that that is why it rains. We come closer to understanding the causes of supply regions by understanding, first, that economic forces originating in import-replacing cities shape economic life outside of cities, and second, that when the force at issue is the power of city markets bearing upon regions that lack import-replacing cities of their own, the results are specialized regions. We come closer to understanding why supply regions persist if we reflect that given forces lack the power to reverse their own effects. Quite other forces must come into play. Ibn Khaldun, a Tunisian scholar and historian, back in 1381 explained that the Bedouins of the desert who sold animal products and grain to urban people would remain economically dependent "as long as they live in the desert and have not acquired . . . control of the cities." True to a point. But he might have added: "—or as long as they do not create a city of their own."

The second flaw of the efficiency argument is that supply economies are not efficient in any case. That is why they are commonly so poor or else are subsidized. To be sure, their specialties are sometimes (not always) efficiently produced. But that is not the same as saying these economies are efficient. An economy that contains few different sorts of niches for people's differing skills, interests and imaginations is not efficient. An economy that is unresourceful and unadaptable is not efficient. An economy that can fill few of the needs of its own people and producers is not efficient. To say that the economy of Uruguay, "the Switzerland of South America," was more efficient because more specialized than the economy of Switzerland is to stand reality on its head.

Although supply regions are warped into their specialized and unbalanced forms by distant cities, those distant cities are powerless to straighten them out. Only cities of their own can do that service for supply regions. Historically, many supply regions have been cradles of import-replacing cities. And as we can observe today, Hong Hong, Singapore and Seoul—unlike Montevideo, Havana and Wellington—have managed to transcend their once limited functions as administrative and distributive centers for supply regions. Now they provide markets for supply regions.

FIVE

Regions
Workers Abandon

Since 1921, Wales has lost a third of its population. Its countryside is dotted with deserted cottages; fields lie unused where
gardens and grain used to grow or sheep grazed. Whole hamlets
have vanished, the buildings crumbled, burned out or pulled
down, their traces left for future archaeologists to rediscover and
perhaps to wonder or conjecture over. The rural Welsh left because they were fed up with the poverty and narrowness of the
old supply economy in which they were trapped. The chief settlement, the economically inert little city of Cardiff, offered few
opportunities, and so, most people seeking city work or better
incomes left Wales entirely.

Just so, large sections of Sicily and Spain that once were heavily
populated now lie almost empty. Even in rich countries there are
abandoned regions. I come from one such, a stagnated anthracite
coal supply region in northeastern Pennsylvania; its two chief
settlements, Scranton and Wilkes-Barre, are less populated today
than when I was a child in the 1920s, and even then people in
search of city jobs were beginning to leave: usually for New York
and its region if they came from around Scranton, or for Philadelphia and its region if they were from Wilkes-Barre. In Ontario,
outside the city region of Toronto are many settlements now so
deserted by the young and the middle-aged that "the old [are]
looking after the old."

The difference between stagnant regions that lose populations and stagnant regions where people stay put is simply that people from places like Scranton, Wales and the deserted parts of Ontario can have realistic hopes of doing better somewhere else and have the means to get there, while people in such stagnant places as Haiti, where most people stay put, lack a way of getting out or a place to go to. Ethiopia, like Haiti, is one of the poorest countries in the world today, yet almost nobody leaves Ethiopia to take jobs in distant cities, for Ethiopians have no places to go and no means of escape. The same is true of many people in regions from which some citizens actually do break away: the Caribbean islands are an example, along with parts of Latin America, India, the Middle East and the Mediterranean countries of Africa. If people in all stagnant regions were to have ample access to city work, no matter how distant, we may be reasonably sure that virtually all poor, stagnant regions in the world today would be losing populations at a great rate.

This is not to say that people in stagnant regions have little attachment to them or that most people actually like migrating. Especially if one must leave a familiar culture for a strange one or put oneself at a great distance from home and family, emigration to escape poverty and lack of opportunity must be a painful and bitter choice between the lesser of two evils.

What I am concerned with here is not the destinations of migrants, but rather the regions they abandon and how these regions are affected by people leaving. The most striking fact is that abandonment has no effect upon stagnant economies—other than to shrink them. Take old Bardou, for example. For almost seventy years—long enough, one would suppose, for a shrinking population to alter the nature of Bardou's economy if it could— people kept trickling away to take jobs in distant Paris. As the population diminished, so did Bardou's economy, but otherwise nothing changed. Of course, the people who got to Paris totally tranformed their own economic lives, but those left behind remained in the usual poverty—which is why they kept on leaving. In rural Wales as well, those who stayed on stayed poor, no matter how many of their neighbors left; that is why they kept on leaving. Sicily, for all its abandoned farms and depopulated settlements, is still poor and still has high unemployment. When places people abandon do come to economic life again, it is owing to reasons other than desertions, reasons such as the transplanted work that some of the current inhabitants of Bardou have brought along with them.

I have been arguing that the only forces which transform regional economies, whether for better or for worse, are the five great forces which originate in import-replacing cities: their markets, jobs, technology, transplants and capital; and that when one of these forces reaches disproportionately into distant regions that lack import-replacing cities of their own, the result is bizarre and unbalanced. In the case of regions that people abandon, the disproportionate force is, of course, the pull of distant city jobs. This force can depopulate a region, but it cannot do anything to transform the region's economy.

To be sure, migrants from abandoned regions often send home money from their distant city jobs, and temporary migrants, when they return, often bring back savings. Over the past thirty years, tens of millions of workers have left poor villages in stagnant regions of Egypt, Turkey, Italy, Greece, Yugoslavia, Morocco, Algeria, Spain, Portugal and the Azores to work on contract in cities and city regions of northern Europe. Most have had dependents at home. In the aggregate, the remittances they have sent back have not been paltry. In Turkey and Yugoslavia, for example, migrants' remittances in many years are reported to have been the largest single sources of foreign funds, exceeding those countries' earnings from their leading exports of goods or from tourism. Yet when workers have returned, their villages have proved no better able to support them than when they left. In 1974, when unemployment rose abruptly and appreciably in northern Europe for the first time since World War II, and large numbers of "guest workers" lost their jobs and flooded home— half a million from West Germany alone—the returning workers returned to the same unemployment and underemployment they had left. It was the same story six years later, when northern European unemployment rose again and many migrant workers returned home.

Offhand one might assume that at least the additional incomes which abandoned regions receive from their migrants would change their economies, perhaps even set them on the road to development, but in real life that does not happen. Remittances, while they last, do alleviate poverty in abandoned regions, just as any forms of transfer payments from rich to poor regions alleviate poverty while they last. The money buys imports for people and institutions which they would otherwise have to go without, but that is all it does. Loss of workers' remittances has imposed import austerity in Yugoslavia and has even played its part in the country's difficulties in meeting loan obligations. Yet even though remittances were large enough to make such differences, they did nothing to convert stagnation to development.

Consider, in this light, a village named Napizaro in a poor region of central Mexico, several hundred miles to the northwest of Mexico City. For about forty years Napizaro has been heavily subsidized by migrant workers. Almost everyone in the region containing Napizaro used to live by farming, and many still do—mostly subsistence farming, although some practice a bit of cash cropping. The families who depend only on subsistence farming are known locally, for good reason, as the *morosos*, those without hope. Their lives are inconceivably grim. But a couple of generations ago a new factor entered the lives of some of these people: the pull of jobs in the United States, distant jobs that, as it happens, were illegal as well because it is hard to crack the American immigration barriers. Some took seasonal agricultural jobs but others found year-round work in such cities as Houston and Los Angeles. It is on jobs in Los Angeles that Napizaro has come to depend.

Today Napizaro is as prosperous a settlement as can be found in its entire region. The village's twelve hundred people live, for the most part, in comfortable brick houses with pretty patios and TV antennas. The community has street lights, a modern infirmary, a community center, and a new bull ring named The North Hollywood in honor of the industrial section of Los Angeles, some fifteen hundred miles away, from which this prosperity comes.

At any given time, more than three quarters of the men are away, working in North Hollywood. For all its amenities, Napizaro is described by an observer as a sad settlement where leave-takings are sorrowful and absences long, and where women live dreary, lonely lives. Because the men can seldom afford time off from the factories of North Hollywood and because trips home are expensive, they are often gone for years at a stretch. The money they send back home buys more than it would in Los Angeles. For example, a new brick house in Napizaro in 1980 cost only $6,000, most of that accounted for by its imported components, because do-it-yourself construction, barter of labor, and the extremely low local wages keep the rest of the cost low. An equivalent house in Los Angeles would be many times as expensive, quite apart from the price of Los Angeles land. The street lighting, infirmary and other public improvements were financed one at a time over the years by the men's self-imposed taxes on their wages. After the bull ring was finished, the men put their tax money into a fund to buy imported pipes, pumps and other equipment for a water-supply system.

When the young men of Napizaro reach working age they are given an orientation course in what lies in store for them in the factories. The teacher is an elderly man, retired after decades of work in North Hollywood. The men currently at work there arrange jobs for the newcomers. One of the enterprises receiving them is a clothing factory founded by a Napizaro migrant himself who has run it successfully for many years.

Naturally, the men of Napizaro have considered founding a factory right at home, a plausible notion at first thought because, among them, they already have the skills and experience to set up a clothing factory, manage it, operate it, train new workers and find wholesale buyers. But reluctantly they have abandoned the idea. A factory in Napizaro could not pay a living wage if, indeed, it could be started at all. The skills and experience the men have acquired in Los Angeles are usable only in the context of a city economy with its symbiotic nests of suppliers and its markets, not in this economically barren region. One and the same lack—a vigorous city right in the region—forces the men to find work far away and also makes it impossible for them to start an industrial plant of their own, at home.

Mexico City is no help. Mexico is a big country and Napizaro lies far outside the region Mexico City embraces, so far outside that the economy of Mexico City hardly touches upon this region at all. For economic purposes, Mexico City is more remote than Los Angeles, which at least provides a steady supply of work.

After forty years of remittances, then, remittances used responsibly, thriftily and cooperatively, the fact remains that if the remittances were to stop, Napizaro would swiftly sink back into the grim poverty it knew before the migrations and remittances began. Or more likely, its people would have to abandon the region entirely. For the fact is that despite the money sent back from Los Angeles and the television sets and other imports it buys, economic life in the region—ways of making a living right there—remain quite as unchanged and unchanging as economic life in old Bardou.

Workers from many poor regions entertain dreams of setting up businesses in their home villages, but even when these projects entail much simpler endeavors than starting a factory they tend to be hopeless. An Egyptian social worker in Rotterdam who helps immigrant workers there and takes an interest in following their fortunes says that even such uncomplicated plans as a one-man taxi service or a new retail store back home seldom work out. The taxi, bought with the savings of years of frugal living in Rotterdam and imported into a poor village in North Africa or southern Europe eventually breaks down beyond repair, and in the meantime it hasn't earned its owner enough to finance a replacement. The village store fails. The trouble is that the rural economies from which these ambitious migrants come and to which they return are too stagnant and inflexible to make room for new activities. The forces that actually do cause formerly stagnant regions to expand economically do not touch these places.

The only dreams that tend to work out successfully, the Rotterdam social worker says, involve tractors. Migrants who have bought tractors with their savings frequently earn enough back at home (by raising cash crops for distant city markets) to justify the investment and improve their own lot. But then, he adds sadly, the tractors put manual laborers out of work and increase pressure on them to leave for jobs, if they are lucky enough to get them, in distant cities like Rotterdam.

In the Italian film *Bread and Chocolate*, which depicts the

loneliness, discrimination, exploitation, dead-end jobs and painful cultural dislocations Italian workers endure when they take
jobs in Swiss cities and city regions, one of the characters, instead
of blaming Switzerland and the Swiss, exclaims, "Blame Italy
that forces us to emigrate." He was getting close, but not close
enough. After all, the north of Italy is not the source of streams
of Italian workers abandoning their regions. On the contrary—
for generations, Milan, Florence, Bologna and their great networks of abutting and overlapping city regions have been accepting an enormous share of southern Italians and Sicilians seeking
escape from poverty, and have helped them do just that.

This is not a problem that can be usefully understood as a
"national" problem or as a deficiency of Italy's "national economy," or as a European Economic Community problem either.
To think of it in such terms is obfuscating, merely fuzzes over
the reality that, specifically, southern Italy and Sicily, like Wales,
lack vigorous import-replacing cities of their own. Understanding
that fact does not present us with a solution or prescription, but
it is an indispensable first step. At least it tells us that remedies
which don't address the real lack—some of which I shall discuss
in the next three chapters—are beside the point, and why little is
to be hoped of them while time slips by and profound stagnation
continues.

SIX

Technology and Clearances

In city regions, improved productivity of rural workers is a direct response to the fact that workers are leaving the land for other occupations. Not so in economies distant from cities, economies that lack import-replacing cities of their own. There, improved productivity has nothing to do with the pull of alternate livelihoods; instead it can make people redundant and leave them in the lurch.

The principles at work in these bizarre and unbalanced regional economies can be illustrated by the Scottish Highland clearances, which began in 1792, lasted about half a century and converted a poor subsistence agricultural region into a not quite so poor supply region. The instrument that propelled these events happened to be a new breed of sheep.

Before the clearances the Highlanders kept small native sheep hardly larger than dogs, with fleece that looked like hair and was useless to city manufacturers. The sheep are described as having been half starved owing to the hard fact that the Highlanders themselves needed every scrap of agriculturally usable land for their own food. Unpastured, the sheep fended for themselves in bogs and other leftover waste space. The creatures that were to displace those sheep, and most of the Highlanders along with them, had been created by a talented breeder in the Border country to the south. His end product, the Cheviot (or the Great Sheep, as it was to be called in the Highlands) had become a success on

Border farms and in England; in 1790 it was experimentally introduced into the Highlands with the object of learning whether it
could stand the more rigorous climate there. It could. After two
years' trial the British Wool Society, an organization dominated
by London wool buyers and large English sheep raisers, offered
to provide flocks at nominal cost to all Scottish lairds "who aspire
to the character of being active and intelligent." There were many
lairds poor and bankrupt enough, says John Prebble, the Canadian-
Scottish economic historian of the Highlands, "to see in this the
perfect description of themselves," and they seized upon the offer.

Raising and shearing the Great Sheep required very few workers, but what the sheep did need was pasture. Not only were the
indigenous subsistence farmers and their families thus unnecessary for the work, they were in the way. The clearance of them
from the land to make way for pasture was brutal. "So that the
Scottish lairds might lease their glens and braes to sheep-farmers
from the Lowlands and England," Prebble explains, "they cleared
the crofts of men, women and children, using police and soldiers
where necessary . . . bayonet, truncheon and fire were used to
drive them from their homes. It has been said that the Clearances
are now far enough away from us to be decently forgotten. But the
hills are still empty . . . The chiefs remain, in Edinburgh and London, but the people are gone."

Sir John Sinclair, the Scot who first brought the Great Sheep
into the Highlands during the brief experimental period, pleaded
for a policy different from the barbaric clearances. He had envisioned slower and more considerate change. His plan was to
encourage small tenants to join their land, hire from among themselves herdsmen in common, and buy small flocks for themselves
at the nominal price. In short, he proposed producers' cooperatives. The possibility went untried, chiefly, Prebble says, because
of the isolation, ignorance and disorganization of the clansmen,
and their traditional habits of deferring to the paternalism of the
lairds, along with the desperation and demoralization of the lairds
themselves, who had been defeated in their uprising against
England in 1745, had suffered under the brutal occupation that
followed and were themselves poverty-stricken in their obsolete,
wholly rural economy.

Had Sir John's scheme been adopted, the clearances would have been more humane (we may hope) and perhaps more gradual. But clearances would nevertheless have had to take place. Once the new animal husbandry was adopted, producers' cooperatives would have had quite as little need for abundant labor as the lairds and their lessees, and quite as great a need for pasture. The inherent requirements of the change mandated clearances, no matter who might own and tend the flocks or receive the income. The people who actually did remain at work in the Highlands after the clearances were over and done with were economically better off than Highlanders had been in the past. The lairds profited most, but shepherds and shearers and their families were a bit better off as well. They had reliable incomes and were not constantly living on the brink of famine. If we fix our eyes only upon the region itself, we must conclude that rural productivity had risen, and with it, rural wealth.

But as for the people left in the lurch, of course their wealth hadn't risen; they were worse off. Many died of the starvation, diseases and other hardships accompanying and following the evictions. Some Highlanders migrated to the nearest cities, Glasgow and Edinburgh, but Glasgow and Edinburgh were themselves poor places with stagnant economies. They could offer only poverty and idleness in slums, where tuberculosis rates are believed to have been then, and were for long afterward, the highest in the world. A few drifted south into London. Some migrated to Ulster, joining Border Scots who had been transported there by the English authorities during the seventeenth-century Border pacifications, dispossessing native Irish of their lands—the results of which are still not "now far enough away from us to be decently forgotten." Some were absorbed into regiments of Highlanders in the British army, in which they and their descendants served notably in the conquests of India. Some were sold by their lairds as indentured servants to those plantation owners in the West Indies and South Carolina who had use for Scottish overseers of their black slaves. Many emigrated to Canada, especially Nova Scotia, where they resumed subsistence farming, and in due course added sheep raising as a cash crop. In due course, too, they and Tory immigrants from New England who had fled the American

Revolution helped dispossess and evict French-speaking Acadians from the land—who of course had previously dispossessed Indians. In all these trains of dislocations and make-do, city jobs and alternate nonurban livelihoods played virtually no part.

The enormous difference between clearances in a poor country like Scotland and a rich country like the United States is this: rich countries can afford doles. But apart from this difference, the consequences of a bizarre imbalance between improved rural productivity and availability of alternate city livelihoods are not that different in rich and poor countries.

The United States has had its great agricultural clearance too, in the South, which until the 1930s was the most backward part of the country. Former President Jimmy Carter, describing his boyhood on a farm in Georgia, has said, "it more nearly resembled farm life of fully 2,000 years ago than farm life today," which may be an exaggeration but not necessarily so if he was thinking of an ancient Italian farm. What Carter meant was that almost all the work in his youth had to be done by animals and human beings with little help from machines. The mule, and the man, woman or child with the hoe, were the indispensables. Because their productivity was low, hard though they worked, Southern farmers were poor; because of their poverty they could not afford equipment to improve their productivity.

To break this circle, the national government provided money and improved agricultural methods to Southern farms. Distant cities played their part by having previously developed: they produced the necessary equipment, and also, through their tax yields, provided the necessary money. Price supports guaranteed Southern farmers a dependable floor under the prices for their staple cash crops; they received subsidies for withdrawing portions of their land from agriculture, low-interest loans for rural electrification, and intensive assistance from government-employed experts on erosion control, fertilization, crop diversification. The subsidies tied to acreage automatically benefited the larger landholders most; these were also the farmers able to make most rapid and effective use of capital-intensive, labor-saving equipment. Thus landholders, and most especially large landholders, could begin to afford equipment they had previously gone without.

The technology that promptly began revolutionizing farm life for the Carters, their hired hands and millions of other people in the South was not revolutionary in the sense of being innovative or unprecedented. The mechanical cultivators, seeders, fertilizer spreaders, harvesters, choppers, sprayers, the electric chain saws, pumps, incubators, drying fans, conveyors and loaders, the fertilizers, the refrigerating systems, the tractors, trucks and educational farm journals, and almost all the other large and small items that went into transforming Southern agriculture during the next several decades consisted of equipment, materials and methods developed in cities and city regions of the North and first put to work there, or of relatively minor adaptations and modifications of those methods and equipment. The instruments had already been extended into supply regions of the West. But during the period when grain growers on the prairies and vegetable and fruit growers in valleys of the Far West were getting tractors, trucks, combines, seeders, sprayers and other equipment, vigorous Western and Northern cities were well able to provide alternate livelihoods to people who were not needed in those supply regions.

When finally the technology was put to work in Southern agriculture, yields increased stupendously. Of course, so did the productivity of farmers and their hired helpers. Therefore surplus hired hands were laid off and sharecroppers let go. Tenants' and small-holders' farms were incorporated into larger farms, but minus the tenants and small holders themselves. In Georgia, Henry Grady's and the Carters' state, there had been about 1.5 million farmers and farm workers in 1930. Fifty years later there were only about 225,000, and more than 300,000 farms had been consolidated into fewer than 70,000. Agriculture today occupies only 4 percent of workers in the state, whereas in Carter's boyhood it had occupied more than half. While these changes were taking place in Georgia, much the same changes were occurring in East Texas, Louisiana, Missouri, Arkansas, Mississippi, Alabama, Florida, Tennessee, Kentucky, South Carolina, North Carolina and Virginia. Over all this territory, farm workers and their families were being cleared from the land as productivity and yields soared.

Where did they and their families go? Because the clearances had begun on the threshold of World War II, the first to be cleared were soon absorbed. Young farm people not drafted into the armed forces rapidly found work in war production and service jobs, and so did many of their elders, in such cities as San Francisco, Oakland, Los Angeles, Seattle, Chicago, Gary, Indianapolis, Detroit, Cleveland, Cincinnati, Pittsburgh, Philadelphia, Baltimore, Wilmington, Camden, Boston, Buffalo, Newark, New York . . . Black workers, who formed a high proportion of those displaced, were snapped up by shipyards, steel mills and construction firms, among others, although they had previously been discriminated against in those occupations, as well as in many of the factories and retail stores and other service enterprises where they found wartime employment. But once the war ended, new jobs, especially for black workers, did not increase in concert with clearances from the land; and many black workers who had found wartime city employment were laid off as returned soldiers were given preference or as enterprises converted from military to civilian production.

Nevertheless, the clearances not only continued but accelerated, especially between 1945 and 1960. Some who were displaced remained in the South on pocket-sized bits of land from which they eked out a living, frequently with assistance from welfare payments; these cul-de-sacs of rural poverty are numerous still. Some found jobs in Southern cities and in industries transplanted to the South from Northern cities and their regions. But Southern cities and industries could not begin to provide work and incomes for all the people who had been cleared from the land. Most who were displaced migrated to cities anyhow—where else?—and especially to the distant cities in the North and Far West which had afforded work and incomes to newcomers in the past, including many migrants from overseas.

But now something unprecedented was happening in America. Cities were no longer generating sufficient jobs and incomes for people leaving the land. Indeed, at the very time the great Southern clearance was occurring, many once vigorous American cities were stagnating economically, and in the years since the great clearance, many have actually been contracting and decaying economically. Therefore, to this day, no work has materialized for millions of displaced Southern rural workers and their descendants. From their point of view they were left in the lurch, discarded after generations of hard, ill-paid work, when the revolutionized agriculture no longer had need for them. From the point of view of the cities to which they were drawn, the migrants and their descendants presented a huge economic burden. It is a burden to house them, educate them, police them and provide them welfare and other social services.

What began as a successful exercise in agricultural improvement has had these side effects precisely because the improvement, like the Scottish clearances, was quite unrelated to the complete panoply of city economic forces. Instead, a few unbalanced strands of city energy—city technology accompanied by city-derived capital—reached into distant regions and distorted them gravely. Much of the increased productivity and wealth attendant on this agricultural revolution has proved to be illusory from a national viewpoint. The costs of idleness and unproductivity of displaced people, along with the accompanying poverty, demoralization, violence, drug addiction and crime, are incalculable but they are enormous.

Within the South, those working in the revolutionized agriculture are better off than formerly, just as those still at work in rural Scotland after the clearances were better off than formerly. Both the landowners and hired hands in the new Southern agriculture earn more than before. They work shorter hours, at easier jobs. Cotton picking by hand is miserable labor; driving a cotton picker is not. Were it not for the missing link, the missing alternative productive livelihoods, this would be a happy story. But as it is, the Southern agricultural revolution was a profoundly arbitrary occurrence, propelled from outside and, as it happened, from an outside unable to cope with its consequences.

The situation in clearance regions is exactly the opposite of what happens in regions being abandoned by workers in favor of distant city jobs, for just as the causes of the two phenomena are different, so are the results. When technology, reaching out from distant cities, clears a region of much of its population, the people who must leave the land are often worse off than before, but those who remain at work there are better off. Regions whose people simply leave for city work present a mirror image: those who leave improve their economic lot but, as explained in the preceding chapter, those who stay do not.

This suggests, of course, that to improve everyone's lot—that of those who leave and that of those who stay—the two kinds of events, abandonments and clearances, ought to happen in the same places at the same times. Exactly this does happen in city regions where some people leave for city jobs while technology improves the rural productivity and yields of others, as happened in Shinohata. But in other types of regions, economic forces from cities seldom dovetail that neatly. If rural people who escaped poverty by leaving Wales or old Bardou had had to wait until clearances uprooted them, they would be waiting still. What happens in city regions happens precisely because they *are* city regions; what happens in abandoned or cleared regions happens because they are not city regions, and yet unbalanced forces from distant cities touch them.

Sir John Sinclair and his plan for considerate change in the Highlands remind one of the American inventor of the mechanical cotton picker. He did not release his invention until the Great Depression of the 1930s was over, and even then authorized its introduction only at a measured pace. Yet its use at all mandated clearances.

Improved rural productivity and improved rural yields are not the same things, but as a practical matter they might as well be. High yields and thrifty, effective use of labor go hand in hand in agriculture. That is why the most thoroughly rural countries, those in which as much as 80 percent of the people work the land, are paradoxically the hungriest, and why countries in which a small proportion of the population devotes itself to growing food are paradoxically the best fed. In practice, it seems that every measure for increasing agricultural yields also reduces need for agricultural labor, or to turn the thought about, that every measure for saving agricultural labor also increases yields. So simple and rudimentary a device as a bicycle water pump, powered by human muscles, can appreciably increase yields in fields where irrigation water has formerly been drawn by hand; but one single such pump eliminates about two thousand work days annually, takes the place of about seven workers. It is the same with virtually every other measure that effectively increases yields; it simultaneously cuts labor.

In the Soviet Union, agricultural yields are a scandal. Regions that could be among the great breadbaskets of the world do not feed even the country's own population adequately. Year after year the Soviet Union buys millions of bushels of wheat from Canada, grown on lands climatically not that different from Soviet wheat lands, and many years the Soviet Union buys from the United States as well. Nor is Soviet production of meat, vegetables, fruit, poultry and dairy products ample by standards of advanced economies. Rural productivity in the Soviet Union is a scandal too, even though attempts at improving it eat up disproportionate shares of Soviet capital and wealth; the country sinks about a quarter of its annual capital investments into agriculture and has done so for decades. The disappointing results are commonly attributed to inept planning, bureaucratic snarls, poor transport, lackadaisical and uncaring workers, the vagaries of the weather, and the fact that people in socialized farming do not stand or fall by what they themselves make of their land and its possibilities and do not invest their own pride and planning in it. The last reason is obviously important, since it is a fact that the small private plots permitted many collective farmers yield a disproportionately large share of agricultural produce. Everyone, inside the Soviet Union and outside, who has examined the workings of Soviet collective and state farms has economic horror stories to relate, stories which often appear as criticisms in the Soviet press: fertilizer that doesn't arrive when it is time to apply it; fertilizer spreaders that are broken down or missing if the fertilizer actually does arrive at the correct time; herds increased at the very time feed is lacking to support the animals; work crews assigned where they aren't needed while other pressing needs are neglected; transport that doesn't materialize while harvests rot; crops ordained for regions where the growing season is too short for them; and so on.

But let us look at this scandalous situation from a slightly different point of view. Suppose the country's agricultural yields and productivity were to increase. If the improvements were really significant, tens of millions of Soviet farm workers would automatically become redundant. At present a constant stream of rural people, mostly young people just reaching working age, already leave the land for alternate jobs, but they are as nothing compared with the exodus required if productivity and yields were to rise significantly. Were productivity increased to only half that of American farmers, some 40 million people out of the present Soviet rural population of 100 million would become redundant. Where would they go? What would they do? The Soviet Union has relatively few cities for a nation of its size, and among them, no vigorous import-replacing cities or significant city regions. The present stream of young people leaving the land is all these Soviet cities can absorb. Where shortages of Soviet labor occur, those shortages are not in cities; indeed, as it is, underemployment is a chronic problem in the country's medium-sized and small cities.

I am not suggesting that the Soviet authorities have deliberately kept agricultural productivity low, much less deliberately kept yields low. On the contrary; such a supposition would not jibe with the exorbitant investments the government sinks into agriculture for the express purpose of trying to improve yields and productivity. For another thing, I doubt that Soviet policy makers understand, any better than American policy makers have understood, the vital connections between agricultural yields and productivity on the one hand, and the availability or unavailability of city jobs on the other hand, much less the connection of the latter with the import-replacing process in cities.

What I am saying, rather, is that because these vital connections do exist, it follows that in any nation where sufficient productive city work is lacking, improvements in rural yields and productivity must leave large numbers of workers idle and redundant, or else rural yields and productivity must remain low. There are no other possibilities than these two. In the United States, this inexorability has worked itself out in the first way. In the Soviet Union it has worked itself out in the second way.

In poor, predominantly rural countries the connection is not understood either, and because it is not, too simplistic a view of how these countries can be helped has often wreaked havoc. On the surface, it seems plausible that both the poverty and hunger of poor rural people can be ameliorated if their yields are increased. What could be more straightforward? This has been the theory behind the aid programs called the Green Revolution, bringing improved seeds, technology and methods to poor rural regions. In its own terms, like the Scottish clearances in theirs, or the Southern American agricultural revolution in its own terms, the Green Revolution in poor and backward countries has had successes, sometimes great successes. But because of the links between improved yields and thriftier use of labor, the Green Revolution has displaced and dislocated people—the more successful, the more it has displaced and dislocated—and all too seldom have alternate productive city livelihoods been available to them. Like evicted Highlanders who turned to Edinburgh and Glasgow and found only poverty and idleness there, Third World people displaced by the Green Revolution crowd into cities whose own poor and stagnant economies have little to offer.

Sometimes, instead of crowding into cities, they stay on the land anyhow, and that can be worse. In Java, improved yields began with better seeds and with two relatively minor mechanical aids: the bicycle-powered water pump and the mechanical tiller. But just one pump and one tiller, taken together, make about fourteen workers redundant at the same time that they increase yields. The redundant workers of Java have tended to stay on the land, moving up into hills, extending subsistence farming into what had previously been forested slopes. To use that land agriculturally has been disastrous; deforestation has led to erosion, and to flash floods in rainy seasons and drought at other times because the vanishing forests no longer act like sponges. As eroded hillsides become useless, the displaced farmers move still farther up the mountains, deforesting still more land.

In Africa, the Green Revolution has yielded considerable new wealth in cash crops, such as peanuts in West Africa and coffee and tea in East Africa, but where the new farming has been most successful it has often led to more malnutrition. Women, the traditional subsistence farmers in much of Africa, are redundant in the new mechanized agriculture. Yet they have no alternate livelihoods and they must somehow try to feed their families on plots seriously reduced in size.

Disasters such as these few examples I have mentioned, along with failures of industrialization schemes promoted in the 1950s and 1960s, led policy makers of the World Bank to rethink their aid and loan policies for poor countries and to adopt a new approach beginning in 1968. Previously the bank had concentrated on financing dams, electric generators, roads, communications and the like. These were intended as a foundation for industrialization—not industrialization in the way it is created by import-replacing cities, but industrialization in the form of transplanted factories of multinational corporations and complete "import substitution" factories analogous to those of the Uruguayan fiasco. The industries frequently failed to materialize; the ovens were built but the loaves didn't jump into them, as one consultant put it. And when they did materialize, the work and incomes provided were pathetically small relative to the need, and of course had nothing to do with what happens in economies producing amply and diversely for themselves as well as others.

The bank's reconsidered approach, largely worked out by Robert McNamara, the former U.S. Secretary of Defense who was appointed president of the bank in 1968, was to concentrate heavily on improvements to rural life with the object of keeeping rural people in their villages instead of displacing them. This was the approach also advocated by the late Gunnar Myrdal, the famous Swedish expert on poverty and poor nations. Myrdal's hope lay in the idea that there must be some way to improve yields of poor villagers and yet, at the same time, keep their agriculture very labor-intensive. Neither Myrdal nor anyone else, however, has found empirical means of accomplishing this. As a policy it was a wish, a problem that has remained without a solution.

The World Bank could not find a solution to it either. In practice, the best that could be done along these lines was to introduce any improved agricultural methods or devices gently, gently, and with such glacial slowness that they made little difference in yields. This of course tended to produce a harvest of disappointment and frustration that so little gain was coming of so much implied promise.

McNamara's solution was to sidestep the whole knotty question of yields and productivity. He decreed, instead, that improved yields were not basic to combating village poverty. He ordained that the basics, instead, were health, education, nutrition, housing and reduced birth rates. Under a doctrine called "basic necessities" the bank turned to making low-interest loans and no-interest loans to poor countries for these purposes. Meanwhile, in some unspecified way, these basic necessities were supposed to pay off in development and the ability of development to expand wealth. That last notion was important because theoretically it justified the bank's mission as a development agency and lender, not a philanthropy.

The cost of basic necessities as defined by McNamara did not come cheap. In 1968, at the time the change in policy was made, the bank's outstanding loans totaled $1 billion. By 1980, the year McNamara retired, the loans had increased to $11.5 billion. Not all of that went for investments in rural health, education, nutrition, housing and birth control. Almost a third of the bank's financing continued to go into electric power projects and other programs classified as industrial, but it was the new programs for rural village improvement that caused the loans to soar, the more astonishingly when we realize that, in addition to the loans made by the World Bank itself, commercial banks made loans of $90 billion during the same period to augment the financing required for the World Bank's projects and programs. In 1980 the bank went to its member countries with a request for still larger capitalization; they agreed to provide another $25 billion.

These loans can be repaid if, and only if, yields in poor, predominantly agricultural countries are to increase substantially and if distant solvent markets for the increased yields are to be found as well. This, of course, brings us right back to the insoluble problem swept aside by the doctrine of "basic necessities," the question of how to increase yields substantially and yet avoid making many rural people redundant.

In the event, the loans are not repayable. The policy has converted client countries into vast charity wards. While this may or may not be justifiable as philanthropy, it is not my definition of meaningful economic development. Nor is it what was ostensibly offered to poor countries, told as they were that money they borrowed to carry out World Bank programs was money to buy development of their economies.

The hard truth is that there is no decent way of overcoming rural poverty where people have no access to productive city jobs. That was true in the days of the Scottish clearances and is true still. It has been true in the case of the rich United States and is equally true in the case of the World Bank's poor clients. Plenty of technology, including inexpensive, adaptable, intermediate and small technology is available for improving rural yields and productivity of rural workers. But what is not available, where they are needed most, are adaptable, vigorous import-replacing cities. In their absence, technology arbitrarily arriving from distant cities is not a blessing but a curse, and the economic wealth it creates is always in part illusory, sometimes wholly so.

SEVEN

Transplant Regions

The standard diagnosis of the trouble with supply regions, abandoned regions and clearance regions, and of stagnant and declining cities as well, is "not enough industry"; the standard prescription, "attract industry." What are these industries that can be lured and hooked? Where do they come from and why? For the most part they are industries that originally developed in cities and city regions but have become free to leave those breeding grounds and leap out into distant regions that lack import-replacing cities of their own. They differ from industries that can't leave their own city regions, and they don't have similar effects on economic life or its development.

To see why that is so, let us return to north Georgia, the site of the funeral that Henry Grady described in 1889 to his audiences of Boston and New York industrialists and bankers. In his speech Grady followed up the grim description of the funeral with a jubilant account of marvels and changes. On a more recent visit to the old grave site he found that a marble quarrying company had moved in and was operating the largest marble works in the world, only a few miles away. The iron hills had also been slashed and were swarming with workmen and loud with the din of machinery. Probably—although Grady didn't say—the ore was destined for a steelmaking complex transplanted to Birmingham, Alabama, in the 1870s from Pittsburgh. Forty cotton mills in a near radius of the grave, he went on, were now "weaving infinite cloth that neighboring shops make into countless shirts." Somewhat airily, not specifying locations, he spoke of shoe, nail, carriage and pick-and-shovel factories. Here, one suspects, he was elevating possibilities into accomplished facts, or else touching on examples of transplanted industries that had landed in other regions of the South. However, he became specific again about four coffin factories forty miles from the grave doing such exquisite work "as to tempt the world to die."

The description of the funeral was a description of the region before transplants had begun arriving; then only imports were coming from distant cities and few of those because the region earned so few. The imports, you may remember, didn't come from Atlanta, the nearest city. Neither did the transplanted industries when they turned up.

Grady thought the transplants were correcting not only the region's poverty but the underlying cause of its poverty: the fact that it produced so little for its own people and producers, importing everything from distant cities instead. "That country can now get up as nice a funeral, native and home-made, as you would wish to have," he said. His plea for more transplants was a plea to Northern industrialists to give this region, and the South generally, the power of producing for itself in well-rounded economies.

Transplants from distant cities did keep flowing to north Georgia, primarily textile mills from New England and garment industries, like the shirt factories, from New York, both drawn by cheap labor. Then, later, military installations came, drawn by the political power of Georgia's senators. In due course, along came Lockheed Aircraft among others, a Los Angeles company, which built a factory that produces military aircraft in the town of Marietta, at just about the same distance from the old grave as the factories producing the exquisite coffins of Grady's day. Lockheed's Marietta works may not be the largest thing of its kind in the world, as the marble works had been, but it is one of the largest. It is the biggest manufacturing complex in the entire southeastern part of the United States.

At the time Lockheed was founded and becoming established,

and for a considerable time thereafter, it had to have a city economy, and not just any city economy but one that specifically contained goods and services the fledgling enterprise needed. Even
Atlanta wouldn't have served this purpose, much less Marietta.
The company's founder, Allen Loughhead, designed his first
plane in the late 1920s, and then had to scramble in the Los
Angeles economy for hundreds of things to make it with: tools
of many types, aluminum sheets, wiring, wheel parts, bearings,
electroplating and printing services, and so on. Not all the things
he required were made in Los Angeles but many were; and for
those items that were not, he could draw on distributors, agents
and importers who were also right there. As for things that
couldn't be gotten at all, or not the way he wanted them, there
were producers in Los Angeles capable of making them according to his specifications, like the producers Sabel marveled at in
northern Italy. Loughhead also had to scramble in the city economy for skilled people he required: draftsmen, mechanics, assistant
designers, and so on. Oddly enough, for a time he even had to
depend on Los Angeles consumers; he supported himself while
he worked on his first design, lined up his requirements, and
found potential customers and financing, by selling sightseeing
flights to Los Angeles residents and tourists. But even if he had
been able to skip that bit of improvisation, he needed the Los
Angeles economy. No amount of financing could have overcome
the drains on his own energy, the time lost, the mistakes, delays
and failures to make things mesh which would have plagued this
complicated endeavor and probably killed it if Loughhead had
tried to begin in an impractical location. As Lockheed became
established and as it expanded, it still needed Los Angeles. It
could expand in Los Angeles or in its nearby hinterland, but it
couldn't move far, being tethered by its relationships to other
producers in that economy. It was also helping to support those
other producers, and helping them to ramify their own capabilities and versatility.

The reason Lockheed was eventually able to rocket a factory
into distant north Georgia was that, as it grew, the company became relatively self-sufficient; it was now able to supply for itself

many of the everyday items, services and skills that it had formerly gotten from outsiders, and it also became so practiced and experienced at commanding what it needed from outsiders that it could acquire those things efficiently, no matter from how great a distance they must come. The head office remained in Los Angeles and much of the company's work was still done there, but as far as many of its operations were concerned, the apron strings could be cut.

In Marietta, Lockheed had no need for the kinds of suppliers and services it could not have dispensed with in Los Angeles. Had it needed such things in Marietta, it couldn't have moved to Marietta. So in Marietta it did not help support other local producers of its requirements; it couldn't and didn't reproduce there, even in microcosm, the sort of economy from which it had been attracted.

It had been the same with the other transplants to the region, right back to Grady's time. The marble works, the mining company, the textile mills, and the shirt and coffin factories had at one time needed the Boston or New York economies in the same way Lockheed later needed Los Angeles, but no longer. Their moves into north Georgia didn't mean they got tools, machines, materials or designs there. Insofar as they didn't provide for themselves, they sent off for what they needed. Furthermore, having already become successful exporters from their former cities, they no longer depended overwhelmingly upon any one locality for their sales.

Alas for Grady's hopes of a region that would take to producing amply and diversely for its own people and producers as well as for others. The wages transplants have brought the region for a century have been welcome because they enable people to import more than they otherwise could, and thus the region imports an even higher proportion and variety of its needs, producers' needs and consumers' needs both, than at the time of the funeral before transplants started arriving. As for the goods the transplants themselves produce, these are overwhelmingly for distant city markets or distant military facilities of the U.S. and foreign governments. Anything produced for local needs is minor, coincidental and narrow in its range. In short, the economy these transplants from distant cities have created in north Georgia is a kind of industrialized supply region, not that different in principle from Uruguay's rurally based supply region.

Furthermore, this industrialized supply region, or transplant region, has an economy as unresilient, fragile and limited as Uruguay's. This began to become apparent in the mid-1970s when north Georgia started suffering serious losses of its older transplants. The textile mills were closing up and leaving, transplanting themselves yet again, this time in search of cheaper labor abroad as well as greater freedom from safety regulations and the costs of equipment the regulations mandated. Remaining in north Georgia, they could no longer successfully meet competition from abroad, so it was either fail and close up or move; either way, close up in north Georgia. As the mills have been moving out, they have left behind them economic vacuums, much as happened in Uruguay when distant city markets were lost, leaving in their wakes only economic vacuums. The transplants, in short, proved to be a barren foundation for indigenous industrial development. When Lockheed eventually closes or transplants its manufacturing again (nothing is permanent), the results will be the same. In its wake, it can leave only an economic vacuum.

What Grady had envisioned in north Georgia was the kind of economic pattern to be found in city regions, but that pattern depends upon industries that are not relatively self-sufficient. When city enterprises transplant themselves into a city's own hinterland, they balance their needs to be close to their suppliers and customers against their conflicting aims of escaping the costs of city space and the congestion or other disadvantages of the city. The balances they strike are reflected in the physical pattern of a city region's industrialization. The transplanted industries typically cluster most thickly just beyond the city and its suburbs, thinning out with distance, here and there forming clots within the region but eventually petering out as the city region's current borders are reached. When branch plants from distant cities are drawn into other city regions by the prosperous markets there, they locate themselves by striking similar balances between the advantages and disadvantages of the city. As a city region becomes dotted with industry, some enterprises can start out in the region itself rather than in the nuclear city or cities, but they too are tethered into the region.

In short, many enterprises that a city generates can move, but can't move far. They are tethered to relationships with other producers or customers or both. This is why, in the aggregate, city regions produce amply and diversely for their own people and producers as well as for others. Conversely, freedom from those relationships, the very freedom that makes an industry capable of moving to a distant region without a city, automatically creates transplant economies that do not produce much for themselves, no matter how successful at attracting industries.

Puerto Rico, although it has been in the business of attracting transplants for only a third as long as north Georgia, has attracted even more of them. For thirty-five years, under a program ironically named Operation Bootstrap, the Puerto Rican government has concentrated on luring, in particular, labor-intensive industries to provide the island with the jobs and wages its own economy does not generate. Inducements have been the beneficent climate, the cheap labor, the well-equipped ports, tax concessions, government-financed labor training programs and government assistance in arranging loans to help industries get sites and finance their relocation costs. As a consequence, the island is dotted with the establishments of famous multinational corporations, along with many lesser-known producers of garments, toys, microprocessors and other light industrial products.

But when transplants leave Puerto Rico in search of still cheaper labor, as they have increasingly done since the early 1970s, they leave behind, like the departing transplants of north Georgia, only economic vacuums, along with soaring unemployment and a population of whom the director of a federal antipoverty program in Ponce says, "We have to get them jobs." No web of symbiotic relationships remains as it does in cities and city regions when some of their industries take off for distant places like Puerto Rico.

The strategy of attracting industry, in the hope that this will reproduce the self-generating and self-ramifying economies that city regions have, has brought disappointment to Ireland, southern Italy, the Canadian Maritime Provinces, and many other places that don't generate many industries of their own but do get them from afar. In Sicily a disillusioned official has called that island's industrial transplants, financed largely by the Italian government at great cost, "cathedrals in a desert." So many multinational corporations have transplanted factory, refinery and chemical works into Greece that air and water pollution have become a disgrace. Nevertheless, at any given time about a third of Greece's young men have been in northern Europe, working at jobs there or trying to find them, while among those at home unemployment and underemployment have continued at a staggering rate, and the country villages of Greece remain woefully poverty-stricken. Wages from the transplants, like the cash crops Greek farmers send to distant city markets, buy imports from distant cities, and these are welcome, since neither Athens nor any other Greek city replaces wide ranges of its imports with local production. If Greek cities had been doing so, they would be generating industries and transplants themselves, instead of trying to rely upon relatively self-sufficient industries spilled out from far distant cities.

Is building a self-generating economy upon a foundation of transplanted industry impossible? Experience would suggest it is, since, historically, supply regions have been the locales in which the vigorous cities of the world have formed and risen— not transplant regions, even though transplant regions go back to Renaissance times, when city textile industries farmed out much of their spinning and weaving work to distant cottagers. However, the experience of Taiwan in our own time shows that the thing is not actually impossible.

The events behind Taiwan's extraordinary and perhaps even unique achievement go back to 1956, when the government there introduced a program called Land to the Tiller. Its purpose, not in itself unusual, was to transfer agricultural soil from the owner-ship of feudal-like landlords to the peasants who worked the land. The government, in paying the expropriated landlords, attached a string to payments, however, a string that converted rural landlords into city capitalists. It stipulated investment of part of the payments in light industry. What kinds and where they would be were left up to the former landlords, as long as the investments were in Taiwan. The place most of the investors chose was Taipei, the capital and largest city: a sensible choice, since it contained both the largest concentration of people and the largest concentration of producers' goods and services (not many, to begin with).

At this time Taiwan was receiving light industrial transplants from distant places, mostly from the United States, much like those Puerto Rico was getting, because in Taiwan, as in Puerto Rico, the big attraction was cheap labor. Taiwan continued to receive such transplants abundantly, but in the meantime something else was happening as well.

Taiwanese who got jobs in transplanted industries learned from that experience how the enterprises were set up and run, just as the men of Napizaro learned from their experience in Los Angeles how garment factories were set up and run. But in Taipei, these experiences and skills were now brought together with indigenous capital; men who first gained experience in transplants managed workshops and factories capitalized by the new local investors in light industry. Some of the young enterprises took on subcontract work for exporters in Hong Kong. Others went into competition with transplants, but since they were anything but self-sufficient, they improvised by getting outsiders—local workshops—to help them out. In this way they stimulated not only the work of local shops but also the formation of new ones, which ramified and multiplied. And in this way, as fast as new niches opened up, Taipei was developing a real foundation for symbiotic and versatile production on its own behalf. The networks of symbiotic enterprises became capable not only of supplying one another, and exporters as well, but also of replacing with their own production some of the producers' goods being imported, as well as some consumers' goods.

As an import-replacing city, which it was within fifteen years, Taipei boomed. Like any import-replacing city, it began generating a city region of its own, and like any import-replacing city it also began generating new capital at a great rate. Not only was the economic development paying for itself as it proceeded, it was generating a surplus. Some of that capital helped afford Taiwan means of financing heavy industry (and much else) in a second city, Kaohsiung—which has also taken to replacing imports, including, of course, and most significantly, imports from Taipei.

All this development and expansion gradually made Taiwan an unsatisfactory locale for transplants from distant cities. "We had a lovely little operation running there for over a decade," an American toy manufacturer complained to a Canadian newspaper correspondent in 1979, "but we had to close it down last year because we couldn't get anyone to work for us. The place has become too damn industrialized and they want too much money."

As for the peasants whose needs for land of their own started this train of events, they now have the benefit of two city regional economies, as well as the alternative of city jobs. "People from all over Taiwan pour into Kaohsiung looking for the good life—jobs, housing, services, department stores, education, hospitals and more—all these things are in good supply by Asian standards," a Canadian correspondent has reported. To his eyes, Kaohsiung was a chaotic city, unhistoric and unattractive but "a place of possibilities and upward mobility, a place where the children of peasants can make a break from the millennia-old curse of being tied to the land."

Instead of paying off the expropriated landlords, the government could, of course, have used equivalent funds to set up light industries itself. But if it had done so, it seems inconceivable that these could have been as improvisational, flexible and diverse as those that actually were set up, or that they could conceivably have given rise to the schools of breakaway firms they have spawned by the thousands as employees, gaining experience, have discovered more niches in the economy, and customers, suppliers and investors for enterprises of their own.

Maybe what happened in Taiwan can't be replicated elsewhere. Maybe the improvisation of city capital that worked there wouldn't work out in another place. But this is the nature of successful economic improvisation of any sort: if it works, it isn't because it is abstractly or theoretically "the right thing" but because it is actually practical for the time, the place, and the resources and opportunities at hand. Successful improvisations give economic life most of its surprises.

Nevertheless, it seems to me that the basic principles behind the Taiwanese experience may in some way or other be transferable. They can be summed up thus: "If our cheap labor can be put to use by foreigners, we should be able to put it to use for ourselves"; and "If foreign transplants give us experience and skills we can use for ourselves, we can try using them as we please." One wonders, for example, what Puerto Ricans might have accomplished if their government had followed up early successes at luring labor-intensive transplants by then getting capital into the hands of Puerto Ricans themselves. As it is, perhaps in another generation Puerto Rico will be seeking transplants from Taipei and Kaohsiung.

One reason the Taiwan experience is probably limited in its application elsewhere is that transplants for regions which lack import-replacing cities of their own aren't all that plentiful. All the places mentioned in this chapter have been unusually successful at attracting industries. Disappointments with results are as nothing compared with disappointments in would-be transplant regions like rural Java or Ghana, where preparations were made for transplants that either didn't take place or arrived so scantily that they made little difference. Disappointments of that sort are what induced the World Bank in 1968 to begin reducing the proportion of its loans designated for power plants and transportation—preparations for transplants—and concentrate instead on village welfare schemes.

So many regions of the world are stagnant and inert, don't generate industries of their own but nevertheless want industry, that the demand for industrial transplants far outruns the supply. To put it the other way, relatively so few cities and city regions generate transplants prolifically that they can't meet the demand. And among transplants that cities do produce, most can't move far. At any given time, only a small fraction of the industries which have been generated are self-sufficient enough to leap into distant regions lacking import-replacing cities of their own. And when we consider that even among these, many are capital-intensive rather than labor-intensive, we must conclude that salvation from transplants is a vain hope for most regions avid to get them as a solution to unemployment.

Even in the United States, domestic demand for transplants now far outruns the supply. Thus situations like these, as reported in a *Wall Street Journal* article, have become commonplace:

> Minnesota's governor . . . is bristling at [South Dakota's] drive to lure Minnesota companies there. More than 60 have moved from Minnesota to South Dakota in recent years . . .
>
> [The governor] has pledged to fight to keep Minnesota business in the state and entice new employers . . .
>
> Economically starving Michigan finds that business-development scouts from Indiana and other states are trying to persuade its companies to relocate. "They're like vultures," one Michigan official says . . . The state is countering by sharply increasing its promotion budget . . . to lure high technology companies . . .
>
> [The entire Midwest] has become a target for recruiters from the Sun Belt and other parts of the country. They are eager to strengthen their states' industrial base by attracting machine-tool and similar companies from the nation's heartland.
>
> The "Silicon Valleys" of both California and Massachusetts are being invaded by out-of-state economic development officials bent on luring away high-tech companies.
>
> "A lot of states are embracing high tech as their savior," says . . . the communications director for the Northeast-Midwest Congressional Coalition, a regional alliance. "The danger is that everyone is going after the same slice of the pie." . . .
>
> Many state and local officials worry that [the competition] will bring a new, damaging round of budget-busting tax breaks and other inducements to attract employers. Such bidding contests have erupted in recent years, notably during the battle among several states to land auto-production plants of foreign companies . . .

Almost two centuries ago, Catherine the Great of Russia had this to say:

> Most of our factories are in Moscow, probably the least advantageous spot in all Russia. It is dreadfully over-populated and the workers become lazy and dissolute. . . . On the other hand, hundreds of small towns are crumbling in ruins. Why not transport a factory to each of them, according to the produce of the district and the quality of the water? The workmen would be more industrious and the towns would flourish.

As was perhaps natural, since Catherine was a monarch, she was thinking of an economy much as if it were an army. If you have a territory and an army, you can deploy the troops where you judge they are needed, never mind if they would rather hang about the glitter and fleshpots of the city.

Since a developing economy is not created in remotely the same way as an army, nor supplied and sustained in the same way either, neither can it be successfully deployed as if it were an army. Nevertheless, not only in the Soviet Union, successor to Catherine's realm, but almost everywhere else in the world, this old and simplistic conception of how to defeat stagnation in the boondocks remains much with us. Catherine was royally untroubled by the hard questions: What if there are too few factories for all those crumbling towns? What happens when the transported factories depart or fail or grow obsolete, what do they leave behind in their company towns? What if the sources of these factories run dry, and new sources don't bubble up?

EIGHT

Capital for Regions Without Cities

The Volta Dam in Ghana, one of the world's great hydroelectric projects, was supposed to supply factories with power. But apart from an American-owned aluminum refinery, whose promised participation supplied the original justification for the dam, almost nothing has materialized to make use of the power, even though it is an extraordinary bargain; the aluminum company gets it at one-tenth the world's average price for industrial electric power. The dam was also supposed to promote irrigated cash cropping, but that scheme proved so impractical that it was dropped. The 80,000 people whose traditional village subsistence economies were wiped out to make room for the dam and its reservoir were resettled on soil so poor that more than half found they could no longer feed themselves and drifted away—most of them, it is believed, to become landless paupers.

Carried away by the power of money to finance great capital undertakings, many people seem to think of such investments as being development itself. Build the dam and you have development! But in real life, build the dam and unless you also have solvent city markets and transplanted industries, you have nothing. The economic pointlessness of the Volta Dam is not all that unusual. "I could cite about forty dams around the world which are completely useless," says a United Nations Food and Agricultural Organization official. Of course, that doesn't mean all dams are useless; many justify themselves by producing power for which there

105

is demand, irrigating crops that can be marketed, controlling floods; we would be badly off without them. However, pointless investments like the Volta Dam do mean that capital, the fifth and last of the great forces unleashed by cities, can be quite as bizarre as any of the other forces when it reaches out in unbalanced fashion beyond cities' own regions.

Cities generate capital as a by-product of successes with new goods and services and replacements of former imports. Normally much of it finds use in cities themselves because cities require capital continually if their enterprises are to keep up-to-date, are to innovate, and are to multiply in numbers and kinds. And city regions need capital too. The changes of recent years in Shinohata, for example, required capital not generated in Shinohata but in the city. But as we have already seen, city-derived capital also reaches out to distant regions; in the form of savings by migrant workers it even reaches into regions people abandon.

Nations depend heavily on cities to yield up more in taxes than the cities get back in governmental goods and services. When the U.S. income tax was first adopted in 1913 (and was still light and touched few taxpayers), a third of the nation's entire yield came from New York State, most of it from New York City, where the economy was very vigorous at the time. Today Bombay is said to yield a third of India's income tax, and Milan a quarter of Italy's. Copenhagen and its region yield up revenues that subsidize housing and other welfare programs which benefit not only people in Copenhagen and its hinterland but the rest of the country. That is why such programs are national rather than local: to iron out regional discrepancies in wealth.

Those are all extreme examples of national financial dependence on single cities and their regions, but even when large numbers of cities share tax loads more equitably among them, as the cities of the United States do today, the fact remains that cities are the milch cows of economic life. The metaphor comes from West Germany, whose officials occasionally grumble, with good reason, that their country is the milch cow of the European Economic Community. However, it is not West Germany as an undifferentiated entity that is milked; rather, it is the country's cities and city regions that yield up surpluses not only for the EEC as a whole but for rural parts of Germany itself, for foreign loans made by German banks, and for the country's contributions to the International Monetary Fund and the World Bank.

In our time, loans, grants and subsidies provided to regions without capital-generating cities of their own have been incomparably more abundant than at any other time in history. And many, many clues in addition to fiascos like the Volta Dam tell us this capital has been wildly disproportionate to the transplants, jobs and markets that cities have been generating. We learn this, for example, from the desperate competition, now occurring almost everywhere, for transplanted industries that are up for grabs, which suggests that investments in capital facilities for transplants to plug into have been far out of proportion to the numbers of transplantable industries generated. The millions of people, from the rural South in the United States to Java, who have been dislocated from the land but have found no productive work and incomes awaiting them in cities tell us that money available for improving agricultural productivity has been out of proportion to the expansion of city jobs.

Nor have cities been shifting their markets in favor of rural goods, expanding their markets, in proportion to the growth of rural output; investments in rural production have outrun the solvent markets of cities. We get that message, for example, from the economic plights of Uruguay and New Zealand. Those countries have been highly efficient producers of food, eminently economical producers, and yet as they have lost former markets they haven't been able to find others to take their places. We get the same message from the government-subsidized competitions between French and American wheat for the grain markets of Egypt, or from the extreme and expensive measures the EEC has adopted to protect Europe's city markets for butter, meat, poultry and other produce from competition by producers outside the EEC. We get the message from the dismay expressed by midwestern American farmers at competition with producers of vegetable oils in Africa, and from their anger that these new competitors have been capitalized with American financial aid. We get the message from the decently understated but very real glee of Canadian prairie farmers when they receive news of crop failures in the Soviet Union or China, and from the protests of Maine potato farmers against U.S. imports of New Brunswick potatoes. When a modern and efficient pulp-and-paper plant in Newfoundland announces it is to close up permanently, removing the economic reason for being of a major settlement in that province, we learn that investment in pulp-and-paper production has outrun solvent city markets for paper.

In somewhat more abstract form, we learn of the same imbalance between capital on the one hand, and city jobs, transplants and markets on the other, from widespread foreign-debt defaults and persisting currency inflations. Many of the foreign debts that can't be repaid were incurred by countries trying to develop their economies. They counted on expansions of markets, jobs and industries—expansion in economic life generally—sufficient to justify their borrowings and to carry the costs. Their lenders counted on expansion too. The hopes proved ungrounded. Similarly, domestic debts that prove to be repayable, if at all, only in intolerably inflated currencies, give us the message that debts incurred by governments for investments in their own persistently poor regions—like the capital poured out over the years by Canada's Department of Regional Economic Expansion—haven't paid off in economic expansion.

All this goes far beyond the mere unbalanced use of capital in this region or that one. What we are learning, rather, is that cities *in total*, have been supplying capital bizarrely out of proportion to their own capacities to generate transplants, jobs and markets, again considered in total. The Volta Dam is merely the caricature of a pervasive situation. Furthermore, this pervasive, generalized imbalance has obviously been intensifying with the passage of decades. That is to say, the more money that has been lent and given, the larger the debt defaults, gluts and doles; the more widespread and unsuccessful the scrambles for transplants; and the more prevalent inflation has become.

In the past, whenever cities took to exporting capital out of proportion to their own continued abilities to generate jobs, industries and markets, they were neglecting their own economies with fatal consequences. For example, imperial Britain became a fabulous exporter of capital for far-flung investments, but in the meantime British cities were gradually stagnating, preparing for themselves a decline so deep it has thus far proved irreversible. Or to take an individual example, Detroit was an enormous exporter of capital during its heyday as headquarters of automobile manufacturing. But coincidentally Detroit, as a city economy, was stagnating. Not only did it stop casting up streams of new kinds of export work and stop replacing wide ranges of its imports, it even failed to maintain its leadership in automotive engineering and methods of production. The heavier capital exports became and the longer they lasted, the worse the imbalance grew between the exported capital and the other forces that those same cities were able to exert to develop and expand economic life.

Thus the generalized and intensifying imbalance we see today is ominous. We must realistically assume that what happened to Detroit and the cities of Britain is being generalized, as it were; that the powerhouses of economic life, the cities, taken in total are gradually winding down their own development, foreshadowing a deep decline for themselves and for all economic life.

But now let us take a stab at trying to see this situation more optimistically. Regions without import-replacing cities of their own have, after all, been benefiting to some degree or other from the unprecedented abundance of loans, grants and subsidies. Suppose those benefits were here and there to spark import-replacing cities into life where they have so far been lacking. In that case, even though many older cities might be succumbing to economic senility, things as a whole would not be so bad. Were new cities abundantly to arise, they would generate new solvent city markets, transplants and potential transplants, abundant new city jobs and incomes, to say nothing of capital for their own continued development. Supply regions that had once been inert, transplant economies, regions that had been cleared or abandoned would soon become well-rounded, prosperous city regions.

Alas, no such widespread wonders are manifest. If they were, obviously Taipei, Kaohsiung, Seoul and Singapore would not be the relative oddities and exceptions that they are. Their analogues would have been popping up in all kinds of places, throughout

South America, Africa, Canada, southern Italy, Scandinavia, India, the Soviet Union, Scotland and northern England, the poorer parts of the United States—everywhere that loans, grants and subsidies have been advanced in such unprecedented abundance, for if loans, grants and subsidies really did stimulate economic life, that is the effect they would be having. In that case, the generalized and intensifying imbalance of city economic forces I have mentioned either would not have emerged at all or would soon have begun righting itself rather than growing worse.

I am going to argue that loans, grants and subsidies sent into regions lacking vigorous cities can shape inert, unbalanced or permanently dependent regions, but are useless for creating self-generating economies—which is to say, useless for creating import-replacing cities. The failure is built into the fact that they *are* loans, grants and subsidies; those golden eggs, being only gold, don't hatch goslings.

Take, for example, the TVA, whose economic effects are now old enough, half a century, for us to see what was not accomplished as well as what was. Furthermore, the economic planning of the region involved and the financing that made it possible were exemplary in their own terms; better are not likely to be found. Nor was the scheme gummed up by political instability, violence, rampant corruption, cultural gaps, terrible historical obstacles, or the like. The failures in this region did not result from gratuitous difficulties or coincidental misfortunes. The Tennessee Valley was no Ghana—although as it happens, the TVA planning supplied the vision that lay behind the planning and financing of the Volta Dam.

The popular designation, TVA, for both the region and its plan, stands for Tennessee Valley Authority, the public body set up by the United States government to make the plan and administer it, and to handle its financing, which was supplied in part by government grants and in part by borrowed funds underwritten by the authority. In turn, the authority took its name from the major river of the region, the Tennessee, a tributary to the Mississippi system. Unlike a city region, TVA is a natural geographic entity, as large as a small nation. It was defined as the watershed of the river and its tributaries, embracing parts of seven states in the Southeast: Tennessee, Kentucky, Virginia, North Carolina, Georgia, Alabama and Mississippi.

Nature was generous to this region, much as Henry Grady observed that nature had been generous to Pickens County, which, as it happens, lies along the region's Georgia fringe. Resources abounded: the magnificent waterways, a warm temperate climate with a long growing season, ample rainfall, naturally fertile soil, timber, minerals, huge deposits of coal close by, extraordinary natural beauty and diversity of landscape. Nor, as such things go, had the region been handicapped or warped socially. People were not under the thumb of great landlords. The proportion of rural families who owned their own land varied from part to part but in most places was high because historically this had not been a locale of plantations worked by slaves. Even the farmers in the corner of Mississippi that lay in the region were small freeholders and always had been. The people, for the most part, had a tradition of self-reliance and hard work, and prided themselves on being neighborly, hospitable and descendants of pioneers. They also prided themselves on being political. Democratic representative government was much alive here. The policies and personalities of candidates for office, who emerged out of the population itself, were taken to be everybody's business and were perennially absorbing and entertaining topics even in the remote hamlets tucked into the folds of hills at the headwaters. All in all, it would seem that both nature and culture had set the scene here for a solid and prosperous economic life.

But in fact, the economy was wretched and growing steadily worse. In 1930 one could have attended a funeral in any number of places throughout the region and mourned it in the same terms Henry Grady had invoked long before in Pickens County. By every statistical measurement of economic well-being—infant mortality rates, disease and chronic-disability rates, nutrition, housing conditions, literacy, incomes—the region as a whole was at the very bottom of the American economy.

The land itself was in process of being destroyed. Crop yields had steadily grown poorer because soil fertility had been leached away by unremitting cultivation with little or no fertilization. Hills were scarred with the deep, raw gullies of erosion. Farmers, desperate for fresh cropland, but possessing no tradition of terracing, simply deforested slopes and plowed them; in the foothills and mountains of the headwaters they sometimes girdled the trees and planted between their leafless trunks. Aptly they called these makeshift fields "deadenings." Because of practices like these, floods in the valley lands were growing worse. Even the scant industry was remarkably destructive. The worst example was a copper smelter in a Tennessee hamlet called Ducktown, where fumes had killed every trace of vegetation over thousands of acres.

Apart from farms and small rural hamlets, the region contained an ample scattering of poor market and service towns and a few more impressive places known as cities: administrative, educational and depot centers. They produced little. Except for the occasional smelters, sawmills or transplanted textile and furniture factories, there was little industry of any sort. What there was employed few people, tended to be technologically backward and paid badly.

Neither the poverty of the economy nor its backwardness was actually surprising, considering the fact that the entire region lacked an import-replacing city and never had had one.

What to begin with? Starting in 1933, TVA began with everything at once, rapidly, energetically and efficiently. At the heart of its planning was construction of dams: to control floods, to improve river navigation, to produce electricity, and as a bonus from the reservoirs, to provide waterfronts for recreational use and for drawing tourists and their money into the region.

The electricity was to be used, among other things, for manufacturing fertilizer and to supply farms with power. Taken together, fertilizer and power were intended to increase farm yields which, in their turn, would improve nutrition, earn cash and permit marginal cropland to be withdrawn from cultivation and reforested. The electricity was also intended to attract industries and so redress the region's lack of balance between manufacturing and agriculture.

Far from marching in like grand Pooh Bah's, ordering people

about, the TVA administrators and experts worked sensitively and respectfully. For example, the agricultural experts sought out farmers who were willing to chance unfamiliar soil-building crops, such as alfalfa, and also to risk investment of their labor in contour plowing and other soil-saving techniques, and who would agree that if they were given free fertilizer, they would use it as recommended and then, when their neighbors saw the results, teach them how to use it. Cooperative self-help of all sorts was emphasized and depended upon. As soon as the first electricity became available, rural electric cooperatives were formed to buy power and distribute it to farms and hamlets. People were helped to form school-improvement committees, nutrition and home-canning classes, boys' and girls' clubs, handicraft cooperatives; they participated in starting and running sanitation and health campaigns, libraries, sports groups.

Remarkably swiftly the fertility of leached, eroded and misused farmland was rebuilt, barren hillsides reforested, floods brought under control, roads built, hookworm and malaria eradicated, new schools built and transportation to them provided, public parks created for camping, fishing, boating and swimming, model housing tracts constructed, water-supply and sanitation systems built. The industrial strategy worked brilliantly too. As fast as electricity became available, TVA sought out and found transplants. Voracious users of power led the way, notably aluminum refineries and fertilizer and other chemical plants; upon the outbreak of World War II, factories to produce armaments and explosives multiplied, and before the war had ended, the model town of Oak Ridge, Tennessee, was built to produce atomic bombs. Employment—on construction work, in transplanted industries and in administrative and public service jobs—combined with increased farm prosperity and benefited the market towns and stagnant little cities. People had more money to spend in them.

At the hub of all this was the pleasant and sleepy little city of Knoxville, Tennessee, site of the University of Tennessee and also headquarters of TVA, which made it, in effect, capital of the region.

Within a decade of the time work had begun, the region possessed new industries, new markets—particularly for its electric power—new jobs, new technology and of course much new capital. In sum, the plan had called up all the forces that cities generate, and it had used them in reasonable balance with one another. As much as such a thing is possible to do, the planners had created a facsimile of a city region: an artificial city region. All it lacked was an import-replacing city. That lack remained; neither Knoxville nor any other city of the region took to casting up streams of new export work or replacing wide ranges of its imports with local production. The legend of TVA—the memory that it was magnificently successful at saving the land, imaginative and humane in finding ways to overcome poverty and backwardness—is the legend of TVA's first decade, the period during which it constructed an artificial city region. Much of the good it wrought in that period still remains and will long remain.

Being an artificial city region, however, the area didn't proceed to work like a true city region. No significant numbers and kinds of city jobs turned up there. In the absence of even a single export-generating and import-replacing city, there was no way that such city jobs could turn up. Far from producing amply and diversely for its own producers and people as well as for others, the region continued to depend on importing almost everything or else going without. It could not be otherwise, given the lack of an import-replacing city. Local city markets did not shift their purchases significantly and expand, and so did not force the diversification of rural work typical of city regions. New industries weren't generated in significant numbers or varieties, so industries had to continue being attracted from distant places. Streams of new kinds of export work weren't being created, other than the work brought by transplants or military producers. Nearly everything continued to be financed with capital generated elsewhere.

All these economic omissions meant that by default TVA had to depend ever more heavily upon an outstanding asset it did possess, just as if it were an ordinary, unbalanced supply region. In the case of TVA the one great asset was not a crop or an ore bed but the capacity to produce electric power.

Although so much had been accomplished while the region was being remade, much poverty also remained. This had not seemed too serious at first. Given the fact that so much had improved so swiftly, much else was excused on grounds that the scheme was still young; it was more or less taken for granted that economic diversification and expansion, already so evident, would continue further under its own momentum.

This didn't happen. The lack of city jobs told. So did lack of production for local use and the lethargy of local markets. By 1964, people in the countryside and in still dismally poor little settlements in Knoxville's immediate hinterland were so badly off that President Lyndon Johnson made a special trip to that area to tell people he recognized their persistent poverty, sympathized with it, and was having the locality officially designated a depressed area so it would be eligible for extra transfer payments to alleviate poverty and for other special funds. (Incredibly, only a year later, Johnson was euphorically announcing that when the United States had won the war in Vietnam it would reconstruct that country's economy by means of TVA planning, and he followed up by sending the former chairman of TVA, David Lilienthal, to Vietnam to start devising a preliminary plan.) In 1970 a U.S. government medical survey identified the portion of Mississippi that lies in TVA territory as being at the very bottom of the entire country as to family incomes and severity of public-health and medical-care deficiencies. In 1976, when General Motors built a new automobile factory in Decatur, Alabama, the site of many TVA transplanted industries, some 40,000 people applied for the 1,400 jobs available. In 1978 an environmental battle involving a dam twenty-five miles from Knoxville brought to light the fact that people in this still badly depressed area favored the dam, no matter how damaging to the environment, because they saw it as their last and only hope for employment.

Because of realities such as these, and because the region hadn't been generating other kinds of export work and yet must import heavily or go without, TVA had had no choice except to concentrate on producing and selling electricity. Directly and indirectly, this asset underpinned the entire artificial city region and its standard of living. Therefore, from 1945 on, the authority concentrated on production of electricity to hold poverty at bay as best it could. During the 1945–1955 decade, production of electric power doubled. It doubled again in the next decade; doubled yet again in the next. The plan for 1975–1985 set forth another doubling still, but this would not be possible. In sum, once the region had attained its early illusory look of being a well-rounded economy, with every passing decade it became economically more and more unbalanced.

The expansion of power production soon outran the capacities of the dams. So the authority added immense coal-fired generators; by 1970, 80 percent of the total electric power was being generated by coal. For reasons I shall touch on in a moment, this expansion could not continue indefinitely at feasible cost, so the authority turned to nuclear power generation. By 1979 it had seven nuclear plants either operating or under construction, sufficient to make it the largest producer of nuclear power in the country, in addition to being the largest producer of water-generated electricity, as well as of coal-generated electricity. Customers of this stupendous output consisted of 50 rural electric cooperatives and 110 municipal systems (those within the region servicing many transplanted factories as well as residential users), and 50 special users. The special users are the customers for which TVA has kept doubling output: extraordinarily voracious users of power, which in the nature of things are limited in numbers and kinds. The largest is NASA (the National Aeronautics and Space Administration), followed by Alcoa (the Aluminum Company of America). Among the others, military production looms large.

Unlike sugar cane or nickel, electricity can be produced one way or another almost anywhere. Therefore TVA's one great economic asset is not electricity per se, but cheap electricity. Cost is of the essence. In the beginning, when the power was being produced by the rivers only, the cost of TVA electricity was only half that prevailing in the United States generally, and less than half the cost in the most urbanized parts of the country. This was the saving that brought transplants to the region as fast as dams were ready to serve them. Most of the expenses to acquire land for the dams and their reservoirs and for engineering and constructing them were charged not against power production, but against costs of flood control, navigation improvement, soil conservation and recreation, and so were many of the costs of maintaining and operating the dams. For those purposes, various grants were available. The electricity was regarded as a by-product, and it could be sold cheaply because of this arrangement in cost accounting.

But the advantageous accounting did not apply to electric generators, for which no case could be made that electricity was merely a by-product. Therefore, by the time coal-fired, steam-generating electric plants loomed large in the region's total power output, TVA could offer customers only a 30 percent cost advantage, the pooled margin from both coal and hydroelectric generators. Nuclear power turned out to be anything but cheap. It was so expensive, in fact, that its costs, together with static markets for power, have now impelled TVA to cancel or indefinitely defer an additional eight nuclear power plants it had planned and on some of which it had started work.

When its marginal cost advantage began to shrink, the authority sought ways of evading the facts. For one thing, it proceeded to plan and construct more dams and to get the customary other-purpose grants for them, even though in reality the dams lacked other purposes and, worse yet, were destroying prime farmland, timber and scenic beauty to no purpose other than to produce power. To get away with this, the authority—as its general manager admitted in court on one occasion—had to falsify reports on the purposes and the environmental effects of the projects. The coal the authority bought came principally from suppliers who strip-mined in the mountains of Kentucky and West Virginia, northeast of the region. The scale and ruthlessness of the strip mining were fully in keeping with the prodigious power production that the coal fed. Topsoil and forests were ravaged, valleys choked with debris. Floods grew in fury, compounding the damage. The authority's coal suppliers were accomplishing, even more thoroughly, a type of ruin that it had taken poor farmers more than a century to achieve. For as long as it could manage to do so, the authority resisted legislation, regulations, court actions and public pressure aimed at requiring its suppliers to repair their depredations; reclamation would raise the price of coal, hence the price of electricity TVA could offer transplanted industries. Finally, after battles lasting for years, environmentalists forced the authority to set reclamation standards for its coal suppliers. Then the authority failed to enforce the standards. More court battles followed. When the federal government mandated scrubbers (which cost about $1 million each) to diminish air pollutants, the authority resisted complying with that, again because to do so would somewhat raise the costs of power and make winning new transplants for the region harder. Although one can't be sure, it now seems that environmentalists have won the battles of scrubbers for the stacks and reclamation for the strip mines.

But as for the region's own grotesque economy, nothing has been corrected. It was so poor in the first place because it lacked an import-replacing city, which it still lacks. It is reaching the end of the line with respect to what can be done by drawing on distant capital, distant markets and transplants from distant places for its output of power. The next stage in its history will most likely be the usual stagnation and gradually deepening poverty of an unbalanced supply region that has run its course, gone as far as it can with a stunted economy, although the authority now sees an expanding future for itself, as an institution, in lending its experts to backward countries. They have advised Brazil, Turkey and Bangladesh on their development, and in 1982 signed an agreement with the U.S. Agency for International Development to assist energy projects in the Philippines, Indonesia, Egypt, the Sudan and Latin America.

At a time when criticism of TVA was reaching one of its crescendos during the 1970s, the chairman happened to be a man who had taken part in the enterprise from the beginning, having been one of the first TVA employees in that legendary first decade. Confronted with evidence of the damage TVA had begun causing, he replied, "I wouldn't say we're doing things that aren't wrong, but if we are, we're not doing it willingly."

There spoke a man caught in an economic trap. His mandate from the beginning had been to help overcome a region's poverty.

He had been working as best he could with what the region has, and lacking an import-replacing city, it has surprisingly little. The only dismal alternative to the dismal course the authority did take would have been to preside over a region that workers abandoned in large numbers for jobs in distant cities—if they could find them.

But how did it happen that no import-replacing city was catalyzed in this region so bountifully benefited by the capital goods that loans, grants and subsidies can buy? For an answer we must understand that whenever and wherever import-replacing cities do rise and flourish, imported goods and services play three different roles in their economies. For one, cities put their imports to use, consume them, just as any settlement does.

But as far as development of their economies is concerned, that is the least of the roles imports play in cities. They also represent "things earned by city export work." This is basic. The very process of earning imports develops a city's economy, for earning imports requires versatility at production and improvisation. That is to say, the earning process itself promotes and supports the symbiotic nests of suppliers and producers that are all-important to a city's economy. As the export work that a city casts up ramifies and diversifies, so do these local producers ramify and diversify, and so do the imports the city is earning automatically diversify in service to diversifying production. The process of earning imports is thus crucial for bringing a vigorous city to birth and life, and remains crucial for continued development. Development cannot be given. It has to be *done*. It is a process, not a collection of capital goods.

The third role imports play in a city is, of course, to serve as candidates for replacements with local production. But that can't occur in an economically feasible way, indeed cannot be done at all, without a foundation of versatility laid down by the earlier process of earning the imports.

Enormous quantities of imports and vast varieties of them came into the TVA region during the period when it was being remade, and have been coming in ever since. But no significant variety or quantity of those imports was earned there by city work. How could it be? The imports were gifts financed by grants and subsidies, or were extended on credit thanks to the borrowings the authority underwrote. Even the loans weren't supported by city work or repaid from earnings of city work; sales of power paid the interest and paid back the principal of the chief loans. Agricultural earnings paid back others. In sum, earnings of city work could not figure at all, by definition, in the case of imported goods acquired through grants and subsidies; they did not figure, either, in the case of goods and services the region got on credit.

Here it is useful to remember what happened in Taipei during that city's recent extraordinary economic development. Taiwan was a beneficiary of loans, grants and subsidies from the United States, but it wasn't those that brought about Taipei's development as an import-replacing city. Something else entirely was happening in the city itself, where imports of sewing machines, machine tools, dies, raw materials, building materials, and so on, were being earned by the work of city enterprises, most of them small and improvisational. Unimpressive as those earnings were in comparison with the great, splendid funds of capital goods that can so swiftly be financed by big borrowings, grants and subsidies, those scrabbly city earnings were what counted in Taipei's development as a ramifying, versatile producer and, subsequently, in its region's development. It was the imports earned by city work, not the unearned ones, that powered development there.

In the TVA region there had been no intent to catalyze city economies, for that was not thought of as being basic at all. And indeed, no existing settlement in the region would have seemed particularly promising. But suppose the intent had existed, along with a reasonably promising candidate for an import-replacing city—*then* would bountiful loans, grants and subsidies have promoted such an economy?

Experience in real life tells us, again, that the answer is no. To take one example, since 1950 the Italian government has poured in loans, grants and subsidies to build roads, power plants, schools, housing, attract industries, subsidize agriculture, and so on, in the southern part of the country, the place from which those sad migrant workers depicted in *Bread and Chocolate* have poured.

In particular, industrial transplants were located at Bari on the Adriatic, and in the close vicinity of Naples—some of them financed at great cost by the government's own industry-creating arm—with the intent of helping Bari and Naples develop economically. The general aim of the planning, both rural and urban, was to close the economic gap between the poor, predominantly rural south and the prosperous urbanized north. But Naples and Bari have remained much as they were, their economies essentially unchanged by the unearned imports that came in the form of bestowed factories while, ironically, cities in the north that were earning imports were becoming more versatile in the process.

Luigi Barzini, the Italian essayist and journalist, has summed up the profoundly disappointing results. To be sure, just as in the case of TVA, southern Italy got important benefits from what the loans, grants and subsidies bought in the way of imports and expertise. Barzini speaks of the astonishing "science fiction air" imparted by all the new facilities, but also the equally astonishing superficiality of the changes: ". . . the ancient desperate poverty *still* remains. In many villages only old people and children live—and wretchedly at that . . . the countryside is empty." Furthermore, even though the construction work itself, the remaking itself, provided employment, and even though the industries brought in do provide jobs the region didn't have before, the economic gap between the rich north of the country and the poor south has not narrowed. On the contrary, it has actually widened. "If the hopes are borne in mind," says Barzini, "the policy must be called a resounding, expensive failure . . . and, what is worse, an historical opportunity lost forever."

In southern Italy, just as in TVA, there was the early, wonderfully hopeful period of change, followed by anticlimax. Everyone, says Barzini, including those who made the plans, is in agreement that some kind of opportunity was somehow muffed, but blame revolves around the questions of how the loans, grants and subsidies might have been better spent, and these are bootless questions. Actually, they probably did as much good as they could.

People who remember the youthful TVA and then observe what it has become may tend to think of the scheme as having been betrayed in some way. But the legendary TVA and the current TVA are one and the same. The fact that loans, grants and subsidies were poured into southern Italy and the fact that it still remains a region workers abandon for distant city jobs, if they can find them, are not contradictory but complementary facts.

It is important, then, for us to understand the distinction between what development loans, grants and subsidies can do and what they cannot do. They can bring very swift, needed changes, and produce real improvements immediately when they are well used. But the spending of the loans, grants and subsidies is the *whole* improvement to be expected. The rest is anticlimax, inertia and profound continued dependency on expansionary forces, usually inadequate, from distant cities. This is the miserable denouement the Algerian revolutionary leader Ahmed Ben Bella was describing when he bitterly summed up, in 1981, the experience of the Third World with a quarter of a century's development loans, grants and subsidies. "The north imposes its patterns and standards on us. We are importing more factories and more tools, but also more wheat and food products, and we are becoming increasingly more dependent."

He is quite right, but this is no cynical or uncaring plot on the part of "the north." The results are built into the nature of the transactions themselves. Poor regions of rich countries get the same results from such transactions as poor countries do.

Once we understand why unearned imports, whatever other usefulness they may have, are beside the point for catalyzing real economic development, we can understand, also, why the remittances that migrant workers send back to their poor home regions do so little to transform economic life there. Not having been earned right there, by city work, these benefits can play no part in economic life other than temporarily alleviating poverty. It is the same with all transfer payments from rich to poor regions. They alleviate poverty but inherently can do nothing to overcome the causes of poverty.

If our present cities and the civilizations utterly depending on them are destined to die away, as so many cities and their civilizations have in the past, perhaps our most impressive memorials will prove to be our dams. The roads won't last. They are too badly built. But the dams, silted up and overgrown, even though cracked and crumbled beneath, will be immense, mute marvels. "What were these people up to?" my imaginery diggers of the future will ask themselves. "Incredible! They even went so far as to build these things in places that seem to have been hardly touched by anything else they had. Maybe it was a cult for the purpose of propitiating or invoking mysterious powers." Too simple a picture of us, but not so wrong in principle.

NINE

Bypassed Places

Economies that have previously served city markets or have sent out people to city jobs or have received city technology, city transplants or city money, can eventually lose those ties to cities. If they do, their people sink into lives of rural subsistence. But as they adjust to sheer subsistence, they shed or lose many former practices and skills. For instance, in Egypt making paper from papyrus plants was an ancient and well-established practice. As late as the time of the Roman Empire, paper was a major export of Egypt. But then, when almost all Egypt collapsed into rural subsistence life, papermaking was abandoned. Unless one is Japanese, the last thing one needs in a subsistence economy is paper. Even the variety of papyrus from which paper can be made became extinct in Egypt. Today nobody would know how the thing was done were it not for a modern scholar in Cairo, Hassan Ragab, who reintroduced the plant to the Nile from specimens he found growing on riverbanks in Sudan and then after years of trial and error reinvented the craft. His organization, the Papyrus Institute, has once again begun exporting paper to distant cities in Europe and America, where it has found small, specialized markets because, although it is very expensive, it is incomparably more durable than any other paper known.

Back in the early 1930s I spent some time in an American subsistence economy that had proceeded to shed and lose traditional practices and skills after it had lost almost all contact and interchange with the economies of cities. The place was a hamlet which I am going to call Henry for purposes of preserving its anonymity. Henry consisted of a scattering of farms unconnected by roads, tucked into mountain folds in western North Carolina, at an outermost edge of what was to become the TVA region. In the case of Henry, no momentous events like the fall of empire or the disintegration of cities had cut its economic ties. Migration, followed by isolation, had done the job. Henry had been retrogressing economically in perfect peace and tranquillity.

Its people were of British descent. In America they had first settled in eastern Carolina, then had pushed westward through the mountains to find fresh land, ending up near the headwaters of the Cane River, a lovely place of majestic folded hills, hardwood forests and loud, tumbling creeks. My aunt, Martha Robison, had been sent there from Pennsylvania in 1923 as a field worker of the Presbyterian Board of Home Missions. At the time she arrived, Henry had been all but cut off from the economies of cities for about a century and a half. Although the little county seat and market town was only twelve miles distant, most people from Henry had never been there, and those who had gone went seldom, by foot or muleback. The track was almost impossible to negotiate with a wagon; indeed, wagons were one of many things people in Henry did without.

One of my aunt's tasks there was to see to construction of a church, financed of course from distant cities in the North. One of the farmers donated, as a site, a beautiful knoll beside the river and my aunt suggested the building be made of fine large stones which were already quarried, as it were, needing little dressing, there for the taking in the creek and river beds. No, said the community elders, it was a pretty idea but not possible. Mortar, they explained, holds only very small stones and they pointed out that chimneys are always made of little stones for that reason. Furthermore, even with little stones, they said, one can go only so far. Entire walls and buildings of stone would not be safe.

These people came of a parent culture that had not only reared stone parish churches from time immemorial, but great cathedrals. Even in eighteenth-century tidewater and piedmont Carolina their ancestors must have been acquainted with masonry buildings. But having lost the practice of construction with stone, people had lost the memory of it, too, over the generations, and having lost the memory, lost belief in the possibility—until a mason arrived from the nearest city, Asheville, and got them started on a church of small stones. The next building they put up, a house for my aunt after her wood cottage burned, was of large stones, and so was the next, a community party, craft and library center. The buildings still stand: the church of little stones, the others of large ones.

When the forebears of the people of Henry arrived in their mountain pocket, they brought with them a rich economic heritage of products and skills: among them, spinning and weaving, loom construction, cabinetmaking, corn milling, house and watermill construction, dairying, poultry and hog raising, gardening, whiskey distilling, hound breeding, molasses making from sorghum cane, basket weaving, biscuit baking, music making with violins . . . They also brought along with them the practice and habit of trade which, over the course of a century and a half, had become for the most part a habit of barter. The owner of the water wheel took a measure of corn or four eggs to pay for grinding a sack of corn; the man who made the best chairs got a basket of laboriously gathered chinquipin nuts or a rag rug.

Actually, the people of Henry did not totally depend on what they could produce for themselves. They grew a few fields of tobacco to earn cash, and except in lean years there were always some surplus jugs of sorghum molasses. The tobacco and molasses were not sold to people in nearby hamlets, because people there had as little cash as people in Henry itself and anyhow produced the same things. By way of muleback, the tobacco got to the county seat and from there to factories in eastern North Carolina, and the molasses was consumed in the county seat itself. In return, Henry got a few precious imports from the outside world: heavy workshoes, denim overalls, some metal tools, ammunition for the aged shotguns that put squirrels in the dinner pots, and Sunday outfits cherished for a lifetime. Cash was so scarce that the snapping of a pitchfork or the rusting of a plow posed a serious financial crisis.

That meager trade with the outside world was as nothing com-

pared with the land and labor that people in Henry put into providing for their needs directly. Once one has seen how demanding
it is for people to provide from a rural economy almost everything
they need for their survival, and how precarious such a life is, it
is not hard to understand why old practices drop away, leaving
only those absolutely necessary. In Henry everything took so much
work and time, and there were so few aids to help the work along.
Without good saws, the work of collecting and cutting the great
piles of wood needed to boil sorghum juice into molasses, a very
important staple of the diet, occupied entire families for weeks.
The sorghum mill itself, an ancient relic made of an iron pressing-
chamber and a cogwheeled screw powered by a circling, plodding
mule, was shared among three hamlets, each family waiting its
turn, an anxious time for those who wondered if they would get
it before the winter freeze.

People in Henry had been sliding backward economically, and
in 1923 were still in process of doing so. Crafts that had been their
heritage were decaying, and some were being lost. One elderly woman still knew how to make baskets and how to find and
prepare the vines, reeds, splints and dyes for them. Many knew
how to make candles, but the time and work required made
candles a luxury; they were disappearing as families learned to go
without them and make do with firelight. Weaving had degen-
erated because, in the press of demands imposed by sheer survival,
people had long since stopped making looms, and nobody any
longer knew how. Old looms, mostly from the early nineteenth
century, were still in use for weaving blankets and cloth for skirts
and cloaks, but the looms were repaired so ineptly that the weaving was no longer of good quality, too fragile in some spots, too
thick in others, lumpy and unraveling at the selvages. Only one
woman any longer churned butter, and few kept cows; dairy
products were all but disappearing from the diet.

Part of the trouble was the degeneration of agriculture. When
old land wore out, deadenings of the sort I described in the previous chapter were contrived for makeshift new cornfields, and
as erosion destroyed a deadening, a new one was cut higher in
the forest. This practice, or some version of it, is very common in
subsistence farming and is not always destructive; soil scientists

call it shifting agriculture. But when the land happens to be hilly and wooded, as the land in Henry was above the narrow valley, shifting agriculture can destroy it permanently. Historically, shifting agriculture has been responsible for widespread deforestation and loss of soil in Spain, China and the Middle East, and is today a chief cause of destruction of tropical forests. When people in Henry took to encroaching ever farther into the mountain forests with their deadenings, they were behaving as people of many bypassed subsistence cultures have behaved, and as many do today under the pressure to survive.

People in Henry worked hard, took their responsibilities seriously, were thrifty, using and reusing everything until it was totally worn out (including the land), and they were bright and full of curiosity, as intelligent as any of us. They were a far cry from the feckless and loutish hillbillies of the comic strips and jokes. Yet, between the degeneration of the soil and the loss of older skills and crafts, Henry's economy in the 1920s had become thinner, poorer and more primitive than that of their own ancestors. Their subsistence life was not a demonstration, as romantics like to think, of how economic life begins, but rather of how it decays and peters out.

Once Henry's ties to cities began to be re-established its economy started slowly to improve and to rediversify somewhat. The old crafts that were on the brink of disappearing were retrieved. My aunt, with the help of her city mission board, found city markets for baskets, handwoven wool and linen, rag rugs, and the traditional chairs and brooms which were two products still being made splendidly. The basket maker acquired an apprentice. The looms, with outside help, were mended properly.

While in most of America the Great Depression brought hard times, in Henry the economy was improving as the hamlet started to emerge from its Long Subsistence Depression. A new road helped. When the paving came through late in the 1920s and occasional trucks and cars came by, some of the young men hitched rides. Two or three of these adventurers hit upon seasonal jobs for themselves in the coal mines of West Virginia. Within a few years, Depression notwithstanding, most Henry families with a son eighteen or nineteen years old, who had remained strong and in good health, were getting a little income from the mines. Later, with the war, the income came from the U.S. Army instead. After the war, young people began abandoning Henry permanently for distant city jobs. In the late 1960s a few city people established summer and weekend houses, but so much of the former population has left that as a community Henry now has little vitality. We may mourn the disappearance of the old subsistence life with its bypassed, interesting ways. But the people who had to live that life in Henry welcomed every link with cities they could grasp. Those links were new in one sense, but in another sense not new at all. Back in history, these people's ancestors had had such links and had lost them as they became economically isolated.

It may well be that no pristine economies remain on earth today to show us the dawn of creative economic life. To be sure, the very few hunting-and-gathering societies to be found here and there are primitive and seemingly unchanging. Yet they generally have weapons, traps, utensils, building methods, ornaments and, often, musical instruments that speak to us clearly of the facts of invention and change once-upon-a-time. Like Henry, or like subsistence Egypt, those hunting-and-gathering societies may be more primitive than their own ancestral economies, may demonstrate to us endings rather than beginnings. Even a band of wild-plant gatherers who possess no tools whatever (just such a band has been found in a jungle fastness of the Philippines) pose a puzzle that speaks more logically of decline than dawn. Somehow at some time the forebears of that band traveled over the sea, an achievement they could hardly have pulled off totally barehanded. Most likely, after migration they deteriorated economically in isolation.

Be that as it may, virtually all people in the bypassed subsistence economies to be found today—in the poverty-stricken rural backwaters of India, China, Southeast Asia, the Middle East, Africa and Latin America—are living in economies that tell us of inventive and creative pasts. Among them are the *morosos*, those without hope, of Napizaro's region in Mexico. Behind these people lie histories of connections with developing economies, of which they still retain bits, fragments and residues.

Consider, for example, Ethiopia. A map showing the typical

settlement on arable lands is so thickly and continuously sprinkled with dots representing dwellings that it looks superficially like a case of stupendous suburban sprawl spilled out through a nation half again as large as France. But except for Addis Ababa and Azmara, neither of which has much of an economy, this vast rash of settlement is rural and more thoroughly severed from contact with cities than Henry at its most isolated. To be sure, hides, cotton and coffee leave the country, but that production for distant city markets is as nothing compared to the land and labor rural Ethiopians devote to their direct battle for survival from the land. Nine tenths of Ethiopia's 30 million people are subsistence farmers or herdsmen. In 1973, a year when the rainfall dropped below normal, more than 100,000 Ethiopians starved to death, an event of which the outside world was hardly aware, and even in the best of years countless Ethiopians go hungry.

Urban energy of any sort, whether from within Ethiopia or outside it, simply does not touch millions of these huts or garden plots. This is an economy left almost entirely by cities to its own devices. Yet the fact remains that this is anything but a pristine economy. Ethiopia was not always bypassed by cities. Long ago it was tied into the urban life of ancient Egypt. Just how that connection came about and how it worked has vanished from memory in both Egypt and Ethiopia, but the fact that there was a connection is certain because Ethiopia's culture is derived from Egypt's in the same sense that America's culture is derived from Europe's, and Japan's from China's. Later on, Ethiopia in its own right became an empire of wealth, power and consequence for its time. But Ethiopia was already stagnating and its wealth evaporating when Rome was being founded. The poor and backward life to be found there today is the end product of a thinned and decadent economic life, a long, long period of arrested development.

The fact of Ethiopia's stagnation is not in itself remarkable. Ethiopia suffered the typical fate of empires, then and now. What is remarkable, rather, is that once this economy had lost its cities and city ties, it has remained bypassed by cities for so long. To get some conception of how long, consider that if the site of old Bardou were to have been bypassed by cities as long as most of Ethiopia has been, beginning at the time the Roman iron mines at the site were abandoned, Bardou would remain bypassed today and the people of that hamlet would still have ahead of them at least a thousand more years of utter economic stagnation. Obviously, the state of being bypassed can continue interminably in an economy that loses its own cities and for which distant cities find little or no use.

By no means have all currently bypassed economies lost their ties with cities long ago. For instance, in some regions of central Africa a generation ago people raised cash crops or worked mines for distant city markets, as colonial subjects of Great Britain and Belgium. The political ties have been severed and in some cases the economic ties as well. Political and military violence and uproars currently make it impossible to get crops to market, and breakdowns of former depot services have imposed economic isolation on country people who have wholly fallen back on subsistence life. What else? Perhaps this change is only temporary, but perhaps not.

What has happened to those outposts of empire in Africa in our own time is not so different, in principle, from what happened in outposts of the Western Roman Empire when the legions pulled out of Britain or when the iron mines at the site of Bardou were being abandoned. The Roman economy left its residues in much of Europe, more residues in some parts than in others, but as Europe sank into subsistence life, think how much was shed and lost and then totally forgotten. The very practice of rotating crops was dropped under the press of survival, then actually forgotten as a possibility. Metal agricultural tools wore out and went unreplaced, the crafts of making them having been dropped and forgotten. As bread baking was abandoned, gruel became the common cereal food of Europe. Whole ranges of manufactured and craft goods disappeared from economic life; so did well-woven cloth (except in one small enclave of the Low Countries where the skill was retained), dyed stuffs, cheap mass-produced pottery, manuscripts, glassware. Living more primitively off fragments they retained in their decayed subsistence life, people were living, even though badly, off a more creative past. In Rome itself in the sixth century, people were literally living off economic fragments and residues from the past as they pillaged hinges from

doors and pipes from fountains to get bits of metal for an economic life no longer organized to mine and smelt ore.

I have argued that all developing economic life depends on city
economies; it depends on them by definition because, wherever
economic life is developing, the very process itself creates cities
and has probably always done so, even though some of those
cities—like cities of the Hopewell Culture of the North American
Indians which had vanished before the time of Columbus, or cities
of the Olmec Culture in Mexico, lost even earlier—would seem
strange indeed to us. I have also argued that all expanding economic life depends on working links with cities. If this is correct,
then it follows that no subsistence economy that uses the products
and practices of economic inventiveness, no matter how residual
and fragmentary, can be thought of as being truly alien to city
life. Somewhere, sometime, it had links to creative cities, however briefly, however tenuously, however long ago.

It might seem to follow from this that re-establishing links with
city economies is not, in principle, alien to bypassed subsistence
economies, but that is not necessarily so. If the specific cities that
re-establish links with bypassed subsistence economies are of a
different culture, they can be disastrously alien to subsistence
economies.

The hamlet of Henry was fortunate that the cities which in-
tervened in its economy, re-establishing ever stronger links after
1923, were not of alien culture. This has been the good fortune,
too, of Japanese subsistence communities, or subsistence-supply
communities like old Shinohata. It had also been the good fortune of most but not all subsistence settlements in Europe: cities
re-establishing links with bypassed subsistence life came out of
the same culture as the rural settlements they were transforming.

When the contrary occurs, the re-established links with creative economic life are all too seldom a boon. To remain bypassed
and ignored by alien cities can be a mercy. The North American
Indians would have been far better off had they not been im-
pinged upon by alien Europeans, with their distant city markets
for furs, and then their own ideas of how to use the Indians' lands.
The Irish, it seems to me, would have been far better off had they
been bypassed by the English of Cromwell's time and the sub-

sequent two centuries. Today the Burmese, having severed old colonial ties with Europe, have adamantly refused offers of loans, grants or subsidies from anywhere, and their rulers have forbidden most external trade, although smuggling and black markets do flourish. The Burmese not only produce little today for distant markets, they produce less plentifully and less diversely even for themselves than they did as a colonial economy or, apparently, than they did in long-gone days when they themselves had a creative and inventive economic life. The Burmese today have sunk, for the most part, into rural subsistence life and by all accounts are poorer than in the past, with a more primitive economy, though apparently they think they are better off for having been bypassed by distant alien cities. Perhaps they are right. An alternative, of course, would be for them to develop not in alien ways but in their own manner, as Europe and Japan did.

After the disintegration of the Western Roman Empire, Europe escaped the sort of interminable stagnation Ethiopia has experienced, owing to the formation of European medieval cities. But it was probably touch and go. A new city, to form, needs one or more older cities with which to begin its initial trade (as we shall see in the next chapter). Luckily for Europe, there was a scruffy little settlement on the mud flats and marshes at the head of the Adriatic which discovered, during the very depths of the Dark Ages, when the rest of Europe was still decaying and deteriorating, that there was a city market for salt, then timber, in Constantinople. But Venice, the pioneer city of the European economy, did not remain a mere supply depot. By diversifying its own production, starting on the base of that trade in salt and timber, it proceeded to develop and, thereby, to provide a Venetian city market for depot settlements of the north and west—which then built up city production of their own, each in its turn. As the cities of Europe, passing on the spark of creative economic life from one to another, multiplied, they also drew into their trade the subsistence life about them and transformed it. Old Bardou was one of the last, anachronistic remnants in Europe of the time when all Europe had been bypassed.

Often enough, all the cities of an empire have stagnated in succession, while in the decay and wreckage of the dying economies no new, young cities have been simultaneously arising to compensate for those losses. City death, without new city life, occurred in the Western Roman Empire, and *later* in the Eastern Roman Empire. Given what Constantinople meant to Venice, we can be grateful for that fact of *later*. So far, going back and back to Neolithic times, there seems never to have been a simultaneous deadening of cities over the entire world, and thus no period in which all economic life consisted of bypassed, subsistence life. While Addis Ababa was dying, Rome was rising. While the great cities of China were stagnating, Venice was rising. No doubt in future (provided, of course, there is a future for a world booby-trapped with nuclear weapons), people will remark that while the cities of Great Britain were dying those of Japan were rising.

But suppose, hypothetically, that the world were to behave like a single sluggish empire in decline. Such a thing could happen if cities in too many places stagnated simultaneously or in quick succession. Or it could happen if the world were to become, in fact, one single sluggish empire.

If global city stagnation ever does occur, it will inexorably cause economic life everywhere to stagnate and deteriorate, and there will be no way out: no existing vigorous cities to intervene, no young cities arising while they still have opportunity to do so. If that were to happen, we may be sure that as the practice of developing city economies vanished, the memory of how the thing is done would vanish too, and after that, belief that it could be done by perfectly ordinary people would no longer be credited as a possibility. Indeed, it is not credited as a possibility in much of the world even today. Isolated Henry, old Bardou, eventually even Ethiopia would become the norm. Everywhere, all would become *morosos*, those without hope. We all have our nightmares about the future of economic life; that one is mine.

TEN

Why Backward Cities Need One Another

The Shah of Iran wanted an economy like America's, Japan's and northern Europe's. He thought he could have it if he had the same kind of equipment they had. So he set about getting it, advised by people nicknamed *masachuseti* by an Iranian sociologist, meaning technocrats equipped with an education and outlook popularly associated there with the Massachusetts Institute of Technology, where indeed many of the Shah's economic and technical experts had been trained.

A helicopter factory the government ordered in 1975 for the venerable city of Isfahan illustrates what was actually taking place and where, when the Shah imagined he was buying development. A contract to design a new nineteen-seat helicopter and to build and equip a factory to produce it was negotiated with an American corporation, Textron, along with a second contract agreeing to pay Textron for training the Iranian mechanics who would build and service the helicopters and the pilots who would fly them. Contracts like this were usual. Iran had entered into them with firms in Europe and Japan, as well as in the United States, for fertilizer factories, cement plants, steelworks, power plants, hospitals, automotive works, even entire agricultural villages. Some facilities were meant to produce primarily for Iran's domestic needs. Others, like the helicopter factory, were intended to produce both for the domestic economy and for export. Iran paid for these with oil, the idea being that by the time the oil ran out, Iran would no longer need to import sophisticated manufactured goods, would produce most of its own food, and would have alternate exports in place of oil—in short, a well-rounded, self-generating economy producing amply and diversely for itself as well as for others. That was the theory.

Textron, as its name suggests, began life as a textile factory but it had become a diversified conglomerate by buying up other enterprises, among them Bell Helicopter, formerly Bell Aircraft of Buffalo, New York, which was transplanted to Fort Worth, Texas. Bell was experienced at handling big, complex projects competently, which is why Textron got the contract; the Shah and his *masachuseti* did not want the project to bog down in the sort of confusion, waste and ineptitude that Uruguay had experienced when it tried to establish a manufacturing economy. Textron set up a new subsidiary, Bell Operations, in Euless, Texas, not far from the parent Bell company, to devote itself to this one job. While engineers in Euless worked out the design of the new helicopter and began work on designing the factory itself, other Bell engineers and management people set up a headquarters in Isfahan to prepare for the work there. The factory was to be a vast installation, comprising fifty buildings.

In due course, Bell Operations let the contract to build the factory to Jones Construction Company of Charlotte, North Carolina, another competent and experienced firm. Jones Construction subcontracted out the various specialties involved. For example, the Howard P. Foley Company of Washington, D.C., was responsible for design, supervision and purchase of electrical equipment. The purchase orders, sent from a Foley branch office in Dallas, Texas, went to six electrical wholesalers such as Graybar Electric Company of New York City, which, through a branch office in Dallas, ordered machinery, parts and materials from a bewildering array of manufacturers, large and small: for example, electrical substations from Dis-Tran Products of Alexandria, Louisiana, and electrical switching gear from General Electric Company, which produced it in four different factories, located in Texas, North Carolina, Illinois and Iowa. Dis-Tran and General Electric were only two of more than ninety manufacturers from which Graybar bought its share of the Isfahan work. All those ninety, in their turn, drew on hosts of their own suppliers for materials, parts and tools. It was the same with the multitude of manufacturers who filled orders from the five other wholesalers like Graybar.

Another major specialty, heating, air conditioning and plumbing, was subcontracted by Jones Construction to the Sam P. Wallace Company of Dallas. Wallace drew from 150 manufacturers, firms such as Texas Automatic Sprinklers, which custom-designed and made the fire-protection sprinkler heads, in its turn, of course, drawing upon its own suppliers of tools, materials and services, just as the 149 other Wallace subcontractors were doing.

To arrange transportation to Isfahan of all these components and much, much more, Jones Construction and the Wallace and Foley companies jointly hired a freight forwarder, Daniel F. Young, Inc., which set up an office for the purpose in a suburb of Fort Worth. Young scheduled and coordinated collection of goods into shipping lots at the ports of Houston, New Orleans, Charleston, Norfolk, Baltimore and New York. For the ocean leg of the transport, Young used four shipping lines, and here at last we find an Iranian involvement. Chief among the carriers, taking on factory cargo at one or another American port every two weeks, month after month, was Iran Express: 49 percent owned by the Ulterwyk Corporation of Tampa, Florida, and 51 percent owned by Iran. Iran also held majority ownership in two of the other three cargo lines.

Although hundreds of similar contracts running into the tens of billions of dollars were carried to completion, the Textron contracts were not. In August 1978, when the factory was nearly a third finished, violent demonstrations against the Shah erupted in Isfahan. A bus for Bell employees was bombed, but martial law was declared and construction continued. However, at about this same time the government was finding it had overcommitted its oil revenues, which were what still paid for everything Iran was buying from abroad. To get more foreign exchange, the government turned to borrowing against future oil revenues, and to cover its ballooning expenses within the country, it had taken to printing money at such a rate that prices were skyrocketing and Iran's indigenous commerce was collapsing.

In October 1978 Iran fell behind on its payments to Textron. As soon as payments stopped, Textron halted the work. All the way down the line, from the Euless drafting rooms of Bell Operations to the punch-press floors of obscure sub-sub-sub-sub-subcontractors in Chicago, Brooklyn and Philadelphia, workers were laid off, while in executive suites and clerical departments other American workers turned to hustling up new customers and selling to scrap and surplus-goods dealers equipment already manufactured but not yet dispatched to Isfahan. Bell tentatively considered plans to produce the helicopter itself or in partnership with another foreign customer if one could be found. Two months after payments and work stopped, and shortly before the Shah was deposed, the Iranian government officially canceled the Textron contracts.

At about the same time that the Iranian government was having second thoughts on this project, a visiting reporter from *The New Yorker* magazine was interviewing a high school teacher, a devout Muslim, who had been one of the leaders of the anti-Shah demonstrations in Isfahan. The reporter, after first listening to the man's descriptions of political repression and growing social disorganization, introduced the subject of the economy. He asked the teacher, who had graduated from the University of Teheran fifteen years before, whether it was not true, nevertheless, that in those fifteen years Iran "had taken large strides toward economic development."

No, said the teacher, "I have to say with great sorrow that our economic growth is based on a windfall called oil. If we consider where we are, and then where the progressive states like Japan are, we realize how little we have accomplished. When I think of Japan I think of a verse:

"Leila and I were fellow travellers on the road of life;
She reached her home, and I am still a vagabond."

But still, the reporter pressed him, even if some other countries had done better than Iran, "Iran had done quite well."

"What we see here is inflation," the teacher answered. "Prices for food have gone way up. What we see is the depletion of our oil reserves . . . What we see is an agriculture worth zero . . . Our industry is just an assembly line for products made in other countries . . ." At this point one of the listeners to the interview offered the reporter an apple. "He began to peel it for me," wrote the reporter, "but at the first stroke of the knife the blade separated from its handle. He held out the broken knife. 'There you see it all,' he said in disgust. 'Our country owns twenty-five per cent of Krupp in Germany, but in Iran we can't even produce a knife that cuts an apple.' "

The choice of the knife to caricature the gulf between the producers' goods Iran was buying and those it was capable of making was well taken. To be able to develop and make producers' goods is at the very heart of economic life, and to be able to make knives, various cutting edges, is basic to developing and making producers' as well as consumers' goods. An economy that isn't turning out for itself increasingly wide ranges of producers' goods is not making "large strides toward development," no matter what it is buying. One might as well infer that an oil tycoon, because he can buy paintings and sculptures, has become an artist.

Insofar as any development was involved in what the Shah was buying, it was all taking place somewhere else, not in Iran. Although the Shah's factories had (at first) all been earned by Iran, unlike facilities financed on credit or by grants and subsidies, they hadn't been earned by Iranian city work, and the earning had thus done nothing for Iran's capacity to build up versatile and productive city economies or, it follows, to generate city regions. Therefore, the purchases had only reinforced the country's already grotesque and unbalanced supply economy with its dependence on oil.

The Shah was not the first autocratic ruler to think he could buy development in a big way. Early in the eighteenth century Peter the Great tried to purchase a developed economy for Russia by buying producers' goods and expertise from Holland and other highly developed economies of the time. Assisted and advised by Western-trained experts, the *masachuseti* of his day, Peter bought hundreds of facilities from Western Europe, ranging from iron foundries and canal locks to ribbon factories and a model capital city, St. Petersburg, now Leningrad. Peter was much admired in Western Europe for his modernization of Russia, just as the Shah was admired in many circles for his modernization of Iran. In Peter's case, the money came from taxes imposed on his subjects, mainly falling on the peasantry since most of Russia's production was rural. In spite of all the money spent, and all the trappings of progress it purchased, the Russian economy did not thereupon proceed to act like the economies Peter was under the illusion he was duplicating. Like the Shah, he thought of development as a collection of things for producing, not as a process of change. The process itself was something he could not buy, nor Western Europe sell. Western Europe, engaged in the process, continued to develop economically in many-sided ways, while Russia, lacking complex city economies, continued stunted and stultified. Thus in the years that followed Peter's purchases, the economic gap between the West European economies and Russia's did not narrow as Peter had anticipated, but widened.

Development is a do-it-yourself process; for any economy it is either do it yourself or don't develop. All of today's highly developed economies were backward at one time, yet transcended that condition. Their accumulated experience demonstrates how the thing is actually done. Historically, we find two major patterns, or motifs: reliance of backward cities upon one another, and economic improvisation. The Shah and Peter and their advisers were as far off the track as it is possible to be, trying as they did to wrest development from their simplistic two-way trade with much more advanced economies, and relying as they did upon already developed methods and products, thereby short-cutting indigenous trial, error and improvisation.

In the previous chapter I noted that for new cities to arise and flourish, they must find solvent markets for their initial work in already existing cities. Yet it is fatal if backward cities confine themselves to that kind of trade, for such trade is only a springboard for embarking on a different type of intercity trade: trade with cities in much the same circumstances and stage of development as themselves. This means that backward cities must trade most heavily with other backward cities. Otherwise, the gulf between what they import and what they can replace with their own production is too great to be bridged. In effect, this is what the angry teacher in Isfahan was complaining of, and he was right.

In Europe the development process that eluded Peter when he bought its artifacts had been pioneered by Venice, which used its simple advanced-backward trade with Contantinople to launch itself into many new ventures. The creators of Venice, the Veneti, are now thought to have taken up life on the mud flats and marshes at the head of the Adriatic as a refuge from plunder and turmoil; whatever the circumstances, by the sixth century there they were, and there they took to using the shallows of the sea to produce salt by evaporation. At first they probably produced it only for themselves, but salt was a valuable commodity and a solvent market for it existed in Constantinople, which was not only an imperial administrative center but a major hub of trade and also a major producer and distributor of city-made necessities and luxuries of the time. What the Veneti took in return for the salt we do not know: perhaps rugs, glassware, luxurious cloth and jewels, goods we know later Venetians prized. Almost certainly they bought metal woodcutting tools, for these were essential to shipbuilding and for developing a subsequent major export to Constantinople, timber.

Embryonic Venice, then, had these assets to start with: natural resources to sell, a solvent distant city market to buy them, and hence a way of earning city-made imports from a more highly advanced economy. In sum, it had exactly what any supply region had then or has now.

Let us suppose that Venice had continued to concentrate on this simple two-way trade with more advanced Constantinople. In that case Venice would not have developed its own city economy. Any crude city-made goods that Venice might have produced— imitations of Constantinople's least sophisticated products— would have been of no interest in Constantinople. Nor could embryonic Venice, in these circumstances, have replaced wide ranges of its imports from Constantinople with its own production. The gulf between most of what it could buy and what it could produce was too great to be bridged. What Venice needed was a market for such city-made goods as it actually could manage to produce. Only then could it start its development process.

Venice did indeed develop: by acting like Constantinople without Constantinople's economy. This may seem laughable, that a primitive little settlement of fishermen, salt evaporators and loggers at the back of nowhere could start behaving like rich and mighty Constantinople at the very hub of things; but it did. The means Venice used was to launch itself into trade with other backward settlements in not too different circumstances from its own, settlements that needed whatever imitations of Constantinople goods Venice was capable of producing. For those settlements, Venice represented a small solvent market for resource goods and raw materials, just as Constantinople provided such a market for Venice.

Venice, in addition to selling simple (at this stage) craft goods of its own, could also re-export some of the luxuries it obtained from Constantinople, customers for these being magnates in the castles and manors of feudal Europe. In return for both kinds of products—its own and Constantinople's—Venice took such resource goods as leather, wool, tin, copper, furs, horn, amber, iron . . . materials it could incorporate into its own slowly ramifying collection of manufactures.

It was all slow going. The backward economies Venice was dealing with were starting from almost nothing except a harsh subsistence life periodically swept by horrifying famines and so lacking in producers' goods that an iron plow, when it could be found at all, was a treasure for a king's estate. Nevertheless, precisely by using its trade with Constantinople as a springboard for trade with backward settlements, Venice by the tenth century, with an explosively expanding city economy for its time, gradually became capable of sophisticated production on its own behalf and was the major market for European resource goods. Venice, as a shifting, expanding solvent market had thus been transforming bits and pieces of Europe's stagnant subsistence economies into supply regions, just as Constantinople's market had earlier converted the subsistence life of the Veneti into a supply economy with its depot settlement that became Venice.

If the depot settlements in Europe with which Venice dealt had remained content with a simple two-way trade with Venice, they would have had only dead-end supply economies. But instead they took to behaving like Venice. That is, using their Venetian trade as a springboard, they launched into trade with one another. Merchants in Antwerp, besides buying wool and channeling it to Venice, began producing cloth for export to backward London, Paris, Genoa, and soon were trading all over Europe. London, to start with, had little or nothing for Venice because London's first export of any significance seems to have been salt fish, and to jump ahead many centuries for an analogy, that would have been carrying coals to Newcastle. But there were other cities in the continent's interior, selling to Venice and to one another, that were solvent markets for London fish, and in due course English wool destined for the looms of the Lowlands was also being channeled through London. London took to copying, that is, replacing, some of its imports; for example, buying leather goods from Cordova, as Venice itself did, and then subsequently making leather goods, at first with Cordova leather, then also with cheaper and coarser English leather. Although such items were probably of no interest in Venice, they were valued in London itself and in settlements not too different from London.

If these fragile little cities had merely produced exports for one another, they would have developed and expanded their economies very little. Collectively, they would have been somewhat like the fabled town in which people prosper simply by taking in each other's washing. The key to the strengthening, diversification and ramification of their own and the others' economies was the fact that the cities repeatedly replaced, with their own production, imports from one another. They could do this as a practical matter because the gulf between what they were importing from the neighbors and what they themselves could produce was not too great to be bridged. What one backward city can produce, another can likely reproduce.

Mutual city import-replacing stimulated markets for city-made innovations. When cities replace wide ranges of their imports with local production, they do not import less than they otherwise would or could; rather, they shift to other imports in place of those now locally produced. So far I have emphasized the shifts that favor larger solvent city markets for rural goods and resource raw materials. Those shifts are important. But even more important, as far as the development of economic life is concerned, is the fact that cities replacing and hence shifting imports also become exceptionally good markets for new types of goods being produced in other cities. They become exceptionally good markets for innovations because they can afford them. In this way import-replacing cities stimulate sales of new kinds of export work being cast up in other cities. This mechanism is the means by which streams of innovations are injected into everyday economic life. Then in their turn they are replaced with local production, opening up new city markets for still more innovations.

What this means is that the trade among vigorously developing cities is volatile, continually changing in content as cities create new kinds of exports for one another, and then in due course repeatedly replace many of them. So it was with the development of the backward cities of Europe. They were forever producing new exports for one another—bells, dyes, buckles, parchment, lace, carding combs, needles, painted cabinetwork, ceramics, brushes, cutlery, paper, sieves and riddles, sweetmeats, elixirs, files, pitchforks, sextants—replacing them with local production, becoming customers for still more innovations. They were developing on one another's shoulders.

This was the process that had made Europe's cities highly developed for their time by Peter the Great's day, and it was the process that continued thereafter and that Peter could not buy by simply purchasing some of the results of the process. To this day Russia engages only very partially and haltingly in this development process. Soviet cities produce exports for one another, but replace few of those goods with products of their own. To rulers who want to know and control, as far as they can, what is going to be produced five years in the future and where it is going to be produced and how, and then five years beyond that, and so on, volatile intercity trade, forever unpredictably and opportunistically changing in content, represents sheer chaos. Of course it is not chaos. It is a complex form of order, akin to organic forms of order typical of all living things, in which instabilities build up (in this case, funds of potentially replaceable imports) followed by corrections, both the instabilities and the corrections being the very stuff of life processes themselves.

The development process of Europe was recapitulated, much more rapidly, in the northern part of the United States, beginning tentatively and spottily during colonial times and then intensifying rapidly after the American Revolution. First came the springboard: the simple two-way trade between American resource depots and much more highly advanced cities in Europe. Boston, which started by exporting timber in the form of clapboards, and fish, and Philadelphia which exported grain, were the first American cities to start wriggling, like Venice, out of this simple two-way, dead-end form of trade. Even as colonial cities they began trying to behave like the cities of Europe. That is, they began copying their simpler imports from Europe and exporting these to one another and to other backward settlements, and replacing their imports from one another. What one backward city can produce, another can likely reproduce. This was displeasing to England, which wanted the colonies not only as resource suppliers but also as captive customers for English manufacturers and merchants. In contrast to Boston and Philadelphia, New York (furs) was economically docile. Immediately following the Revolution, however, New York was drawn fully into the volatile little network of backward intercity trade that had been pioneered in Boston and Philadelphia. New York's postrevolutionary establishment and economy proved so hospitable to entrepreneurs generating exports for other backward cities, and replacing imports from them, that in little more than a generation the city had developed a greater diversity of manufactures than either Boston or Philadelphia, and soon a greater volume as well. As new cities like Cincinnati, Pittsburgh and Chicago formed, they entered the network of volatile trade. When the discovery of gold in California resulted in the formation of San Francisco in 1849, it behaved like the cities of Europe and the U.S. North. Loosely speaking, it played the economic role of Venice in the Far West, much as Boston and Philadelphia had played that role in the East.

In the South, cities behaved differently. Charleston, Savannah, Richmond, St. Augustine and Williamsburg, rather than concentrating upon trade with one another, confined themselves for the most part to simple two-way, dead-end trade, first with much more highly advanced European cities, and later with more highly advanced cities of the American North as well. They channeled out agricultural cash crops, received in return manufactured city goods, and did not use this trade as a springboard to launch themselves into volatile trade with one another. Consequently, they did not develop their own economies. When Atlanta formed as a depot (cotton), there was thus no network of volatile intercity trade in its part of the country. This was the Atlanta of Henry Grady, through which Northern imports for the funeral in Pickens County were channeled but which did not produce any of the goods itself.

One is reminded of Montevideo in Uruguay and Buenos Aires, located right across the Rio de la Plata from each other, and with no end of other economically backward settlements up and down the coast, all of which have solipsistically concentrated on their own simple dead-end trade with much more highly advanced economies. Because these cities have not developed on one another's shoulders, they have not developed. Backward cities need one another.

When Japan began developing its modern economy in the 1870s, Japanese cities behaved like those of Europe and the American North. They used their international trade in silk as a springboard for intensified and ramifying trade with one another. Tokyo played the role of Venice. Instead of remaining content with what its silk exports would buy from more highly advanced economies, it copied such imports as it could and exported them to other Japanese cities, which in turn did not remain content with that trade, but replaced many of Tokyo's new exports to them with their own production and cast up new exports to sell to Tokyo as well. Because Japanese cities replaced imports from one another—what one backward city can produce, another can likely reproduce—they continually served as excellent markets for still newer kinds of exports from one another, and in this fashion developed on one another's shoulders. From the very beginning of Japan's modern development, trade in new products (new to Japan) among Japanese cities has been far more intensively pursued than foreign trade. This still remains true. Thus, in 1980 Japan was exceeded only by the United States in the proportion of its total trade that is domestic, a Japanese achievement more remarkable than America's considering the fact that so many American resource goods are produced domestically while Japan must import most raw materials. Japan's success as an international exporter of manufactured goods is a by-product of the volatile trade among Japanese cities. That is to say, goods and services first produced for internal use in Japanese cities and city regions, and for producers and consumers in other Japanese cities, subsequently become foreign exports. Exported Japanese robot tools, for example, were first produced for, and put to use by, producers in Japan. This is a pattern of development Japan has consistently used, beginning with its first imitations of Western goods; just so, today a highly developed Japan is its own first and best customer for innovations.

Hong Kong only two generations ago was an economically backward colonial depot city. While it is still a colony in name, economically it is anything but. It has played the role of Venice on the Pacific Rim, exporting its producers' goods and services to Singapore, Seoul, Taipei, in return buying products of cheap labor for incorporating into its own products and export contracts. But the Pacific Rim cities, like the cities of Europe, have not been content with simple two-way trade, whether with Hong Kong or other more highly developed cities, and in addition have concentrated heavily on trade both with one another and with more backward settlements, in the way that Taipei, for example, trades heavily with Kaohsiung, which in turn has replaced wide ranges of its imports from Taipei, in the process becoming, of course, an excellent customer for newer Taipei exports to it.

Economic development in the United States was rapid in comparison with what happened in Europe. Japan's modern development occurred more rapidly still, and that of the Pacific Rim has been, so far, most rapid of all. This suggests that some, perhaps many currently backward economies could develop rapidly indeed if their cities were to use their trade with more advanced economies only as a springboard for volatile trade with one another. But that process, the actual process of developing, is thwarted when backward cities or their nations try to rely instead upon simpler two-way, dead-end trade with more advanced economies, whether by buying "development" as the Shah and Peter did, or by acquiring "development" on credit or through gifts.

The second major pattern, or motif, to be found historically in the actual development of backward economic life is improvisation. Here again, the Shah and Peter and their advisers were off the track with their acceptance of ready-made schemes of producing predetermined choices of products.

Backward cities that have actually developed have combined even their outright imitations of imported goods with their own improvised means of producing them. An example is the fashion in which enterprises in Tokyo at the turn of the century developed indigenous manufacturing of bicycles (see Chapter 2). Not only did Japan acquire bicycle manufacturing and develop its own producers' goods for the purpose as it went along, it also acquired an improvised method for reproducing other types of complex imported goods symbiotically in groups of individually small and simple factories, a method put to use for manufacturing sewing machines, for example, and later radios and electrical goods. A modern derivative of the system, used by the great Nissan automobile works with its close clusters of suppliers who make daily and even hourly deliveries of what is needed for assembly at the time, has recently become the subject of much study and admiration on the part of American industrialists. At the time when the Japanese developed their own bicycle manufacturing, the bicycles they imported were being made in highly integrated, huge, complete factories in America, as the sewing machines also were. Had the Japanese tried to import complete factories for these purposes, whether by buying them outright or obtaining them on credit, they would have lost the opportunity of developing their own producers' goods and production methods, and the bicycles, sewing machines, and so on, would have been more expensive as well, probably too expensive for Japanese to buy. Instead they used their trade with currently more advanced economies only as a springboard for their own development.

The backward cities of medieval Europe had to improvise because they had little choice. Backward cities today must improvise just as surely because, for one thing, they have to cut costs in comparison with more advanced economies. To put it another way, they have to bring the price of what they make into the range of what their own people and enterprises—and people and enterprises in other backward cities—can afford. One advantage they usually have is cheap labor, but this is a practical advantage only in cases where labor-intensive methods of production can be improvised as more economical substitutes, for capital-intensive methods being used to produce imports they buy from more highly advanced economies. Smallness of enterprises, as in the Japanese bicycle-manufacturing development, is an asset because smallness cuts down administrative and other overhead costs both in individual enterprises and in the aggregate, in comparison with the overhead costs of large operations. Improvised materials often cut costs by letting producers put to use what is at hand or can be gotten cheaply, rather than slavishly imitating the materials that more advanced, richer economies happen to be using at the time, or even other backward economies. That is what the craftsmen of medieval London did when they began using British leather to imitate objects of much finer Cordovan leather. That is what enterprises in Hong Kong did when they manufactured cloth shoes in styles imitating leather shoes.

Tariffs are of course means by which backward economies have often helped give their manufacturers a start (and in the next chapter I shall explain the circumstances under which tariffs are necessary, and why). But tariffs come out of consumers' pockets, and there is a limit to what consumers can bear, as Uruguay discovered when its consumers could not afford the protected products of Uruguayan manufacturers, nor bear the taxes and inflation on which subsidies to manufacturing rested.

Apart from the direct practical advantages of improvisation, the practice itself fosters a state of mind essential to all economic development, no matter what stage development has reached at the time. The practice of improvising, in itself, fosters delight in pulling it off successfully and, most important, faith in the idea that if one improvisation doesn't work out, another likely can be found—that will. Invention, practical problem solving, improvisation and innovation are all part and parcel of one another. To go back to the bicycle, for example, the many improvements in Europe and America that made it a practical vehicle instead of merely an awkward toy or clumsy curiosity consisted of a long, long series of improvisations, each added to imitations of what had already been achieved. Makers and tinkerers, using the means at their command in their own economies at the time, came up with ball bearings, roller bearings, pneumatic tires, chain-and-sprocket drives, differential gears, the tubular metal frame in place of the solid metal frame, caliper brakes, brake cables, drum brakes, back-pedaling brakes, and in a sense they even partially reinvented the wheel itself, gaining unprecedented lightness and strength with unprecedented economy of materials from an unprecedented way of spoking the wheel asymmetrically.

These improvisations developed for the bicycle turned out to have ramifying uses. They underlie, in good part, the development of tractors, automobiles and airplanes, as well as the more obvious instances of motorcycles and mopeds. Bicycle improvisations formed new markets for new types of lubricants and steel alloys, which also had ramifying uses. Innovations today remain essentially improvisational, as all of us know who held our breath wondering if the ceramic tiles improvised for the space shuttle would do their job and not fall off. All innovations, all new ways of economizing on materials, including energy, are inescapably masses of improvisations and experiments, some successful and some not, combined with imitations of what has already been achieved.

Thus, to buy a developed economy as the Shah or Peter tried to do or as Saudi Arabia is attempting to do as this is written, or to sell or give the trappings of progress to backward economies under the pretense of bestowing development, fails to work not only because the development, such as it is, takes place somewhere else entirely, but because the transactions denigrate and discourage rather than foster a basic practice of all true and creative development work.

Successful improvisation implies, among other things, appropriate technology for the circumstances at hand. "Appropriate technology" nowadays is a rather fashionable phrase carrying connotations of suitable devices for the rural poor. Unfortunately, many such devices turn out to be profoundly inappropriate— not because they don't work but because they work too well. For example, development of a bicycle-powered spinning wheel, a nice improvisation, was sponsored by the government of India, and proved to be a great success in the sense that one villager, equipped with it, can spin as much as twelve workers using traditional wheels. But the effect of this is devastating to India's poor villages. Solvent markets for cloth of hand-spun Indian yarn, which is exported to rich countries, are not expanding at any such rate. Most Indians themselves wear cloth of machine-spun fibers, which are much cheaper; they can't afford cloth of hand-spun yarn even when it is made by the bicycle-powered wheel and ill-paid workers. The new wheel thus simply displaces poor village spinners who have no alternate work or incomes. Therefore, having sponsored development of the wheel, the government cannot promote its use.

Inappropriate though much theoretically appropriate rural village technology has proved to be, much ingenuity is expended in its cause. Inventions for this purpose have a romantic appeal, it seems, for the same people who romanticize subsistence farming. But the ingenuity spent on such devices is misdirected because it puts the cart before the horse; that is, it is directed toward improvements in rural productivity which inherently cannot be feasible economically without prior city development.

Consider, for example, a marvelous economic hothouse of improvisation and ingenuity located on a tropical savannah of the Orinoco River basin in Colombia, more than three hundred miles from the nearest town. The project is run by a young engineer from Bogotá, Colombia's capital and principal city, which is economically much like Montevideo in Uruguay, being profoundly dependent on simple dead-end, two-way, advanced-backward trade. The Bogotá engineer is helped by a full-time team of seven technicians, with additional part-time advice from twenty other engineers and assorted experts back in Bogotá. They get their financing from the Colombian government, the United Nations Development Program and the Dutch government.

One of the team's innovations is a windmill with vanes so sensitive and adjustable that they spin in a breeze of less than four miles an hour, with each windmill being capable of pumping nearly 4,000 gallons of water a day. The successful model is the sixty-sixth windmill tried. The team started with the kind that used to be employed for pumping water on Midwestern American farms, but the savannah winds were so light that those windmills worked only four months of the year. Then the team tried designs based on a type of mill used on Crete, where winds are also light, and after much trial and error made a version with canvas blades that worked perfectly and was cheap. But it wouldn't do either, owing to the grass fires that sweep the savannah. At long last they developed the successful model, which has aluminum blades based on an airfoil developed for the U.S. space program. Unfortunately, in light of what Colombian farmers in the region, living mainly by subsistence agriculture, can pay, it is prohibitive. Mass-produced, even as a nonprofit item, it would cost some $500.

Other contrivances include a solar hot-water heater made from burned-out fluorescent light tubes; a small hydroelectric generator that requires a dam less than four feet high to produce sufficient electricity for a small institutional building such as a primary school; a manual sugar-cane press suitable for one-family use; and a bicycle-powered cassava-root shredder that enables one worker to shred as much cassava root as twenty workers using traditional methods.

The project, for all its successes, has reached an impasse, not because the devices don't work but for the usual obdurate reasons. Although the region for which they have been developed is only now being settled, and therefore introduction of the devices will not displace existing workers and already traditional arrangements, the settlers can't afford them. The very reason the land has been opened for settlement by the Colombian government is that so many poor subsistence farmers elsewhere in the country can no longer make even a subsistence living in older regions. And since there are no alternative jobs and incomes awaiting them in cities, they were allowed to homestead in what was formerly tropical wilderness. The poverty of the settlers, and the thin economic base available to them, prevent this rural technology program from becoming self-supporting, as was intended. The original idea was that poor subsistence farmers, with little or nothing to export to solvent markets, could themselves comprise a market for the manufactured goods that would be produced locally.

But since some of the materials must inescapably be imported into the region—subsistence farmers can't produce bicycle parts, generators, aluminum, glass tubes, and the like—regional self-support of the factory is not possible. Seeking a way out, the engineer in charge has played with the idea of supporting the factory, paying for its necessary imports, by finding export markets for its products in tropical agricultural regions elsewhere, in other parts of Latin America and on farms in Sri Lanka, Indonesia and Africa. But the trouble with that idea is that poor farmers in the putative export markets can't afford the devices either. What is worse, in those markets the even more troubling problem would arise of what to do with rural workers displaced by the devices. Equipment like this might make good sense on the farms of tropical city regions. But tropical city regions are nowadays rare, and if they did exist, their people would certainly not send to the back of beyond in the Orinoco basin to get their windmills, generators, presses and cassava shredders. Their own cities would produce them.

One economic surprise has been imbedded in this Colombian project. Rather to the embarrassment of the inventors, one gathers, the solar hot-water heater made from burned-out fluorescent light tubes has actually become a commercial success in a small way; to their embarrassment because the success has not occurred in the rural world. The device has been put to use in new apartment buildings in Medellin, a small city about two hundred miles northwest of Bogotá, and in apartments in the capital city itself. Conceivably, this is the sort of ingenious improvisation a backward city might well export to other backward cities. More important, it is also the kind of thing that could be replaced with local production in customer backward cities because what one backward city can produce another can likely reproduce. To be sure, if the device were to become a success of any significance, the supplies of burned-out fluorescent tubes would soon become inadequate. Good. Then something else would have to be improvised in their stead. Just so does economic life develop.

The mind boggles to think what people as resourceful and indefatigable at improvising as these young Colombians might do were they to put their minds to appropriate technology for their own backward cities' economies and for trade with other backward cities. Paradoxically, appropriate technology for backward cities can sometimes be the most radical and freshest technology. That is because new things—like solar heating, for example—tend to start with new simplicities. Backward cities, in the nature of things lack some of the great overburdens of elaborated and rococo ways of doing things which have evolved in advanced cities: overburdens that can stifle and discourage fresh departures simply because the existing ways exist, and because so much has been invested in them.

The more that economic life, taken in general, has developed at a given time, however, the better for backward cities in volatile trade with one another. They have a flying start. The Tokyo bicycle-parts makers and assemblers, despite the fact that they had to improvise their own methods of developing, did not have to invent the bicycle. The Colombian engineers and technicians did not have to dream up the idea of storing hot water (and what a strange, radical idea that was originally), nor did they have to invent glass tubing. This is the chief reason for why there has been a pattern of speed-up in backward cities' development between the time of Venice and the time of Hong Kong.

If one wanted to define economic development in a single word, that word would be "improvisation." But infeasible improvisation is fruitless, so it would be more accurate to say that development is a process of continually improvising in a context that makes injecting improvisations into everyday economic life feasible. Cities in volatile trade with one another create that context. Nothing else does, which is why backward cities need one another.

ELEVEN

Faulty Feedback to Cities

We must suppose that the very earliest proto-cities and cities, trading with one another in prehistoric times, bartered the obsidian, copper, shells, animals, horn, pigments, rushes or other goods of their territories they had to trade. Unmediated by currency, bartered goods would have fluctuated sensitively in value relative to one another. An item in high demand would command good volumes and varieties of imports for a settlement, but if demand fell off as additional sources of supply or substitutes were found, the superseded product would command diminishing imports, just as a falling currency does. Then the settlement exporting it would be in trouble unless it hustled up something else worth trading or else imitated on its own behalf some of the artifacts it had formerly imported, a process we call "economic borrowing" when we find evidence of it in prehistoric times.

Once cities invented currencies, at first each had its own; at any rate, the very early city-states of which we have knowledge in Mediterranean Europe, the Near East, China and India created their own currencies and circulated them in trade. Their coinages were typically based on metals with widely accepted intrinsic values. But even so, the coins, like much later paper currencies based on a gold or silver standard, necessarily fluctuated with respect to the goods or labor they could command in given cities at given times. Grain cost more in a city-state that had suffered bad crops than if it was gotten in one where the harvest had been good.

Iron swords diminished the value set on bronze swords. Perhaps pottery had once upon a time diminished the value set on skulls.

After an ancient city-state had been conquered by a more powerful neighbor and thus converted to a provincial city, or after it had voluntarily surrendered much of its sovereignty to a federation, it seems typically to have continued, nevertheless, to mint and circulate a currency of its own. Even the Roman Empire only gradually eliminated the non-Roman currencies of its conquered provinces and dependencies; only later still, in an unsuccessful effort to combat inflation at the time of Diocletian did Rome decree standardized prices, which is to say really rigidly standardized currency values, throughout its realm.

In early medieval Europe, city currencies once again became the norm, not the exception. Venice welcomed and used imperial Byzantine coinage because of its trade with the Eastern Empire, but Venice circulated its own currency as well. The cities that rose in the wake of Venice and extended their own volatile trading networks also commonly created their own currencies. For example, the north German and Baltic cities of the Hanseatic League were united in many common purposes but they had no league currency. Member cities created their own, as well as devising instruments comparable to our letters of credit and certificates of deposit for use in their intercity, multicurrency trading.

Medieval city currencies of Europe persisted into Renaissance times, and indeed multiplied as European economic life itself developed with the multiplying of cities. Even currencies that did not originate in cities proper such as Florence, Genoa or Amsterdam must often have worked much as if they were the currencies of city-states because the principalities doing the minting were often so small themselves. For instance, the currency of Brandenburg was the currency of Berlin, that of Saxony the currency of Dresden, that of the Dukedom of Milan the currency of Milan, and so on. Many such currencies persisted even into recent times. German monetary union was not instituted until 1857, as a precursor to formation of the German Empire. Except during one brief and ill-fated experience with centralized government inspired by the French Revolution, Swiss cities, as cantons, retained the power to create their own currencies until after 1848.

Today we take it for granted that the elimination of multitudinous currencies in favor of fewer national or imperial currencies represents economic progress and promotes the stability of economic life. But this conventional belief is at least worth questioning in view of the function that currencies serve as economic feedback controls. ·I am going to argue that national or imperial currencies give faulty and destructive feedback to city economies and that this in turn leads to profound structural economic flaws, some of which cannot be overcome no matter how hard we try.

As we all know, when a nation's currency declines in value relative to currencies of other nations with which it trades, theoretically the very decline itself ought to help correct the nation's economy. Automatically its exports become cheaper to customer nations, hence its export sales should increase; and at the same time, its imports automatically become more expensive, and this should help its own manufacturers. Theoretically, then, a declining national currency ought to work automatically like both an export subsidy and a tariff, coming into play precisely when a nation begins to run a deficit in its international balance of payments because it is exporting too little and importing too much. Furthermore, this automatic export subsidy and tariff ought to remain in play precisely as long as it is needed, no longer. If that were indeed the effect that national-currency fluctuations had, they would be elegant examples of feedback control, registering that a correction is necessary and, at the same time, triggering the appropriate correction.

To understand why national currencies don't actually perform that constructive function, we need to understand how feedback controls work. First of all, it is of the essence that the feedback information governs a responding mechanism. For example, in our breathing, a momentary rise in the level of carbon dioxide in the bloodstream automatically triggers off the brain stem's breathing center to shoot a message to the diaphragm to contract and allow the lungs to fill again. In this case the triggering information is the amount of carbon dioxide in the blood, and the responding mechanism is the diaphragm. As organisms, we depend on vast arrays of feedback controls, each working so appropriately and automatically that we are unaware we have them until researchers tell us so. Unstable systems require continual corrections and adjustments, otherwise they would soon succumb to their own instabilities.

Without having called them feedback controls, I have already mentioned many in this book. For instance, when new enterprises in a city multiply and diversify rapidly, the information feeds back in the form of crowding, inconvenience and increasing competition for city space; it triggers off the appropriate correction: some enterprises move out of the city into the region, although still within reach of the city services and markets they require. Similarly, the information that city jobs and markets have simultaneously increased feeds back into the system in the form of rural labor shortages in a city's own hinterland. That triggers the appropriate correction: use of rural labor-saving equipment, or development of it if need be. City regions are the outcomes of many different corrections triggered by many different inputs of feedback information. To be sure, the corrections are not wholly automatic, but then, neither is our breathing. We can hold our breath—within limits.

Feedback controls always work on their own terms regardless of what we might prefer. For example, when a government prints money exuberantly, the information feeds back into the system and triggers the appropriate correction: a given unit of money buys less. Wishes for a different correction, economic expansion, don't avail; expansion is a different response, under quite different controls. Analogically, the common thermostat works beautifully at its own corrective task of registering changes in temperature and triggering the appropriate corrections, but it is futile to wish that it would govern the speed of a rotary mill because that is the task we want done; however, a different feedback control does exactly that. In short, feedback controls are built right into the systems they correct, and the corrections they trigger are not discretionary. They are precisely to the point, and the point is always the specific correction of results of specific previous happenings.

The trouble with national currencies as constructive feedback controls is not that they are feeble at the job. They are anything but that. Those dreary little columns of international exchange-rate figures in the back pages of newspapers, creeping from day to day in this direction or that with their little fractions of percentage points, can represent power of life or death over entire industries. A gradually accruing 10 percent rise in the value of the English pound in 1979 and 1980 forced the major producers of English china and earthenware to lay off workers, and put several of the smaller producers out of business altogether, priced out of foreign markets which, until then, had remained strong for these wares. The rising pound was simultaneously pricing the wares out of their domestic markets too, as foreign imports became cheaper. The chairman of the largest producer, Wedgwood, blamed the rise of the pound on a combination of North Sea oil production off Scotland, which had improved Great Britain's balance of trade, and the government's policy of setting interest rates high in order to try to improve the economy by attracting foreign capital. He was probably right. For his own enterprise the consequences were massive layoffs and a decision on the part of the company that for its own survival it must transplant much of its production permanently out of Britain, into customer nations.

Currencies are powerful carriers of feedback information, then, and potent triggers of adjustments, but in their own terms. National currencies register, above all, consolidated information on a nation's international trade. When net international exports of goods or services rise, relative to those of other nations, the currency, being in demand, rises in value; when exports fall off, it declines in value. International imports and exports of capital work in just the opposite way. If a country has been importing more capital than it has exported (by borrowing abroad, for example), the value of its currency is automatically bolstered. Conversely, if it has exported more capital than it has been importing (by lending, making gifts, paying interest on prior foreign loans, exporting the profits of foreign-owned industries), the value of its currency is automatically depressed to that extent. This is why imports of foreign capital into Britain (stimulated by rising interest rates there) and the production of North Sea oil, improving Britain's balance of international trade, were acting in concert to raise the value of the pound.

The reverse effects of movements of capital do not long over-rule a currency's feedback concerning international trade in goods and services. That factor dominates over the long term. For example, suppose a nation borrows heavily abroad to develop its economy. Its currency's value is automatically bolstered from the very fact of the borrowing itself. But then suppose that the development schemes do not pay off in expanded international exports of goods and services, or else in replaced foreign imports. The currency must then decline. The cost of interest on the loan, which seemed so feasible when the loan itself was bolstering the debtor nation's currency, becomes devastating as the currency declines. That is why heavy international borrowing that does not pay off in a heavily improved balance of trade for the debtor nation can abruptly bankrupt a country unless its lenders agree to keep lending to it and to ease up on repayments and interest. The threat then, of course, becomes bankruptcy for the lenders.

Because currency feedback information is so potent, and because so often the information is not what governments want to hear, nations commonly go to extravagant lengths to try to block off or resist the information. Furthermore, when the information does come through—as sooner or later it always does, no matter what the evasions—the effects can be inappropriate, to say the least, as they were in the English Midlands, where most of the nation's potteries are located. Unemployment was already high in England generally and very high in the Midlands; the country was already suffering from declining exports of its manufactures, and had been for decades. But those realities were overridden by the other realities of the North Sea oil and the imports of foreign capital being stimulated by the interest rates offered.

National currencies, then, are potent feedback but impotent at triggering appropriate corrections. To picture how such a thing can be, imagine a group of people who are all properly equipped with diaphragms and lungs but who share only one single brain-stem breathing center. In this goofy arrangement, the breathing center would receive consolidated feedback on the carbon-dioxide level of the whole group without discriminating among the individuals producing it. Everybody's diaphragm would thus be triggered to contract at the same time. But suppose some of those people were sleeping, while others were playing tennis. Suppose some were reading about feedback controls, while others were chopping wood. Some would have to halt what they were doing and subside into a lower common denominator of activity. Worse yet, suppose some were swimming and diving, and for some reason, such as the breaking of the surf, had no control over the timing of their submersions. Imagine what would happen to them. In such an arrangement, feedback control would be working perfectly on its own terms but the results would be devastating because of a flaw designed right into the system.

I have had to propose a preposterous situation because systems as structurally flawed as this don't exist in nature; they wouldn't last. Nor do they exist in the machines we deliberately design to incorporate mechanical, chemical or electronic feedback controls; machines this badly conceived wouldn't work. Nations, from this point of view, don't work either, yet do exist.

Nations are flawed in this way because they are not discrete economic units, although intellectually we pretend that they are and compile statistics about them based on that goofy premise. Nations include, among other things in their economic grab bags, differing city economies that need different corrections at given times, and yet all share a currency that gives all of them the same information at a given time. The consolidated information is bad specific information for them even with respect to their foreign trade, and it is no information at all with respect to their trade with one another, as opposed to their international trade. Yet this wretched feedback is powerful stuff.

Because currency feedback, at bottom, all has to do with imports and exports and the balance or lack of balance between them, the appropriate responding mechanisms for such information are cities and their regions. Cities are the specific economic units that can replace imports with their own production, and the specific units that cast up streams of new kinds of exports. It is bootless to suppose that amorphous, undifferentiated statistical collections of a nation's economies perform those functions, because they don't.

Ideally, at a time when a city's exports are doing well, it needs

MARKETS
JOBS
TECHNOLOGY
TRANSPLANTS
CAPITAL

JAMES THIN PENGUIN BOOKSHOP
WAVERLEY MARKET
EDINBURGH

5.95

TOTAL   5.95

CASH TENDERED   6.00
CHANGE DUE   .05

2 1 20/05/86 19:34

CALL AGAIN SOON

to receive as wide a range and as great a volume of earned imports as it can, especially from other cities, because those funds of earned imports are the grist the city must have for its vital process of import-replacing. Conversely, at a time when its exports are in decline, imports should ideally become expensive because to escape decline from diminishing export work a city desperately needs to replace wide ranges of its imports with local production. It also needs maximum stimulation for tentative new types of export work it may soon be capable of casting up. In other words, with falling exports a city needs a declining currency working like an automatic tariff and an automatic export subsidy—but only for as long as they are necessary. Once its exports are doing well, it needs a rising currency to earn the maximum variety and quantity of imports it can. Individual city currencies indeed serve as elegant feedback controls because they trigger specifically appropriate corrections to specific responding mechanisms.

This is a built-in design advantage that many cities of the past had but which almost none have now. Singapore and Hong Kong, which are oddities today, have their own currencies and so they possess this built-in advantage. They have no need of tariffs or export subsidies. Their currencies serve those functions when needed, but only as long as needed. Detroit, on the other hand, has no such advantage. When its export work first began to decline it got no feedback, so Detroit merely declined, uncorrected.

The flawed and inappropriate feedback that cities get from consolidated national currencies works itself out differently, depending upon the international trade of their countries taken as a whole. Three main kinds of difficulties arise, which I shall take up one at a time.

If a nation's international trade is predominantly in rural or resource goods, those exports and the feedback information they bring in falsify and contradict the realities of city trade and production. Uruguay and its city are an example. The international value of Uruguay's currency during the entire formative period of that nation's economy rested wholly on the country's exports of meat, wool, leather and a few other rurally produced goods. Since Uruguay did well with these foreign exports, foreign imports were relatively cheap, with the result that Montevideo, the country's chief city, did not take to replacing wide ranges of these plentiful imports with its own production. The more Uruguay's currency rose in value and purchasing power as the nation's trade in rural goods built up, the cheaper the foreign imports became. In short, Montevideo was getting potent information on the state of Uruguay's international trade, which is all a national currency can convey. But Montevideo was not getting feedback on its own trade. Montevideo was not producing those exports nor earning those imports, but living on the country's rural work at one remove.

When Uruguay's foreign markets declined, beginning in the 1950s, Uruguay's currency inexorably began to decline in relative value. For a time the government bolstered the currency by borrowing, with the result that imports kept flowing in during the 1960s, but this couldn't last because the projects for which the government borrowed were not, in fact, reversing the country's worsening balance of trade. Finally the feedback from the falling currency came in loud, clear and unmistakably: "Uruguay, you aren't producing enough salable exports," it said. "You can't continue buying all those imports."

At long last, Montevideo itself was getting accurate feedback about its own economy, which had never been creative or productive. But by the time the message came through, it was too late to be helpful. Montevideo could not respond appropriately. Its capacity to respond was atrophied. During all those years when the city had been living off the nation's rural earnings it had failed to build up its own capacities to produce, so it had no foundations of producers' goods and services, no foundations of skills, none of the versatility at producing which it needed to take advantage of the automatic tariff and automatic export subsidy with which it was now being presented. In Uruguay, figuratively speaking, the carbon-dioxide level rose, and the fact that it had risen was registered clearly by the country's declining currency. But with no corrective capacities to trigger off, the rise merely proved fatal. Uncorrected, the economy collapsed.

Currency feedback that erroneously tells a city its export trade is in fine shape, as Uruguay's currency erroneously once told Montevideo, need not always be fatal. Such erroneous feedback can sometimes be overcome by tariffs, which is how the young United States, for example, evaded the consequences of faulty feedback to its young cities.

When the American colonies won their independence and for almost a century afterward, the international trade of the United States was similar to Uruguay's—overwhelmingly rural. The South contributed most heavily to this trade with its valuable tobacco and indigo, and later cotton. But in the North as well, international exports were primarily natural resources and agricultural goods: fur, fish, timber, grain. The city-made exports that the little Northern cities produced for one another were useless in foreign trade because they included nothing that European cities didn't already make themselves more cheaply. Indeed, foreign manufactured imports, all earned by the rural exports of the country, were for the most part too cheap for American cities to replace with their own production, thanks to the buying power abroad of the country's currency. That doesn't mean they were so cheap that all Americans could afford them, but they were cheaper than the same things produced domestically. Imports would remain relatively cheap and plentiful unless and until American exports were to fall drastically in value and volume, and just as in Uruguay, that couldn't and wouldn't happen as long as the nation's international trade in rural exports held up. Meanwhile, imports were coming in, not earned by city production and deadening city production. The little American cities had quickly reached a dead end economically.

The situation was thought of not as a feedback flaw, which it was, but as the plight of American manufacturing. However, the response was germane because it countermanded the feedback American cities were receiving. Beginning in 1816, the federal government began enacting the first of many tariff measures intended not to raise revenue like the country's earlier customs duties, but specifically to make manufactured imports artificially expensive. In effect, the tariffs told city people and producers what, in fact, was actually true of their own city economies: You aren't producing exports, so you can't afford all these imports you aren't earning. The tariffs worked. The fact that foreign manufactured goods were now less affordable than domestic equivalents stimulated city import-replacing, and the cities' economies developed very rapidly instead of living, at one remove, off the earnings of the rural supply economies of the country.

Unfortunately, when the currency feedback was countermanded, it had to be countermanded for the whole country's economies, rural as well as urban. In the South, where cities did not become productive, the tariffs simply drove up the cost of living without producing the economic benefits they did in the North. The South's rural producers were being robbed of the cheap imports they had actually earned; in effect, they were victimized to subsidize city production. So bitterly was this resented in the South that tariffs were one of the causes of the South's attempted secession from the Union in 1861 and the four-year slaughter that followed.

We may wonder why Southern cities didn't respond to the tariffs constructively, as the Northern cities did. At the time the tariffs were instituted, the Southern cities were already backward relative to Northern cities, and if they were to have been helped, they would have thus needed protection against competition from Northern manufacturers, much as Northern manufacturers needed protection against competition from European manufacturers. Perhaps, had the South not been militarily defeated when it attempted independence, it would subsequently have raised tariff barriers against the North, and in this way, perhaps, encouraged its own city economies.

Southern cities were more backward in 1816, when tariffs came into play, because earlier they had not begun generating such exports as they technically and economically could for one another, and therefore had not started up the volatile little networks of intercity trade to be found in the North. But why the difference? Here I am conjecturing, but it may have been because the Southern trade in tobacco and indigo had become so successful so soon. In the North the poorer foreign earnings of the rural economies may have played a part in triggering Boston and Philadelphia into a certain amount of economic make-do as a supplement to the poorer rural economies they served. Whatever the reason, Boston, Philadelphia and the other Northern cities with which they traded took advantage of the countermanded feedback in a fashion that Charleston and Richmond did not.

Japan, at the time it began developing its modern economy, evaded city-deadening feedback from its currency in much the same fashion as the United States had done earlier. When Japan was opened to international trade at the middle of the last century, and for a long time thereafter, its chief international export was silk, a predominantly rural product, particularly when exported as yarn to places like Lyons and Paterson, New Jersey. Thanks to the silk earnings, Japan was capable of importing such things as bicycles, sewing machines, iron ships and many other foreign manufactures too cheap for Japanese producers to match. They would have remained so if Japan had not countermanded the feedback from its currency by instituting tariffs. The Japanese bicycle-parts producers and assemblers I have previously mentioned were ingenious at cutting costs and in the process supporting development of Japanese producers' goods as well, but they were also getting help, probably indispensable help, from tariffs. However, while Japanese cities were being helped to develop with the aid of tariffs, it is worth noting that, as in America, rural economies were victimized. Dore, in the course of describing Shinohata and the changes it has experienced, speaks poignantly of the sacrifices rural people made by subsidizing city manufacturing, forgoing cheaper foreign imports that the rural work earned. For eighty or ninety years, Dore comments, villages like Shinohata were squeezed in this fashion. Of course, rural Japanese are well off today, he points out, thanks to the development of the country's economy, and have no regrets for policies that aided that development. As for his own feelings about the rural injustices involved, he points out that his actual flesh-and-blood friends belong to the living generation and, emotionally, he can't wish them poorer in favor of predecessors he didn't know and to whom he has no attachment. But even so, he can't help feeling saddened for those predecessors.

Sweden is an example of a small nation that used tariffs to countermand the faulty feedback of its currency. At the time when Swedish tariffs were instituted, about a century ago, the country was an important international exporter of timber, fish and ore, but was relatively poor and backward compared with much of Europe, whose volatile intercity trade Sweden was dilatory at entering. The Swedish tariffs were wide-ranging and stiff, and were even applied (in part out of political pique) against the few Norwegian manufactures of the time, mostly produced in the little city of Bergen. Norway was then part of Sweden's realm, under Swedish rule, and the tariffs directed against its manufactures ultimately led to the secession of Norway in 1905 and its independence.

Many countries whose cities or potential cities today are automatically deadened by the inappropriate feedback they get from rural-based or resource-based currency values are former colonies, but by no means all. Some are decadent, poverty-stricken seats of former empires: Portugal, Turkey. Nor are all poor. The oil-producing nations that are economically backward all have cities afflicted with inappropriate feedback. The way the Shah attempted to overcome the country's backwardness, by buying the artifacts of development, was futile; but reliance on indigenous development combined with free trade would have been futile too.

Tariffs, necessary though they are in nations with undeveloped or long-stagnated cities and appreciable international trade in resources or rural products, are far from an ideal remedy for faulty and deadening feedback to cities. Tariffs create obstacles of their own to volatile intercity trade. They are particularly hazardous for small countries, not only because they invite retaliatory barriers but also because, in the nature of things, the cities of small nations need heavy and volatile trade with cities across national boundaries. And in large nations or small, tariffs victimize rural economies lying outside of city regions. In Canada, most international exports are agricultural or resource goods, and on this trade the international exchange value of Canada's currency—and its ability to command international imports—rests. The city benefiting most from Canadian tariffs is Toronto, and naturally it is hated by Canadians in the supply regions of the country. They call it Hogtown, and see national tariff policies as being rigged to drive up their own costs of living for the benefit of Toronto. They are right; and yet Canada would be an extremely poor and backward country without tariff protection. Nor does it do all that well at city development because of yet another feedback flaw I shall discuss shortly, having to do with relationships among cities in the same nation.

Singapore as a British-ruled colonial city was backward. It might well have continued to be handicapped after its nation, the Federated Malay States, gained independence in 1963, because the country's international exports were primarily rural and resource products such as tin and rubber. However, in 1965 Singapore, with its predominantly Chinese population, was expelled from Malaysia, as the country is now called, because in the eyes of the rural Malay population of the other parts of the country, Singapore was an undesirable foreign body. As a sovereign and independent city-state, Singapore has a currency that reflects its own trade situation. Furthermore, with its expulsion, the anomaly of a shared national "brain stem" vanished. Singapore, for the sake of its own development, doesn't need to cheat the rural Malays of their own rightful import earnings, but neither is it deadened by inappropriate feedback from a generalized Malaysian currency. Singapore has to earn its own imports or it won't have them, and generate its own exports or it won't have them, but appropriate feedback helps it do both and replace imports as well. In feedback terms, Singapore is a nice well-made piece of equipment with a mechanism to carry information and trigger responses (its currency), and a responding mechanism (its capacity to produce), forming a sensitively self-correcting economic unit. Hong Kong is another such unit. And Taiwan and South Korea are not too badly off, either, in the terms I have been discussing, since their international trade does not consist mainly of rural or resource-based exports. Thus these Pacific Rim economies have important built-in structural advantages, lacking in most economies that attempt to develop.

The fact that city-state currencies prevailed widely at times and places where significant development was getting under way suggests that national currencies may be fatally premature in some parts of the world now. South America comes to mind. To be sure, the emergence of sovereign city-states in South America, at the expense of existing national arrangements, is wildly unlikely. But it is also wildly unlikely that the nations of South America are destined to achieve solid economic development or self-correcting economic stability. Those that have not already spiraled into disaster, like Uruguay, are in process of doing so. When an entire continent is in as much economic trouble as South America, it may be that nothing can help short of recapitulating successful development patterns of the past, the alternative being only indefinitely prolonged degeneration, disorganization and oppression.

Once a nation has managed to develop vigorous city economies or has acquired them in the course of political consolidation or military conquest, troubles with faulty feedback are not over but merely take other forms. For these difficulties, not even makeshift remedies such as tariffs are available. Countries with such troubles must simply live with them and ultimately die and decay with them.

One might suppose, offhand, that the currency of a country which enjoys a big international trade in city-made exports, as opposed to rural or resource goods, would be a currency helpful to cities, operating much as Singapore's or Hong Kong's currency does. The difficulty arises from the fact of numerous cities and potential cities, and from the circumstance that cities in trade with one another (as the cities within a nation are if they have developed at all) are like "the creatures of the world" Lao-tzu described some twenty-five hundred years ago:

> . . . some go in front, some follow;
> Some blow hot when others would be blowing cold,
> Some are feeling vigorous just when others are worn out
> Some are loading just when others are delivering . . .

Cities have their own individual timing for replacing imports and also for generating innovative exports. To experience a significant episode of import-replacing, by definition a city must first build up a critical, unstable mass of potentially replaceable imports. The cycle of a vigorous city, one that maintains its vitality generation after generation, seems to run like this: first a period in which it generates diverse exports, in the process earning an increasing diversity and volume of imports; second, as export-generating dies down, a significant explosion of import-replacing (provided a critical mass of replaceable imports has piled up, otherwise the city merely declines); third, a period in which potential new exports, often including innovations, are generated in the city's now greatly enlarged and greatly diversified internal economy; fourth, a period of vigorous export-generating and, it follows, of earning wide ranges and volumes of new, potentially replaceable imports—in other words, a return to the first phase of the cycle and a preparation for repeating the second phase.

In some cities, at some times, one phase follows another very rapidly; in others the changes occur slowly; but rapidly or slowly, this is the cycle that keeps their economies going.

The cycles of cities in volatile trade with one another do not correspond; rather, they intersect constructively at their different phases, some "feeling vigorous just when others are worn out," some "loading just when others are delivering." If all the cities of a nation engaged simultaneously in explosions of import-replacing, the joint economic boom would be horrendous, frantic, probably so impractical as to choke itself off from lack of materials, workers and sheer time to solve practical problems before they became overwhelming. But in any case, such an unbalanced, simultaneous expansion can hardly happen normally because cities require differing phases of one another's cycles. A city in the phase of generating unprecedented exports (unprecedented for that network of cities) or true innovations needs customer cities in the phase of import-replacing because those cities, shifting their import purchases, can afford innovative goods and services and are the best initial customers for them. Potential cities, just getting started, have historically often depended for their chance at life upon older cities replacing imports and shifting their purchases to exotic new goods or to rural supplies that create an opportunity for a depot city to arise and, perhaps, to develop and flourish. "Some go in front, some follow."

Now let us return to the goofy arrangement of different individuals hooked up to one brain-stem breathing center, but this time let us imagine an elephant hooked up with three sheep, two puppy dogs and a rabbit. Whose carbon dioxide level is going to govern the brain-stem trigger?

Whichever city in a nation happens to be contributing most heavily to the international export trade is apt to be the city whose needs are best served by the national currency. The city with that edge probably gets cheaper foreign imports when its own economy can benefit from cheaper imports, and probably gets an automatic tariff and export subsidy (with respect to foreign trade only) just when it needs such help. If one city and its region gets an edge of that sort, even a small edge, we must expect that the advantage will make its economy more vigorous and more successful than that of other cities in the nation. The edge, once gained, must logically be self-intensifying and self-reinforcing because the more economically successful that city is, then the more heavily its production will weigh in the total national production and total foreign trade of the nation's cities. The more heavily it weighs, the more closely the feedback from the national currency will suit that specific city. But it won't coincide with other cities' needs and the timing necessary and natural to them; it may even contradict them outright, certainly must deaden them. Naples has little influence on Italian international trade and hence on the country's currency fluctuations as a consequence of the trade. Milan and the great overlapping conglomerations of city regions of which Milan forms the nucleus have an enormous effect on Italy's international trade. With which city's needs and timing will the national currency's fluctuations best coincide?

What I have just been presenting is a hypothesis. If it is correct, what we should expect to find in a nation with a large international trade in city goods is not a nation of many city regions—as one might offhand expect—but rather a nation with one overwhelmingly important city and city region, along with other cities that are feeble at generating regions of their own. And we should expect that with the passage of time the one "elephant" city would become increasingly dominant economically, and the others increasingly passive and provincial.

That is the pattern the feedback anomaly I have been describing ought logically to produce, and that is indeed the pattern that typically exists and grows more marked with the passage of time. Great Britain, for several centuries, was the pre-eminent example of a country that heavily exported city-produced goods and services. But as the trade built up, London and its city region became ever more important economically, while the second city of Great Britain, Glasgow, failed to generate a city region of any significance, nor did the second city of England itself, Manchester. Birmingham did, but in no way comparable to London's. As for the other cities of Great Britain—Liverpool, Bristol, Edinburgh, Cardiff, Newcastle, Belfast—they became ever more passive and provincial with the passage of time, even during the period in which Britain's foreign trade in city-made goods and services was burgeoning and flourishing. The passage of time simply widened the economic gulf between these cities and London.

In Italy, as time has passed since the unification of the country a century ago, the economic dominance of Milan has grown only more marked, not less so. Even Rome itself has only a meager city region, vanishing a few miles south and east of the city where, immediately, the poor south of Italy begins. In Germany before its postwar partition, Berlin had become ascendant. With most of Berlin gone, West Germany's cities are today more nearly on a footing of equality with one another, but if the usual pattern works itself out, only one among them will eventually possess a strong and intensifying city-region while the others become economically ever more inert and provincial. In France, only Paris has a significant city region now, unlike the country's so-called eight great peripheral cities: Marseilles, Lyons, Strasbourg, Lille, Rouen, Brest, Nantes, Bordeaux.

The pattern is distinctly a national phenomenon. For instance, the Scandinavian countries among them have less than half the population of France, and little more than southern France, which lacks any city region whatever. Yet each of the Scandinavian countries—Finland, Sweden, Norway and Denmark—does manage to have a significant city region. In these small countries, on a small scale, one finds the same pattern as in the larger countries I have mentioned. For example, as Denmark built up its international trade in city-made goods and services, only Copenhagen generated a significant region. Odense, Aarhus, Sönderborg, all are economically passive and provincial. In Sweden, development of Stockholm and its region has not implied comparable development for Gothenburg.

The Netherlands presents an interesting and fortunate variation of the customary pattern. Its two largest cities, Amsterdam and Rotterdam, together with most of the country's small cities and many of its towns, have jointly formed a single overwhelmingly important region which the Dutch call Ring City because the amalgamation of cities and their joint city region encircles a "hole" formed by agricultural land and the inland sea. Partly because the cities originally formed on the coast and other peripheries of the farmland, and partly because the Dutch have had the good sense to save their most fertile land for farming, the cities pushed their regions around the ring, and instead of invading the hole, filled the interstices in the great ring. Although the country's city and city regional development is well distributed in this fashion, rather than occurring in one single lump and leaving the rest of the country relatively poor, the fact of one great city region, Ring City, obtains here too.

I suspect that what is happening in Japan is somewhat similar to what has happened in the Netherlands or in the north of Italy, although the configuration of the great Japanese urbanized region, with Tokyo at its nucleus, resembles neither a ring nor one fat lump, but rather a huge lopsided bow tie with the knot at Nagoya. Tokyo and its region form only a part of this whole, much as Amsterdam and its region form part of Ring City, or Milan and its region part of the heavily urbanized north of Italy. We might logically expect Japanese cities that lie beyond this dominant urbanized region to become relatively inert and economically passive with the passage of time, rather than proceeding to develop vigorously and to generate their own individual city regions. And indeed, there are now unmistakable signs of just that. In the northern part of the central island of Honshu, on the two southern islands of Shinkoku and Kyushu, and on the northern island of Hokkaido, officials now work hard at seeking transplants for their regions, not only Japanese but also foreign transplants, their motive being, according to the *Wall Street Journal*, "familiar to anyone in the U.S. who has watched young people move out of a rural or industrial depressed state, seeking a better life . . . They want jobs for their people. It's that simple." Not quite that simple, for we must ask why the cities of these regions are not developing vigorous economies of their own and transplants for their own hinterlands.

It seems as though, in nations with very different histories, populations and geographical sizes, some force is bent upon transmuting multicity nations into something resembling city-states, that is, states overwhelmingly dominated by one city region and its city or cities. That force, if I am correct, is the faulty feedback exerted by the consolidated national currency.

In a small country, transmutation of the nation into something resembling a city-state is not necessarily destructive. If the country is very small, like Denmark, or if it has a sufficiently huge dominating urban region, like Ring City in the Netherlands, the nation can get along economically with its single elephant city region. But even in small countries, the pattern exacts its penalties. In Denmark, for example, most of the country remains relatively poor and must be heavily subsidized by Copenhagen and its region, creating grave difficulties of a kind I shall explore in the next chapter. Another penalty is that a nation transmuted into something resembling a city-state has almost all its economic eggs in one basket, increasingly so as time passes. As long as the overwhelmingly important city and region of a small country has vigorous trading partners outside the country, it at least has a good chance of maintaining its continued capacity to develop. And indeed, small countries with a high proportion of their international trade made up of city-produced goods and services do tend to be successful and economically resilient. A resilient system is a system getting and acting upon appropriate feedback.

A large nation transmuted into something resembling a city-state is a different matter. The many cities that grow more inert and provincial as time passes don't pull their weight economically. They don't make good domestic customers for the dominant region. As other cities stagnate, the dominant city and region must subsidize them, and the subsidies, being unearned, don't create self-generating growth, so the drain goes on interminably. Ultimately most of the nation becomes incapable of supporting itself, or can do so only badly.

The elephant city-region pattern, even in a small country, can create miserable resentments and exacerbate ethnic bitterness or hatreds. For instance, in Czechoslovakia before World War II, Prague, the city of the Czechs, was dominant and steadily becoming more so. Bratislava, the city of the Slovaks, was relatively inert, relatively provincial, and becoming more so. The Slovaks attributed the difference to political and cultural favoritism on the part of the government. The envy and anger this nurtured helped divide Czechoslovakia during the war and help divide it now. Prague was indeed the more favored city economically, but the favoritism was not of a form that either the Czechs or the Slovaks could actually control. Czechoslovakia was merely conforming to a perfectly typical national economic pattern.

Cities within a nation get no feedback whatever from the national currency with respect to their trade with one another nor their other domestic trade either, for that matter. This means that in a country with very little international trade relative to domestic trade, cities get virtually no feedback. While this lack may not deaden them, neither does it help correct or rejuvenate them when they falter. A physical analogy would be an object in equilibrium on a hill. As long as its equilibrium goes undisturbed, it can get along without feedback and maintain its position. But once it loses its equilibrium, even slightly, it's downhill all the way. Just so, when the decline of a city getting no feedback does begin, the decline typically proceeds thereafter, uncorrected.

Throughout most of the history of the Chinese empire, Chinese cities had no feedback. Chinese tradition has it that the empire was formed of fifty-five provinces, unified under one of them, Ch'in. The provinces, in turn, are reputed to have been formed earlier of some 1,700 little city-states or principalities. That figure may or may not be reasonably true, but the fact that a big unit was made of many smaller units is certainly true. Long before the empire was more or less solidified (it kept being militarily unified, breaking apart, militarily unified, breaking apart, militarily unified, breaking apart), all the bases of China's artistic and material culture were developed: its languages, writing, literature, philosophy, art, music, silk culture and weaving, embroidery, ornamented pottery and other ceramics, very sophisticated metallurgy in both bronze and iron, boats, chariots, bricks, bells, wine, chess, magnets, fishnets and all the other essential fishing and agricultural implements, astronomical observations, codified laws, currencies, and much, much else. Under unification, China has never equaled its earlier fantastic capabilities at development or fulfilled the promise that these imply. So immemorially stagnant did its cities become that by this century some 80 percent of its population was rural, and of course as in all nations with a predominantly rural population, it was poor, hungry and backward. At the least, we may say that a universal currency, hence no feedback, did not help the cities of imperial China and we may surmise it doesn't help them today.

After Rome came to rule most of the world known to Rome, the more centralized the economic control of the empire became, the less feedback the individual cities received. After the Western Empire disintegrated, the Eastern Empire long persisted. It, too, was relatively self-sufficient, trade with Venice notwithstanding, for although that trade loomed large in Venice, it at first figured little in Byzantium. The Ottoman Empire, which took over the ruins of the Byzantine Empire and then extended further, was also relatively self-sufficient, its cities receiving little feedback from the outside world. The historical fates of huge, unified realms don't hold much economic promise, to put it mildly.

The most outstanding modern example of such a realm is the United States. After the tariff policy had overcome the initial feedback flaw that afflicted the country, the United States became a nation in which cities got almost no feedback from their currency on how their own trade was doing. The flourishing Northern cities proceeded to produce for one another and for the country's regions lacking cities, and relatively little for the world outside. Most kinds of foreign imports that arrived were swiftly replaced with local production in this city or that one, and the reproductions, adaptations and improvements were sold as domestic products. The goods and services of their own devising that American cities cast up—often truly unprecedented goods and services, and often solving very important practical problems—went overwhelmingly into domestic trade, too. In time, to be sure, American-manufactured exports, along with services such as engineering and equipment installation, loomed large in some of the countries receiving them (Uruguay for one), but they did not loom large in the total production and trade of American cities. As the American cities burgeoned, the rural international exports which had once so threatened their economies became of little importance relative to total trade. American cities themselves became the chief markets of the country's rural products. The cotton went increasingly to the mill towns of New England in Boston's orbit, and then to transplanted industries sent south from New England. The tobacco went increasingly to American consumers. Beef cattle and hogs went to packing houses in Kansas City and Chicago, then later to rural or small-city packing houses—in either case mainly for consumption within the nation. Ore went to American steel and brass mills, and thence overwhelmingly to American fabricating industries, toolmakers, railway, locomotive and ship builders, automotive manufacturers, and bridge and building contractors. The country's domestic trade came to hover at about 95 percent of the country's total trade, foreign and domestic, and sometimes exceeded that.

With no admonitory feedback from the national currency, American cities flourished mightily, but only up to a point. All cities tend to have their runs of bad economic times for many reasons, ranging from unavoidable hard luck to outright short-sightedness, folly and overspecialization. Furthermore, every city's already established export work dwindles over the course of time owing to replacements in customer cities, transplants to distant regions, and obsolescence. A city that loses export work without compensating for the losses is a city doomed to decline. Such a city needs help and needs it fast, needs the automatic equivalents of tariffs and export subsidies. This no city can get in a country like the United States. Although American cities were able to build up their economies astonishingly with no feedback help (other than the tariffs that countermanded false feedback information), they have had no defenses, no means of self-correction, whenever they have seriously begun to lose important export work.

Today so many American cities are stagnant and in economic decline that the stagnation and decline are acknowledged to be "national" problems. But, taken individually, American cities have been stagnating for a long time now. The first of the major cities to stagnate decisively was probably Pittsburgh, at about the turn of the century. During the eight decades since, city after city has been stagnating and not pulling out of it: little cities like Rochester, Utica, Scranton, Akron, Toledo, Wilmington, Camden; larger cities like Buffalo, Cleveland, Indianapolis, Seattle, Detroit, New York. New York's economy has been declining since at least the 1940s, and yet never did a city have better responsive equipment with which to make corrections than New York then. But the corrections weren't made, and now much of the responsive equipment itself is lost—the versatility at producing, the producers' goods and services, the skills—and much of what remains is not up-to-date, has become obsolescent. One among many symptoms and signs of the city's growing poverty is that today, as an economy, it is too poor even to repair its rundown subway system, water-supply system, roads and bridges, although in the days when the city was economically vigorous it was able, from its own revenues, to carry the capital costs of creating these great systems, and much more.

In the meantime, the Sun Belt cities of the South and West have been rising, and this would be all to the good except that in large part their economic bases consist of military production, and of exports to backward client states like those exports to the Shah's Iran that I have already described. Military production and international trade in sophisticated goods from advanced to backward countries are profoundly dead-end forms of economic activity, as I shall explain in the next chapter. They are not so much expressions of development and expansion as they are means of trying to temporize with economic sluggishness.

Since about 1960 in the United States, the proportion of international to domestic trade has gradually been rising, to about 15 percent in 1980. American exports consist in part of ever more important rural international exports such as soybeans and wheat, while the manufactured exports go mainly to client states, in many cases on credit, and increasingly are military goods. The country's imports largely consist of city-made goods with which American cities can no longer compete in quality or price. Imports from Japan are increasingly made by methods that render American producers' equipment and techniques obsolete. Thus it is not surprising that clamor grows for new tariffs or for negotiated quotas on foreign manufactured goods. But American cities are not suffering from the contradictory currency feedback that tariffs can countermand. They are suffering, rather, from the fact that they don't correct their own economies, and as one after another has stagnated, they have been letting one another down. Tariffs are no remedy for that form of city failure. The little Northern cities of America's infancy, weak and backward though they were, were not letting one another down by letting their own economies slump and become moribund; that is precisely why they could make successful use of tariffs.

One might say—except that it implies an undeserved censoriousness—that American cities have suffered badly from lack of economic discipline: the discipline imposed by currency fluctuations or, if we prefer, the opportunities presented by currency fluctuations. These can make it possible for a city's falterings to be merely temporary. But if uncorrected, faltering becomes final, downhill all the way. The failure is not the fault of the cities, the government, or the American people. It is a structural flaw that comes with the territory. We must be grateful that world government and a world currency are still only dreams.

I do not mean to imply that currency fluctuations are the only determinants of whether a city, and its region if it has developed one, can repeatedly replace imports and generate exports vigorously. The fact that we must inhale and exhale doesn't mean we live on air alone. Other factors are important too. But it still remains that currency fluctuations are a powerful force, a potent form of feedback control, for good, for ill or for nil.

As far as I can see, there are no remedies at a city's or a nation's command, short of separations in the pattern of Singapore, for correcting the flaw I have hypothesized as leading to elephant cities while deadening others, and none for correcting the lack of feedback. But that doesn't mean that nations don't try to remedy, countermand or compensate for the exasperating stagnation of their cities and decline of their economies. They typically try hard and ingeniously to do just those things. But as we shall see, the efforts are worse than futile, for they only deepen and hasten widespread city stagnation and decline, unwittingly piling further structural economic flaws upon the built-in structural flaw of faulty or missing feedback to their cities.

TWELVE

Transactions
of Decline

Successful imperialism wins wealth. Yet, historically, successful empires such as Persia, Rome, Byzantium, Turkey, Spain, Portugal, France, Britain, have not remained rich. Indeed, it seems to be the fate of empires to become too poor to sustain the very costs of empire. The longer an empire holds together, the poorer and more economically backward it tends to become. Imperial powers that are only briefly successful because they lose their colonies and conquests early on, like Germany and Japan, or those that abruptly contract into only a very small home nation, like the Netherlands or Austria, seem to be the luckier ones. Yet if imperialism wins wealth for imperial powers, as it undoubtedly does, how can this be? A paradox.

I am going to argue that the very policies and transactions that are necessary to win, hold and exploit an empire are destructive to an imperial power's own cities and cannot help but lead to their stagnation and decay. Imperial decline is built right into imperial success; the two are part and parcel of each other. Furthermore, the same types of policies and transactions that make the declines of empires inevitable can also speed stagnation and decay in nonimperial powers that adopt them.

I say "speed" stagnation and decay, rather than "cause" stagnation and decay because, as we have seen, cities in nations that preside over numerous cities are handicapped by feedback flaws in any case; those come with the territory. They make it chancy or impossible for cities that begin to decline to reverse themselves (although in a later chapter I shall describe an outstanding exception), and they also hamper or prevent the formation and flourishing of new cities. All this is especially disadvantageous to large countries in need of many city regions. The special policies I am going to explore and the transactions that sustain them are additional to feedback flaws and at least in large part are the responses of governments to failures of cities and the obdurate poverty of regions in which cities persistently fail to develop.

These policies and transactions, no matter what the motives for them, are all killers of city economies. They fall into three main groups: prolonged and unremitting military production; prolonged and unremitting subsidies to poor regions; heavy promotion of trade between advanced and backward economies. Different as these seem superficially, these policies and the transactions that sustain them are similar in the harm they work. To explore how they operate, let us begin with military production.

Unremitting, prolonged military production is an unremitting and voracious feeder upon the earnings of city economies—so much so that, historically, prolonged and unremitting militarism has been impossible for a realm until it has already become reasonably well urbanized. Ancient empires that contained rich, productive cities for their time were economically able to go in for unremitting militarism and typically did just that. However, in the European economic tradition that has shaped so much of the world as we know it, prolonged and unremitting military efforts have been possible only within the past four centuries.

From our perspective, it may seem that European warfare was all but continual during medieval and Renaissance times, but that is not so. For more than a thousand years after the disintegration of Rome, Europe was simply too poor and rural to support uninterrupted military efforts lasting even as long as a few years at a stretch, much less permanent standing military forces. Armies and even navies were sporadically levied, supplied and then disbanded with bewildering rapidity. Mercenaries had to scramble to find employment, first under one warlord, then another. Feudal armies consisted of peasants and yeomen rounded up under noblemen and their knights for short campaigns when they could be spared from the fields. Even though much of the pay of soldiers, such as it was, came to them in the form of opportunities for plunder, the pickings weren't all that rich. When armed bands put themselves on a more permanent footing, as the Crusaders did, they had to fend for themselves much of the time by begging or looting, and in any case drawing upon supplies and equipment first from one domain, then from another, all in all managing so miserably that death from exposure, disease and malnutrition was evidently appalling even for the times.

Under such conditions, military production was sporadic and spasmodic too, oscillating rapidly with production for other needs. We tend to think of insufficient surplus food for armies as being the constraining force on uninterrupted medieval warfare, and so it was, as it would be in any predominantly rural economic life. But sheer inability to afford other kinds of production for the military were constraints as well. After the Fishmongers' Guild in medieval London had contributed a fleet to the Crown to combat pirates, the shipyards quickly reverted to building fishing or merchant vessels. They had to; the country couldn't yet afford to support a royal navy, a permanent customer for military shipping. A saddler in Genoa or a smith in Orléans would likely as lief equip soldiers one month, merchants or pilgrims the next.

Not until the sixteenth century did European realms become economically capable of waging uninterrupted warfare lasting several years at a stretch, Spain taking the lead followed by England and France. In Russia, Ivan the Terrible managed to set up a small, permanent, professional army and equip it with log housing, food, colorful clothing and halberds, battle-axes and spears, but between campaigns these soldiers ran shops (some got rich) in their quarter in Moscow, worked as servants, did gardening for the officers.

Not until the beginning of the seventeenth century was there any power in Europe other than Turkey which could afford a standing army in our sense: effective fighting or garrison forces maintained at strength, and with no other occupation than soldiering even when there was no fighting for them to do at the moment. During that century, unremitting production for permanent military establishments finally emerged, Spain again taking the lead, followed by France and England. The Royal Navy was put on a permanent and well-organized footing; yet even so, for two centuries longer Britain depended partially on privateers, as did rival powers: armed merchant ships, whose functions oscillated between peaceable commercial trading on behalf of their owners and raiding of enemy shipping when that was what their government wanted of them.

The United States, from the time it won independence, was prosperous enough to afford standing naval and army forces, but these were small and so was American military production except at times of war. Most such production was thus undertaken only sporadically and abruptly for specific wars of a few years' duration, and then was equally abruptly dropped.

Starting with the Korean War in 1950, however, America has supported military production that with minor ups and downs has become heavier as time has passed. If we discount the pause of five years after the ending of World War II (a pause during which Marshall Plan aid partially took the place of military production), we can think of military expenditures as being unremitting drains upon the earnings of American cities since early 1941, when lend-lease supply to Britain started.

Military production gives export work to cities, in some cases colossal quantities, and this work, along with its multiplier effect, creates booms. In the case of the United States, the World War II military production boom brought the country bounding out of the Great Depression. Any massive increase in export work, in any settlement, creates a boom there from the combined effect of the soaring export production and its multiplier: the secondary jobs and incomes that arise from serving the workers and their families and from work supplying and servicing the exporting enterprises. It takes a few years for a city or any other settlement to assimilate the multiplier effect from soaring export work, and those few years are years of extraordinary boom. Thus abruptly instituted wartime military production is all boom, to the extent that controls on civilian output and destruction of settlements in the line of fire permit it to be.

It is important to understand, however, that prolonged military production does not create prolonged economic booms. Once the multiplier effects of the military work are assimilated, things settle down. Thereafter any further economic expansion from that source requires the military work itself to be expanded. And once a city, or any other settlement, comes to depend upon prolonged military work as an appreciable, normal part of its economic base, the military production must be maintained indefinitely or the economy shrinks. For example, much the largest employer in the city of Seattle is the Boeing Aircraft Company, which produces commercial aircraft but also depends heavily on contracts for the development and construction of bombers. In the early 1970s when military contracts to Boeing were reduced, Seattle experienced a very severe localized depression. Unemployment rose sharply; retail trade suffered; houses on which people couldn't maintain mortgage payments were foreclosed; emergency feeding stations were set up for people whose large fixed expenses, assumed in better times, left no margin for even bare necessities in hard times. Seattle was losing not only military work but also the multiplier effect of that work. In a few years, contracts to Boeing expanded and things in Seattle returned to normal.

Cities and their regions, being the greatest yielders of revenues in a nation or empire, are capable of supporting heavy and unremitting military production if there are enough of them and they are rich enough. While this drains earnings from cities, it also gives some among them a trade-off in the form of military work upon which, like Seattle, they eventually depend. To sustain that work, city earnings must continually be diverted to the cause; and to expand it, still more earnings must be diverted to the cause.

Almost all the military export work of cities, as well as that of other settlements, consists of goods sent to non-urban destinations. Thus it represents production automatically rendered sterile and useless for the process of import-replacing anywhere in economic life. This is so not only when the military goods are consumed in battle but even when the production is undertaken in time of peace and the goods never used in combat. Furthermore, this is true not only of weapons but of goods no different in kind from civilian production.

To see why this is so, one need only notice the kinds of economies possessed by military bases and garrison towns; they import, but they don't replace wide ranges of their imports with local production. At Camp Lejeune, the great U.S. Marine Corps base in Onslow County, North Carolina, loaded trucks rumble through the gates, bumper to bumper, throughout the cargo receiving hours of the day, bringing in their freights of peanut butter, business machines, dental drills, mattresses, chain-link fencing, shoes, file folders, light bulbs, detergents, cooking ware, spaghetti . . . A rail line interminably drops off its deposits too. This has been going on day after day, year after year, decade after decade—all production irretrievably useless for stimulating or feeding the import-replacing process anywhere, owing to its very destination. It doesn't matter how diverse the imports are, how large the volumes, or over how long a period they are received. Garrisons have functions other than replacing imports; in any case, getting the goods doesn't build up garrisons' versatility at producing, as happens in the case of imports that cities earn.

Like the camp itself, the nearby garrison town, Jacksonville, North Carolina, is not an import-replacing settlement, nor is it a city. The five-mile strip of road between Jacksonville and the camp's main gate is lined with highly decorated bars, night clubs and restaurants, but that doesn't mean Jacksonville is capable of producing neon tubes, red and yellow paint, beer coolers or anything else much. The town rejoices in a number of tattoo parlors and is a consumer of electric tattoo needles and inks imported from New York, but those facts don't render the place economically capable of making these producers' goods for itself.

Camp Lejeune is equipped, among other things, with U.S. Post Exchanges, the retail stores established for the convenience of American military personnel and their families at garrisons and bases, at home and abroad. The pay of the servicemen who patronize the exchanges is financed by distant taxpayers, and insofar as those taxpayers are city people and city enterprises, the goods on the shelves and in the warehouses of the exchanges are actually imports earned in cities—or rather their equivalents in value— which have been lost to cities. By 1970 the PXs throughout the world had become the third largest merchandizing enterprise in the world: a lot of production rendered impotent for import-replacing because of its destinations. Of course, those goods represent only a small fraction and thin variety of what is required for upkeep of people in garrisons.

Weapons help account for the almost incomprehensible sizes of military budgets: the costs of developing and producing tanks, missiles, nuclear bombs and warheads, artillery, machine guns, ammunition, bombing planes, fighter planes, spy planes, missile interceptor planes, military transport planes, helicopters, technical equipment for airfields, spy satellites in space, rocket launchers, battleships, cruisers, aircraft carriers, minelayers, mine sweepers, submarines, destroyers, landing craft, systems for detecting other people's planes and ships . . . But what I have said of the kinds of military supplies similar to civilian goods and services applies more stringently still, if anything, to weapons. Whether their destinations are storage depots, readiness alert stations, training bases, testing or maneuver grounds, patrol units, surveillance centers, naval or air bases, the fact that the weapons are imported to these locales doesn't make the destinations capable of replacing them with local production even if such a thing were wanted, which it isn't. The only exceptions to this rule are instances when arms producers acquire other producers' weapons and then proceed to copy or adapt them, or when weapons, after first being imported from foreign countries, are then built in transplanted factories, the strategy adopted in part by the Shah of Iran. But in the new locales, the production promptly becomes sterile for import-replacing. Although I have used the U.S. military in my examples, garrisons everywhere are not that different, nor are patrol bases, air bases and so on.

In sum, then, to the extent that city earnings support unremitting military production, the programs subtract from cities imports they have earned and translate these, instead, into production imported by settlements that don't and can't replace imports. Cities, some of them, get a trade-off of export work, but to sustain this a nation's or empire's cities must unremittingly surrender earned imports, or rather their equivalents in value. This naturally makes cities poorer customers for one another than they otherwise would be. It also inescapably makes them feebler or more dilatory at replacing imports from one another, or from anywhere else, than they otherwise would be, a deficiency that undermines both their capacities to generate new kinds of goods and services and their capacities to afford problem solving or other innovative exports from one another, even if these are devised. The more heavily cities of a nation or empire lose earnings to pay for military expenditures, and the longer and more unremittingly they lose them, the more heavily they must come to depend on military work they are given in this trade-off, or else not only stagnate but decline as well. These military transactions are thus at the expense of intercity trade and also at the expense of the import-replacing process.

Consider in this light that there are three master characteristics of all developing and expanding economies, three kinds of major changes taking place as they rise and flourish.

First, taken as a whole, economic life becomes more urbanized and less rural. City work and intercity trade show the greatest gains both absolutely and proportionately. Rural production and trade increase as well, but as by-products of the city activity.

Second, as city trade expands, it sparks additional cities into life, mainly in what had been subsistence and supply regions, and draws them into volatile city trading networks.

Third, increased quantities and proportions of all goods and services being produced are imported into cities and become available there to the process of import-replacing. This is a consequence of the two preceding changes and it is also a condition for their continuation.

Those changes are nothing less than economic development and expansion: the very dynamic of development itself, in action.

When economic life is in process of declining and contracting, exactly the opposite changes are occurring.

First, taken as a whole, economic life becomes less urbanized, more rural. City work and intercity trade decline proportionately as a share of total economic activity, while rural production and trade increase their proportionate share.

Second, existing cities stagnate and decline, while insufficient new cities arise to compensate for the losses.

Third, decreased quantities and proportions of all goods and services being produced are imported into cities and thus fall outside the import-replacing process. As cities stagnate and stop replacing imports significantly, even the imports they still receive do not serve import-replacing. This is a consequence of the two preceding great changes.

We can think of that second set of changes or deteriorations of economic life as being the dynamic of decline. They *are* decline, the very ruin itself in action. Those are the changes that reduce formerly developing and expanding economies to inertia, poverty and backwardness, as dwindling varieties and quantities of new kinds of goods and services are cast up and enter everyday economic life, and finally none; and as unsolved, pressing practical problems merely mount up unsolved. When stagnation becomes total, the declined and contracted economic life then lives on residues it retains from former development.

Unremitting and heavy military production is one of the means by which the characteristics of developing economic life are directly converted into the opposite characteristics of degenerating economic life. The transactions involved *are* decline, part of the very process itself in action.

Understanding this helps us understand another paradox associated with decline of empires. War and war production has often stimulated the development of metallurgy, communications, epidemiology, surgery, engineering, chemistry, shipbuilding and navigation, aeronautics, weather forecasting, footgear and other clothing, map making, transport . . . the list could go on and on. This being so, one might suppose that heavily militarized nations or empires would be in a particularly good position to continue in the forefront of economic development, perhaps lead it indefinitely, aided as they are by spin-offs from military work and its pressures to employ innovations.

Yet from ancient to modern times, the very societies that have invested most heavily and most unremittingly in military production have become arrested and grown backward technologically. Military developments do spur civilian economic developments, and conversely, civilian technology spurs military technology but only when production oscillates between the two. That oscillation happens little when military production continues on and on, providing producers with permanent customers for the war goods. But still more important, a stagnating economy becomes poor generally at injecting innovations into everyday economic life, no matter what their source. It is also worth noting that nonmilitary work doesn't need militarism and its pressures in order to develop—witness Switzerland, or Japan in the years since World War II. Cities, not war production, incubate economic life. When militarism feeds unremittingly on the earnings of cities and distorts their normal intercity trade, it retards development, no matter how much ingenuity or research is invoked in its cause. Indeed, the more ingenuity and research, the worse, because those very efforts are expensive drains on city earnings at the cost of intercity trade.

The historical spectacle of economies managing to develop and expand, and then putting their wealth to the service of agony, terror, destruction and bluster is depressing to say the least, and of course nowadays carries with it the ultimate terror of extinction. So why not, as humane and reasonable people are constantly suggesting, redirect national military spending to constructive and kindlier ends . . . think of the good to be done with the money a single battleship costs . . . if it is possible to go to the moon, why can't we solve the easier problems of building for the ill-housed, feeding the hungry, overcoming poverty and fear of poverty . . .

Welfare programs with those aims, and grants and subsidies to bring standards of living and services in poor regions into line with those of prospering city regions unfortunately also work out as transactions of decline. If they are unremitting, they too drain city earnings unremittingly. If they are at all generous, then if anything they are even more voracious feeders on cities than military programs. That is probably one reason why modern welfare states have emerged from economic life even more recently than standing armies or navies. Until a nation has a well-developed and productive city or cities it can't afford appreciable transfer payments and other welfare programs. The welfare state of modern times was not pioneered until a century ago, beginning in Bismarck's then newly unified Germany. Bismarck envisioned universal, centrally administered national insurance for the working classes, but at the time this was neither economically nor politically possible for him to bring off, so the start he made was to promote decentralized joint worker-industry accident insurance funds, expanding, as income permitted, to insurance also covering sickness, disability and old age retirement. From this beginning have come the hundreds of varieties of national insurance, welfare benefits, and special grants and subsidies that are now distributed by most governments able to afford them. (Not all; the Swiss have few and scant national subsidies or grants, since, on the whole, Swiss regions are sufficiently prosperous not to require much aid 'from one another.) Agricultural price supports and other agricultural subsidies are analogous to welfare programs, in drawing upon city regional economies to support poorer regions.

The discrepancy between what any individual city and its region pay toward national or provincial welfare, agricultural and other subsidy programs and what they receive back represents losses of earnings diverted, instead, to other economies that don't replace wide ranges of their imports with local production, for if they did, they would be on the giving rather than the receiving end of such transactions. Thus goods and services the subsidies buy turn up, just as military goods and services do, at destinations which don't and can't replace imports with local production. Nor does receiving subsidies—unearned imports—help them become capable of doing so. Not being earned, these do nothing to promote versatility at producing in subsidized economies. In sum, goods and services sent into subsidized regions are goods and services that fall outside the import-replacing process anywhere.

Cities get an economic trade-off for their subsidy contributions, just as some do for their contributions to military costs. In this case they get orders for consumers' goods from people in settlements and regions who would not otherwise be able to afford the goods, and orders for construction and equipment items from hospitals, schools, universities, water and sewage systems, fire departments, farms, electric utilities and other establishments in subsidized poor regions, orders they otherwise wouldn't get.

Superficially, that suggests a rather wonderful perpetual-motion machine, the subsidy transactions extracting contributions from cities while simultaneously stimulating orders for city export work. Such transactions, it might seem, would need only to be kept going indefinitely and, behold, economic life itself would chug away indefinitely. Just as Marx supposed, it would only be a matter of effectively distributing purchasing power. Demand-side economics would really work. In a perpetual-motion machine of this kind, the significance of city economies would merely be that they are especially good at generating wealth and especially adept at some kinds of production and services.

But that isn't why cities are uniquely necessary to economic life. Their vital functions are to serve as primary developers and primary expanders of economic life, functions that work not in the least like perpetual motion. They require continually repeated inputs of energy in two specific forms: innovations, which at bottom are inputs of human insight; and ample replacements of imports, which at bottom are inputs of the human capacity to make adaptive imitations. The usefulness of cities is that they supply contexts in which those inputs—insights and adaptations—can be successfully injected into everyday economic life.

The trouble, then, with transfer payments and other subsidies as means of keeping economic life chugging away is that, feeding voraciously upon city earnings as they do, they reduce intercity trade in favor of trade between cities and inert economies; divert earned city imports to economies that cannot replace imports; and reduce cities' abilities to serve as good customers for one another's innovations. Subsidies milked from cities are for these reasons profoundly antidevelopment transactions.

When cities and their regions give sporadic emergency aid—for example, as flood, earthquake, fire or war damage relief—the aid is analogous to sporadic military production. It doesn't distort city economies permanently or drain them unremittingly, nor does it make them dependent upon the very work of supplying goods and services for the aid of inert economies as a substitute for volatile intercity trade.

Heavy and unremitting subsidies are transactions of decline, and once adopted the need for them grows greater with time, and the wherewithal for supplying them grows less. When welfare subsidies and their analogs, agricultural subsidies, are first undertaken by careful and responsible governments, they are affordable. Yet remarkably soon—present experience suggests within two generations—the economy of a welfare state itself becomes perilously insecure. The programs turn out to be no longer affordable on their former scale and in their former scope, or else affordable only by means of permanent, not emergency, deficit financing. That is why nations with generous and comprehensive welfare programs must either drastically curtail benefits that were earlier affordable or allow inflation to make the curtailments.

It seems unfair that programs undertaken out of compassion or to combat the injustice of poverty in regions that remain obdurately poor should unwittingly work as instruments for spreading stagnation and deepening poverty. But one might as well say that it isn't fair for unfertilized soil to deplete itself when it is exploited to feed the hungry rather than for less defensible purposes. The soil doesn't know the difference; neither do city economies being drained of the nourishment they need to remain creative and productive.

Furthermore, subsidy programs are not necessarily always compassionate. Empires or large nations plagued with active or latent separatist movements use subsidies to contain restiveness and discontents. Governments use them to stay in office. Empires use them to retain the loyalty of client states when that is necessary or to outbid rival imperial powers. Subsidies, precisely because they are transactions of decline, are economic time bombs. They help buy tranquillity as long as they can be afforded—but no longer. When they must be drastically curtailed, or when inflation renders them meaningless, societies that have depended on them become distraught socially and politically, as Uruguay did. As this is written, French students are rioting because of curtailments of subsidies. Once unremitting subsidies begin, governments have to go to almost any lengths to try to retain them, with minor ups and downs. The alternative becomes repression, which is expensive too and not only in monetary costs.

So far I have mentioned only tax-supported transactions as being drains on city earnings, bestowers of city export work for non-urban destinations in return, subtractors of goods and services from use in the import-replacing process anywhere, and depressors of intercity trade in favor of trade between cities and non-urban economies—in sum, converters of the dynamic of development into the dynamic of decline. But investments can have those same effects, and in addition can promote rural production at the expense of cities and their economic needs.

To understand in principle how investments can operate as transactions of decline, consider what happens when a factory is transplanted from a city or its region into a distant supply or transplant region, or into a region people have been abandoning because it doesn't give them a living. At the site of the transplanted factory, much is imported in its cause: window glass, utility pipes and wires, construction machinery, lathes, looms, refinery tanks or whatever else may be required to build and equip it; also consumers' goods for the construction workers to buy with some of their pay. Those imports have not been earned by the export work of the transplant economy, which is why the financing of transplanted factories is customarily supplied either by the parent company or by distant banks from which it borrows. Transplanted factories are customarily expected to pay back their capital costs and to yield interest and profits as well. If the costs are indeed economically justified, and hence repayable over the course of time, either of two things happens next, or a combination of both.

On the one hand, the repayments, as they come in, can be invested this time around in the city or cities from which the financing came. They can be used, for example, to re-equip an existing city enterprise so that it doesn't become obsolete, or to buy imported materials for a new enterprise that has been successfully launched there and is expanding, or to sustain some innovative work until (perhaps) it proves practical and finds local or export markets, or to feed capital into enterprises replacing imports but needing feeder imports, such as rubber for bicycle tires or leather for bicycle seats. If the repayments are reinvested where the capital first came from, then the transaction of the relocated factory has not depleted the city of those earnings, nor diverted their equivalents in earned imports permanently. The imports have merely been deferred temporarily. The drain is not unremitting. If interest or profits from the investment are also put to use in the city involved—whether to buy consumers' goods there or to finance producers' goods—then the city economy even receives extra imports from its extra earnings.

On the other hand, when the costs of the transplanted factory are returned they can, instead of being reinvested within the city or its region, be reinvested in still another distant transplant, then another, and another, indefinitely. For all practical purposes, the repeated similar investments have drained the city permanently of earnings and of the goods those earnings represent, goods that are also permanently lost to the import-replacing process anywhere. That is investment for production working as a transaction of decline, and in principle that is one reason supply-side economics is a meaningless conception of how economic life chugs on.

The same two possibilities occur when city-derived capital reshapes a supply region in ways expected to pay off. If the repaid investment is then interminably reinvested in similar fashion, this too is a transaction of decline, and if the investments are continually enlarged, they become an ever larger drain on the cities yielding them. Empires are especially prone to these transactions.

The most destructive city-financed investments in rural production are those that finance labor-saving equipment in regions where displaced workers have no access to city jobs near or distant. These investments are, of course, often subsidized; but whether they are or not, city earnings are diverted, and it often follows that more and more city earnings must be diverted to the region to support people there who have been made redundant or to lure in subsidized factory transplants. Investments in clearance regions not only fail to make subsidies unnecessary; they can make further subsidies obligatory, interminably. Of course, cities producing rural labor-saving equipment get a trade-off: sales of equipment. The more city economies stagnate, the more desperately such sales are sought and promoted, no matter how ill-starred a clearance program may be. And like military goods, these goods go to destinations where they cannot be replaced with local production. This, of course, is not the case with rural labor-saving equipment destined for city regions rather than clearance regions.

Sophisticated city-produced goods and services exported to backward cities are sterile also as far as import-replacing is concerned. As we have seen, the gulf between such goods and what backward cities are capable of producing is too great to be bridged, which is why backward cities need volatile trade with one another. The manufactured goods, in all their immense variety and large quantities that showed up decade after decade in Montevideo, were useless for the process of import-replacing anywhere, quite as useless as if they had gone to rural destinations.

When dead-end advanced-backward trade of this kind is pay-as-you-go, as it was during most of Uruguay's history, or as the Shah's purchases were for the most part, then at least the transactions do not drain advanced cities of earnings and the imports those earnings buy. They, or cities with which they trade, get wool, leather, oil, and so on, mainly resource and agricultural goods, which in some cases can even be replaced with city-produced substitutes or incorporated into replaced imports in cities. In other words, at the "advanced" pole of advanced-backward trade, the goods are not necessarily sterile for import-replacing, although they are sterile at the "backward" pole.

However, when advanced-backward trade is maintained on credit instead of being paid for with products of backward economies, the cities at the "advanced" pole of the trade are being drained of earnings. If the loans, even when paid back, are repeatedly renewed in the interests of further advanced-backward trade, cities providing the financing are being drained indefinitely. When the loans are simply unrepayable, or when the trade is financed by grants, the transactions work like subsidies. Earnings of advanced cities are being diverted to inert economies. Advanced-backward trade that depends on credit (largely unrepayable) or grants is no negligible factor in international trade today. By the middle of 1982, U.S. banks' loans to Brazil and Mexico equalled 95 percent of the capital of the nine largest U.S. banks and 74 percent of the capital of the next fifteen largest, according to the *Wall Street Journal*. Of course, that doesn't mean that 95 percent and 74 percent of the banks' lending powers are committed to Brazil and Mexico, since banks lend multiples of their capital. But it is sufficient to cause the banks to crash if the loans are defaulted instead of being interminably renewed. Add the many other U.S. loans for promoting advanced-backward trade, with Argentina, Chile, the Philippines, Venezuela, Spain, Poland, Yugoslavia . . . and one begins to understand what a chimera this trade is unless it is continually fed by city earnings. West European countries, Canada, Japan and the Soviet Union are financing advanced-backward trade on credit as well, on behalf of "sales" of their own products; and the International Monetary Fund and the World Bank are also financing such trade, largely on behalf of "sales" by their contributing nations. Those sales are the trade-offs for cities in these transactions of decline.

Transactions of decline are absolutely necessary to empires. Consider, for example, the kinds of transactions that made possible the British Empire, without which it couldn't have been formed or held together. They are similar to the transactions that made possible the Turkish, Spanish, Portuguese, French and many other empires highly successful in their day. Throughout Britain's period of imperial expansion, England was unremittingly investing, publicly and privately, in the conquest and shaping of far-flung supply regions. The trade-off was expanded British export work for obdurately backward economies, and while most of this was pay-as-you-go, still it represented great and growing shares of British production rendered sterile for import-replacing either in Britain or anywhere else. To maintain the entire political and economic contraption, Britain had to maintain far-flung and numerous garrisons, produce weapons and other supplies for them, and build up and unremittingly sustain its expensive naval power. The trade-off for that was naval and other military work for many British cities and smaller settlements. The cities, as time passed, came increasingly to live on export work to obdurately backward inert economies and on military work, and decreasingly on their trade with one another. These were the cities, as volatile mutual trading partners, that had created the industrial revolution. But gradually their capacity to develop further atrophied. Their existing industries and services became increasingly obsolete, the innovations scant, and their ability to serve as prosperous customers for one another feeble.

All the wealth of the Indies could not compensate for the stagnation and decline of Britain's own cities' economies. But the stagnation and decline were built right into the very transactions necessary to win, hold, administer and exploit the wealth of the Indies. Suppose Britain had been more generous to its empire, giving out grants, lending bountifully to further promote and intensify advanced-backward trade, subsidizing the poor in poor regions? The British Empire would have declined sooner and much, much faster.

From an economic point of view there are two types of empires, which we can think of as the English and the Roman models. In the English model, the imperial power concentrates almost exclusively on winning and holding control over economies more backward than its own. This is what the English did, first gaining and holding contiguous possessions—Wales, Scotland, Ireland—then the far-flung possessions overseas. The conquests of other European powers in Asia, Africa, the Americas and the Middle East were also on this model, the conquered realms being more backward economically than the conquerors'. This is also the model the United States followed in its conquests of Mexican territory, in the conflict between the states when the North retained in the Union the more backward South, the conquests of fragments of the Spanish empire in the Caribbean and Pacific, and in the unsuccessful venture into Vietnam.

The Roman model of imperialism also takes backward economies into the fold, but in addition incorporates and dominates economies as advanced as its own, some more so. That is what Rome did in the course of bringing the entire ancient Mediterranean world under its control. It is what Ferdinand and Isabella of Spain did in first bringing the more economically advanced Moorish portion of Iberia under control of Castile and Aragon. The founding state of China, Ch'in, conquered many economically advanced states and their cities, a process repeated many times in Chinese history when the great unwieldy mass disintegrated, then was reunited again by force of arms. When Russia expanded far into Siberia during the nineteenth century it was following the English model, but when the Soviet Union took East Germany, the small Baltic republics, Czechoslovakia and Hungary under its control after World War II, it was employing the Roman model, these economies—especially Czechoslovakia's and East Germany's—being more advanced than its own.

Successful imperialism on either model drains cities by means of the necessary transactions of decline, the difference being that the Roman model can temporize longer with decline because of its acquisitions of wealth-yielding cities along with backward, inert economies. But either way, the empire's cities are drained in the interests of empire.

Today the Soviet Union and the United States each predicts and anticipates the economic decline of the other. Neither will be disappointed.

The Soviet government ever since the inception of its rule, has been a voracious gobbler of its cities' earnings as fast as they could be earned. It has converted those earnings into extravagant, unremitting (and ineffectual) capital and operating subsidies for agriculture, into industrial investments in rural settings, into national welfare programs, and, of course, into heavy and prolonged militarism for policing its own domains and borders and for its prolonged arms race with the United States. Precious little has been left, either before World War II or afterward, for intercity trade, and little indeed for feeding the processes of city import-replacing. Even if they were allowed to replace imports opportunistically, Soviet cities are so short-changed on the imports they earn that they likely couldn't do so significantly. When the Soviet Union took under its economic control Gdansk, Warsaw, Cracow, Prague, Bratislava, Budapest, part of Berlin and other cities of East Germany, it acquired an additional supply of city earnings to drain for transactions of decline. The chief trade-off for these cities has been export work destined for inert economies in the Soviet Union. Far from continuing to develop, the economies of these cities have been arrested.

The United States, for its part, has been milking its cities and city regions even more prodigiously, a feat possible because, being more numerous, more highly developed and richer, American cities have had more to yield than Soviet cities. Besides being drained for the arms race, they have been contributing their disproportionately large shares to a nationwide pension plan (rapidly approaching insolvency unless the scale and scope of its benefits can be reduced), and to various other domestic subsidies which, by 1976, were being distributed through more than one thousand different federal benefit and grant programs. Foreign loans, public and private, have been promoting advanced-backward trade, and where loans have not been sufficient, grants have been made to the same purpose. American multinational and domestic corporations have engaged in protracted sprees of factory transplanting, by no means always paying off, and many undertaken to cash in on subsidies. The drains on city earnings all add up. American brains and skills haven't unaccountably evaporated, but the contexts in which Americans can expand and develop economic life have been constricting.

The Sun Belt cities are trade-off cities in two senses. Their economic bases consist largely of trade-offs given cities by transactions of decline: military work; goods and services for advanced-backward trade like the goods and services sold to the Shah; and city work financed at one remove by rural subsidies; retirement pensions are also an important economic base for some of them. The trade-offs for the Sun Belt have been financed by draining older cities of their earnings. In effect, one set of cities has been traded off for another set. Sun Belt city prosperity is not a net addition to American economic activity, as it would be if the dynamic of development were responsible for their rise.

Now that so many of America's older cities are in decline and need subsidies themselves to keep going and to contain discontent, support for transactions of decline must, ironically, shift increasingly to the Sun Belt cities. There go their earnings in the cause of more transactions of decline; and yet they must support those transactions—the military work, the subsidies, the advanced-backward trade—or else lose their own economic reasons for being. Transactions of decline are powerful traps.

France has undergone imperial decline like England, through much the same types of transactions. But France has been able, for a time, to temporize with the consequences in an interesting and probably unprecedented way. France is deficient in city regions, so rural France consists largely of supply regions, mainly agricultural. These would be poor indeed were they not heavily subsidized through the agricultural arrangements of the European Economic Community. The cities of West Germany, the Netherlands, North Italy, Belgium and even Denmark and England are all helping to subsidize rural France on a scale that France's own cities couldn't possibly manage, particularly as they themselves are mostly stagnant, which is why France has few city regions. In effect, France has found a variant of the Roman model of empire, since, as a nation, it is draining revenues from economies as advanced as its own, some more so. The sophistication of the arrangement doesn't change the fact that it drains cities of earnings, depresses volatile intercity trade in favor of city trade with inert economies, and subtracts production from any possible use in the import-replacing process—in sum, transactions of decline, in this case at the expense of Western Europe's cities generally.

Britain, having come late into the EEC, had no influence upon its basic arrangements, but it did have an understanding, or so it thought, that the community would undertake regional aid to depressed areas generally. As one commentator has put it: "The British neither benefit from the agricultural policy nor compete industrially as effectively as the Germans. They pay huge amounts into the EEC budget, despite having a per capita income below the EEC average. Naturally, the British want the rules changed. They want spending on agriculture reduced and expenditure on regional assistance, from which they would benefit, raised." When adoption of the regional aid policy Britain wanted was postponed (dropped, really) after Britain had entered the community, Britain attempted to retaliate by blocking an energy policy and a move into the next stage of proposed economic and monetary union. The wrangles of the EEC are to a considerable extent the jockeying of two played-out empires, France and Britain, over which one can more successfully milk the cities of Europe to temporize with its own decline. So far, the French have pulled off the feat and the British have not, but either way, development and expansion of European economic life is sacrificed to transactions of decline.

Today life in most nations that can afford them and many that can't has come to depend heavily on subsidies for inert economies; on advanced-backward trade that drains advanced cities and economically paralyzes backward ones; on vast and unremitting military production and traffic in arms; and on excessive and uneconomical reshapings of rural economies. We seem to have no ways of extricating ourselves from antidevelopment traps because by now so many people, so many enterprises, so many governments and so many once vigorous cities, too, have come to depend on incomes contrived through city-killing policies and transactions.

Transactions of decline have not been adopted because of a lack of concern about development or because governments accept poverty and stagnation. On the contrary, they are meant to foster development and attack poverty. In part, this is true even of military production. Purely for economic reasons, localities and enterprises compete to win military work and lobby to enlarge it. The devil finds work for idle hands. Transactions of decline, no matter which guise they take, are not remedies for stagnation and don't address causes of poverty, yet transactions of decline are precisely what national governments have become well fitted to deliver, and what empires and nations aspiring to empire must deliver.

THIRTEEN

The Predicament

Even as prosperous a country as Japan is troubled with inequalities among its different regions. Central Japan is well equipped with creative, import-replacing cities and their well-diversified regions like the one in which the hamlet of Shinohata is to be found. However, things are different on the northern and southern islands, which form a geographically large part of the nation, contain much of the population and are dotted with long-established hamlets, villages and towns, and some cities as well. Those peripheral cities differ from cities in central Japan. They haven't been good at replacing wide ranges of their city-made imports, which of course come primarily from central Japan. Since they are not import-replacing cities, they haven't generated significant city regions, either. It follows that these peripheral regions do not produce amply and diversely for their own producers and people as well as for others. It also follows that by not shifting to new import purchases as they replace wide ranges of older ones, these peripheral regions are less important markets than they otherwise would be for innovative exports cast up in central Japan's cities.

These are the parts of the country which, not surprisingly, press the government to retain or impose national tariffs on agricultural goods. The hamlet and village economies here are far less complex, diversified and ramified than little Shinohata's. Even the agriculture on these islands is less diversified because what is missing are the explosively shifting purchases of regional import-replacing cities, the purchases that have so stunningly diversified Shinohata's agriculture.

One consequence of the missing import-replacing cities is that a high proportion of young people seeking work must leave these regions entirely. To try to provide more local work, officials in northern and southern Japan behave much like officials in other countries. They compete to lure transplanted industries from distant cities, mainly from cities in central Japan but also increasingly, in recent years, the subsidiaries of foreign corporations. Just as elsewhere in the world, the demand for transplants outruns supply.

To be sure, people in northern and southern Japan are far better off economically than they were in the past. Nevertheless, these are poor economies relative to those of central Japan and have persisted in remaining so. Their troubled officials note that in some mysterious way development has passed them by.

So it has. The solution, of course, would be the emergence of import-replacing cities in these regions too. But this hasn't happened, and as time passes it becomes increasingly unlikely that it will. By now, potential import-replacing cities in the stunted regions would need tariffs or their equivalent on products from the larger and more highly developed cities in central Japan, much as the cities of central Japan themselves once required tariffs to set them going on replacing imports from the then more highly developed cities of America and Europe.

If the northern and southern regions of Japan had their own individualized currencies, they could automatically get equivalents of tariffs and export subsidies (as I explained in the discussion of city feedback in Chapter 11). If their agricultural exports skewed the value of those currencies too heavily, as exports of silk did when Japan was beginning its modern development, actual tariffs would be needed as well. However, both individualized currencies and the power to lay tariffs—if that were necessary initially—would imply new sovereignties, a family of Japanese sovereignties in place of a single unified sovereignty. As it is, the fact of a single unified sovereignty ensures that these regions must remain persistently stunted relative to those of central Japan. Although

Japan is the example I am using, this same analysis applies to all other nations that contain both city regions and persistently stunted regions in which import-replacing cities don't emerge.

In Japan, as elsewhere, regional disparities cause discontent, as well as a feeling in the nation at large that the inequalities must be addressed in some way and redressed as far as possible. Just as elsewhere, the response of the government has been to start heavily subsidizing the peripheral regions. Here we see why nations often first embark upon transactions of decline and why, once begun, those transactions have no ending. They mitigate regional inequalities but can't eliminate the causes.

Between the early 1950s and 1977, national tax rates were reduced every few years in Japan almost as a matter of course. During that period, production of wealth was outpacing demand for national government expenditures. But since 1977, Japanese tax rates have been rising, and so has deficit financing; both are unmistakable evidence that government expenditures have begun outpacing the production of wealth. The chief increases have been for social subsidies, agricultural subsidies, special economic grants, and support of the nationalized railroad system.

While the Japanese have begun increasing domestic subsidies rapidly, they have also increasingly promoted trade with backward countries, not merely in payment for the resource and rural goods the country imports from stunted foreign supply regions, but also to sell these nations sophisticated goods on credit. Cities in central Japan get the usual trade-offs from these transactions: export sales destined for inert economies that can't replace what they are receiving with their own production. Promotion of this dead-end type of trade has become necessary in Japan, as in advanced nations elsewhere, precisely because the cities of central Japan can find too few vigorous, solvent city trading partners, too few both domestically and internationally. But again, once embarked upon, these transactions of decline are not remedies for their cause. They make inert, dependent distant economies more dependent instead of self-developing.

History does not repeat itself in details, but patterns of economic history are so repetitious as to suggest that they are almost laws. If the usual patterns work themselves out, we may anticipate that Japan, with the passage of time, will resort ever more heavily to subsidies for its obdurately stunted regions, will ever more heavily promote its international advanced-backward trade and in due course will adopt prolonged programs of heavy military production. Unlikely as that last now seems, given Japan's pacifist convictions, pressures are mounting right now (in large part, but not entirely, exerted by the United States) to bring Japan's currently small military expenditures up to a level at which they absorb 2.5 percent of national production. This would put Japan in third place among nations in sheer value of military production, behind only the United States and the Soviet Union.

We may also anticipate, if the customary pattern works itself out, that as Japan's various transactions of decline increase in their aggregate weight, Japanese cities, now so creative and vigorous, will gradually stagnate and come to depend more and more on trade-offs from these transactions, rather than on their own and one another's creativity and their volatile mutual trade.

If, a century from now, historians seek a date for the beginnings of Japanese decline, 1977 will serve as well as any. A comparable date in the United States is 1933, when the nation began contending with the persistent poverty of the South by subsidizing it, then other poor regions as well, ever more heavily, followed up in due course by prolonged military production, too, and' promotions of international advanced-backward trade: transactions of decline, one and all. After half a century of this, American cities depend heavily on trade-offs from the transactions, rather than on their own and one another's creativity and their volatile mutual trade.

Transactions of decline, at the time they begin significantly, are interventions, abrupt discontinuities of the kind that put an increasingly unstable situation on a new footing that is temporarily more stable. In nature, for example, stresses and instabilities gradually build up in various portions of the earth's crust. When the accumulating stresses reach a certain point they are abruptly disposed of by a discontinuity, in this case an earthquake or the eruption of a volcano. The same type of phenomenon is at work in human affairs. A city enterprise that moves out because of accumulating stresses—say, congestion, makeshift space, rising costs

—is experiencing an abrupt discontinuity. If the stresses and disadvantages were simply to accumulate indefinitely, unrelieved, the enterprise might well deteriorate to a point of no return. But with a discontinuity it can evade otherwise continuing and mounting stresses and elude deterioration. When a city is losing export work and can't afford its current fund of imports, it can simply deteriorate economically. Or, alternatively, it can be rescued by an abrupt, explosive episode of import-replacing that not only disposes of the accumulating stresses and instabilities but also puts the city on a different and better footing for generating further export work. When surface traffic in a city becomes insupportable and is relieved by a subway, the city has had recourse to discontinuity.

Mathematicians grappling with the difficult and mathematically controversial subject of discontinuities call the type I am dwelling on "bifurcations." What all bifurcations have in common is that they are not first causes, but responses to prior accruing instabilities and stresses; they "fork off," are discontinuous with what has gone immediately before; and they leave things radically changed.

Through nobody's fault but simply in the nature of things, nations are inherently unstable economic systems. Even in the best or luckiest of them much goes awry because import-replacing cities fail to emerge in regions that lack them and need them, and in addition from time to time an existing city falters and doesn't correct its economy, which builds up further instabilities and stresses in the nation as a whole. Even if nations were run by selfless geniuses or by angels, stresses and instabilities from missing or arrantly contradictory feedback would accumulate; they are built into the situation itself.

Here we must stop and ponder for a moment a superficially confusing circumstance. Cities and potential cities have two fundamental, bedrock economic needs. Large nations or empires can serve one of these well, while they are at cross-purposes with respect to the other.

First, as we have seen, from the moment they begin to develop and then forever after, cities need ample, volatile trade with other cities. Large nations can serve this one need well because they can eliminate gratuitous barriers in their domestic trade.

Thus the larger a nation and the more cities it contains, the greater the opportunities for unhindered city trade. This is an asset denied little city-states like Hong Kong or Singapore and small nations like Taiwan, which are inherently so vulnerable to trade barriers raised against them by other nations.

If unhampered trade with one another were all that cities and potential cities needed to flourish, a single world government would be the economic ideal, and almost all the great empires of the past as well as those of recent times would have permanently remained splendid environments for cities. But they didn't, because trading networks of cities are somewhat like baseball or football teams. The players need a team, to be sure, or they can't play at all, but each player on the team also needs to maintain his own skills. If he doesn't and he isn't replaced, the team's performance suffers. If enough players deteriorate individually, the team is shot. It is this second fundamental need of cities, the need to keep themselves up to scratch individually, which nations serve so wretchedly owing to the feedback flaws that come with the territory.

In addition to instabilities and stresses that accumulate in a nation because of persistently stunted regions and because of cases of stagnation among the cities it does have, still further instabilities and stresses accrue because of severe economic depressions, which are exaggerations of the downsides of business cycles, being deeper and more prolonged than recessions.

Nobody knows what causes business cycles, periods of greater and lesser prosperity, but it seems to me there are good reasons for surmising that like virtually everything else in economic life, they are consequences of events in import-replacing cities. For one thing, they are entirely absent in economies that are bypassed by cities, like Henry during the time it simply experienced a long noncyclic period of poverty. They occur, rather, only in well-urbanized economies, reaching inert ones as secondary repercussions from a distance; e.g., a recession in the United States depresses Colombia's coffee-bean earnings.

A second logical reason for supposing a link between business cycles and import-replacing cities is that such cities, themselves, have built-in cycles owing to the peculiar way in which they grow.

At times when a city is replacing wide ranges of imports rapidly in a chain reaction, it expands explosively. But typically those episodes alternate with intervals of lesser expansion or none at all while the city builds up funds of potentially replaceable imports for a future chain reaction of replacements. And, of course, if an import-replacing city becomes so feeble or dilatory at replacing imports that it can't keep its economy up-to-date or maintain it as a good foundation for generating new exports to compensate for its losses of old ones, its economy shrinks and contracts.

If a national economy taken as a whole were to behave like one single, vigorous import-replacing city, it could not avoid having business cycles, and if that single city actually lost its vigor, the nation could not avoid a deep depression that might, but also might not, be self-terminating.

However, most nations contain more than one city, and blocs of nations trading heavily with one another contain numerous cities, many of them import-replacing. Vigorous cities, making up a good team, need to work on differing cycles from one another ("some are loading just when others are delivering"). In a nation or trading bloc of nations with vigorous cities, the individual city cycles are not synchronized. But let us suppose that they are not working perfectly in nonsynchronized fashion—a reasonable supposition if consolidated feedback from national currencies is serving to synchronize the cycles of at least some cities within a trading network. A recession in a nation or bloc of nations would automatically result at times when fewer cities than usual happened to be in process of replacing imports. But it would be self-terminating as soon as some of these cities, currently building up funds of replaceable imports, swung into the import-replacing phase of their cycles. The pauses would be relatively inconsequential, as well as soon over.

In rough fashion, this does seem to jibe with what happens in nations experiencing rapid development and expansion. The downsides of business cycles tend to be soon self-terminating. Furthermore, although they are painful, they are relatively inconsequential from the perspective of the prevailing trend of growing prosperity, development and expansion. That is how it was in Britain, for example, during the time of its rapid industrial development and it was also the situation in the United States until the Great Depression of the 1930s. It has been the situation in Japan for more than thirty years since World War II. It is the situation now in the rapidly developing little nations of the Pacific Rim.

If business cycles are indeed caused as I hypothesize, then the appearance of deep national depressions that are not self-terminating would mean that a nation's cities, taken as a whole, are becoming ominously weak and dilatory at replacing imports: as a group are losing vitality. In that case we must also expect stagflation in due course, that characteristic of poor and backward economies, since a nation in which city economies have been enfeebled is necessarily a nation in process of becoming poor and backward.

Deep, widespread and prolonged international depressions, not soon self-terminating, would logically be signs and symptoms that cities in many, many nations were losing vitality. That is, in fact, a message we are now getting from many other symptoms of trouble, such as growing gluts of rural and resource goods owing to too few solvent city markets; insufficient city enterprises to meet demands for transplants of city work; insufficient city jobs for people who have left the land or been cleared from it.

Whether or not cities are the cause of business cycles as I have reasoned, and whether or not serious losses of city vitality are the cause of deep and prolonged depressions, depressions do add to the other economic instabilities and stresses that accumulate in nations as time passes.

If nothing were done about accumulating instabilities, other than allowing them to continue accumulating with discontents and angers accumulating too, a nation would succumb to its stresses. It would become unworkable as a coherent political unit.

Transactions of decline are a nation's recourse. Like all bifurcations, these transactions are consequences of prior accumulating instabilities. Once we understand this, we can understand that the interplay between nations and their cities occurs in two different stages. During the first stage, instabilities, random failures, inequalities and disparities gradually but inexorably accumulate, owing to faulty feedback given cities and potential cities. In the second stage, transactions of decline temporarily dispose of the stresses. In the first stage, nations are chancy environments for cities. In the second stage they become lethal environments.

Consider the plight this creates for nations, quite as much as for cities. To develop in the first place, and then to continue prospering thereafter, nations must have import-replacing cities and enough of them. Nothing else in their grab bags of economies suffices: not supply regions, not clearance regions, not regions workers abandon, not transplant economies, not artificial city regions, not stagnated cities. Yet to hold themselves together as systems, nations must drain their cities in favor of transactions of decline and must undercut volatile intercity trade in favor of supplying settlements that can't replace imports. In response, city economies stagnate. Stagnating, they undermine the wealth, well-being and capacity to develop further of one another, and of their nations as a whole. In the end, both cities and the nation itself come to ruin.

A group of political scientists associated with Princeton University's Center for Research on World Political Institutions has studied many instances of dissolution or disintegration of sovereign political units—nations, empires, confederations—occurring in recent times or in the past. The object was to discover what common forces, if any, bring about political disintegration. The researchers concluded that the "load" carried by the failed political unit had increased while, at the same time, its "capability" had decreased. But what are "load" and "capability" in the concrete?

"Excessive military commitments" were identified as a usual factor of fatally increased load. The researchers defined "excessive" as prolonged, pointing out that, historically, short wars, taken in themselves only, have not presaged dissolutions (often the contrary: territorial expansions or intensified unity) but that prolonged military burdens often have presaged political failure and disintegration. The other two major components of increasing load that they identified, sometimes accompanying prolonged military burdens but sometimes not, were "substantial increases in political participation on the parts of populations, regions or social strata which previously had been politically passive," and political awareness of "ethnic or linguistic differentiation" among regional groups embraced in the political unit. Either of these, of course, leads to use of subsidies or force to contain discontents. As for decreasing capability, the chief one identified was "prolonged economic decline or stagnation."

We must remember that nations or empires do not get into these predicaments by choice. Circumstances that are built into their territories and that they simply cannot change, try as they may, leave them without choice. Central Japan must subsidize northern and southern Japan because the need is there, and because otherwise inequalities in regional standards of living and disparities in public services would become politically and morally unacceptable. The north of Italy supports the south because the need is so great that it must do so to keep the peace and combat utter economic breakdown in a large part of the country. Germany supports French agricultural regions because if it didn't, the European Economic Community would break down, and France insists on the subsidies as a condition of its membership because otherwise France could not contain the anger of its farmers or the ever simmering threat of separatism in the country's south. Canada frankly calls its systems of national equalization payments to poor provinces the sinews that hold the country together and combats separatist sentiments in Quebec in the same fashion that the English combat separatist feelings in Scotland: by reminding pensioners and other recipients of transfer payments, and beneficiaries of other economic grants, where their money is coming from. Pensioners need those pensions; economically dead villages and towns need their subsidies. The cities of America, including the Sun Belt cities that have prospered as others decline, need the huge trade-offs they get from military work, loan-supported international advanced-backward trade, and domestic subsidy programs.

Furthermore, not to invoke transactions of decline would solve nothing. For the central Japanese not to help their fellow citizens in the peripheral regions, for the north of Italy not to help the south, for the Germans not to help French farmers, for the cities of Canada not to aid the elderly, the sick and the unemployed wherever they may be in the country, for the United States not to produce arms and not to hustle up advanced-backward trade and not to subsidize its regions that have always lacked import-replacing cities or its increasing collection of regions afflicted with decaying cities—those omissions would not dispose of the inequalities, failures, stresses and instabilities the transactions are meant to redress.

Is there any kind of radical intervention or discontinuity other than transactions of decline to which nations might resort, to contend with their inexorable, built-in cumulative instabilities? Theoretically there may be another way out, but only theoretically —for reasons I shall touch on. Nevertheless, let us take a look at this theoretical possibility.

A metaphor used by some mathematicians to illustrate discontinuity is a dog that realizes he is the object of an approaching hostile advance. The dog is just standing around at the time, but the one thing he can't continue to do is just stand around. He must do something radically different: prepare to attack, or run, either of which is a discontinuity.

In principle this is the situation of a nation in which instabilities and stresses have reached a point demanding action. The one thing the nation cannot do is stand around and do nothing. It must either leap to the attack on its difficulties by instituting transactions of decline or else . . . or else what?

Can it run away from the insoluble difficulties that are becoming intolerable? If so, *how* run away from them? Could running away dispose of the accumulating instabilities and stresses, put things actually on a new footing temporarily? We are taught that running away from a problem doesn't solve it. However, in real life it occasionally does, as the metaphor of the dog suggests and as we know from experience if we have ever disposed of a potentially disastrous temptation by running away from it, or in retrospect have sorely wished we had.

The equivalent for a political unit would be to resist the temptation of engaging in transactions of decline by not trying to hold itself together. The radical discontinuity would thus be division of the single sovereignty into a family of smaller sovereignties, not after things had reached a stage of breakdown and disintegration, but long before while things were still going reasonably well. In a national society behaving like this, multiplication of sovereignties by division would be a normal, untraumatic accompaniment of economic development itself, and of the increasing complexity of economic and social life. Some of the sovereignties in the family would in their turn divide as evidence of the need to do so appeared. A nation behaving like this would substitute for one great life force, sheer survival, that other great life force, reproduction. In this utopian fantasy, young sovereignties splitting off from the parent nation would be told, in effect, "Good luck to you in your independence! Now do try your very best to generate [or maintain, as the case might be] a creative city and its region and we'll all be better off. We won't discriminate against you in our trade, and if you should need to raise tariff barriers against our manufactured goods to get a start, we will put up with it without rancor."

A chief advantage, although not the only one, of this unlikely national behavior would be multiplication of currencies. The technical difficulties and inconveniences that would entail are surmountable, increasingly so with the aid of computers, instantaneous communications systems and such devices as credit cards which—even in their current rudimentary and limited uses—are already convenient for simultaneous transactions involving diverse currencies. On my card I can order, say, books from London payable in pounds, shirts from the Boston city region payable in U.S. dollars, and garden seeds payable in my own currency, Canadian dollars, all the transactions being equally convenient as far as I am concerned. Nor would multiple currencies that truly reflected the state of discrete economies be a step backward from national currencies, or internationally pegged currencies, jumbling up as they do apples, oranges and cucumbers in a meaningless chaos, and now and again wildly inflating, then wildly devaluing. On the contrary.

The difficulty, rather, is precisely that multiplicities of currencies imply multiplicities of sovereignties—indeed, would only be cosmetic currencies otherwise, like the Scottish pound, which is the English pound with different pictures. Thus this type of discontinuity as an alternative to transactions of decline would be at the expense of unified nations. It addresses the survival of societies, cultures, civilizations and cities, but at the expense of the nation.

With almost no exceptions, our current nations came into being in the first place through bloody military force. Most have been held together from time to time with bloodshed. Many are still held together so. Nations are not the offspring of Vulcan the smith, or Mercury the messenger and sponsor of the healing arts, much less Ceres the mother of fertility and plenty, and they don't behave as if they were. They behave like the offspring of Mars that they are—and that many of their citizens adore them for being.

The mystique of the nation is the powerful, gruesome glamour of human sacrifice. To betray the nation and its unity is to betray all that shed blood; to do so to be better off economically would seem to render the most glorious pages of national history mere sound and fury. Virtually all national governments, it seems fair to say, and most citizens would sooner decline and decay unified, true to the sacrifices by which their unity was won, than prosper and develop in division. Even separatists, when they manage to gain sovereignties of their own, bitterly resist any further division; perhaps sovereignties with a separatist history most of all. This is why my suggested alternative to transactions of decline is theoretical only.

Even theoretically, what I have suggested is no economic panacea. There is no magic in mere smallness or division of sovereignties *per se*, much less so when they are a last resort after load has outrun a political unit's capability. The world is littered today with the profoundly stagnated and pitiable fragments of stagnated empires, both old and recent. My utopian proposal, in any case, is no substitute for the volatile trade backward cities must develop with one another if they are to develop. Nor is it any substitute for the necessity of vigorous cities remaining creative.

Its virtue, rather, is that it could serve as a way of preventing or evading the decline and decay which otherwise must surely come to the people of any nation who attempt to hold their political unit together with transactions of decline. As such, it would have to be invoked in time, meaning before transactions of decline had already become so well entrenched that they could not be dismantled as a practical matter. And the new sovereignties splitting off—in time—would have to be either already vigorous cities in their own right or else regions with a depot or other promising proto-urban center capable of becoming (with tariff help, if need be) an import-replacing, export-generating city.

From time to time the world casts up new "pattern states." The phrase is Sir George Clark's, an English historian specializing in seventeenth-century Europe who pointed out that the strong monarchy of France's Louis XIV became a pattern state of the time. As a model, it was adopted by Frederick I, the first king of Brandenburg-Prussia, the realm that later became the nucleus of Germany after many wars of unification; and by Charles II and James II in Britain, among others. After the Glorious Revolution and the exile and defeat of the male Stuarts, Britain became the next great influential pattern state, its parliament emulated by many others. Actually the parliaments of Iceland and the Isle of Man are older, but those two political units did not serve as pattern states for others. The rise of the United States as a great and successful republic made that country an influential pattern state, and to some extent it has even served as a model for the European Economic Community, which, at the time of its formation, was commonly explained as being "a United States of Europe." Until recently, many a public figure in Latin America or Africa could gain an ephemeral reputation as a far-sighted statesman by advocating a United-States-of-This or a United-States-of-That. The success of Lenin and his followers in overthrowing the short-lived successor government to the old regime of the Russian Empire and then establishing a mighty socialist government in its stead made the Soviet Union an influential pattern state for revolutionaries and would-be revolutionaries elsewhere. Sweden, owing to its extraordinarily thorough system of transfer payments and other domestic subsidies, has also been an influential pattern state.

So unsatisfactory, in their various ways, have all the existing or old patterns become that nowadays merely the promise of a different dispensation, not the performance, is sufficient for a new pattern to be hailed. Thus Maoist China was briefly influential as a development pattern for the Third World, even though its persuasiveness as a model rested only on wishful thinking, rhetoric and zeal, not on development policies that were even briefly tenable and workable. Mao was enormously successful as a military leader but as an economist he was a disaster, as so many great military leaders or dictators installed by armies tend to be. Perhaps this is because military arts derive from the hunting and raiding life, economics from the making and trading life. Many assumptions, intuitions and virtues that work very well in the one serve badly in the other.

Today both the Soviet Union and China demonstrate to us governments that depend to an extreme degree on transactions of decline to hold the political unit together. Whatever wealth Soviet or Chinese cities create is promptly devoted to subsidies for other parts of the nation and purposes of the state. If my analysis of the deadly interplay between nations and cities is correct, then in the Soviet Union and China we are not seeing the dawns of significant new episodes in the history of economic development, but rather the spectacle of old empires still holding together at all costs. Both realms were on the brink of dissolution when their old regimes proved incapable of carrying the political loads they had assumed, but the new regimes succeeded in reconsolidating them by force of arms. All that has changed significantly is the greater competence, efficiency and ruthlessness which their present regimes have brought to the task of holding these sovereignties together. Just as long-bypassed subsistence economies show us not what the dawn of pristine economic life was like but instead the end products of long stagnation, so do we see in the Soviet Union and China, I think, end products of huge and tenaciously preserved sovereignties.

No pattern state, or rather, pattern family-of-states, now exists for the theoretical possibility I sketched out: the expedient multiplication of sovereignties (not semisovereignties or provinces) from larger ones, as an alternative to transactions of decline. The separation of Norway from Sweden in 1905 was a partial step in that direction, for it occurred before Norway and Sweden were enmeshed in transactions of decline. That was not Sweden's choice; rather, nineteenth-century Norway, although it was very poor, rejected even any beginnings of subsidization and insisted on supporting itself on its own budget. Sweden, for its part, although it accepted the separation unwillingly, did not resort to military force to prevent it; and thereafter, as its former possession developed economically, engaged in volatile intercity trade with it. However, Sweden did not follow up this experience with division by applying it further as an alternative to transactions of decline. Quite the opposite; ironically, insofar as Sweden has become a pattern state, what has been copied is not that solitary example of an alternative to transactions of decline, but rather the country's thoroughgoing use of such transactions domestically. Sweden also augments these nowadays by much promotion of advanced-backward international trade sustained by gifts, credits, and repetitive investments in foreign supply regions by its multinational corporations: transactions that give Stockholm and Gothenburg the usual trade-offs.

Singapore's separation from Malaysia is another small instance of division as an alternative to transactions of decline, having occurred before the Malay States had become enmeshed in such domestic transactions. The separation, as we have seen, gave a former depot city, Singapore, an individualized, appropriate currency of its own; this enabled it to escape both the anomalous position of Montevideo and the need to victimize rural Malaysia with tariffs to evade the anomaly. This small example of a practical approach to a big problem has been ignored, however, by what Clark called "imitative states." One is reminded of how imitative states ignored the Icelandic and Isle of Man parliaments, but heeded Britain's parliamentary system.

If a people were ever to experiment with expedient division of a sovereignty large enough to engage the attention and interest of the world, we must suppose those pioneers would have to possess considerable confidence in their culture and capacities, enough confidence to dispose of centralized control and centralized problem solving. By definition, such people would also have to be politically inventive and capable of evolving their own institutions in both realistic and original fashion. No doubt, if such a pattern were ever to emerge, it would influence less original societies and less confident cultures; if it actually did work out as a successful alternative to transactions of decline, deservedly so.

Since it does seem that sooner or later human beings get around to trying everything within their capacities, no doubt somewhere, sometime, in some culture or civilization this alternative form of discontinuity will be tried—if it really is within human capacities to divide large sovereignties before they have reached a dead end of disarray. In the meantime, things being what they are, we have no choice but to live with our economically deadly predicament as best we can.

FOURTEEN

Drift

A Japanese anthropologist, Tadao Umesao, observes that historically the Japanese have always done better when they drifted in an empirical, practical fashion ("Even during the Meiji revolution, there were no clear goals; no one knew what was going to happen next") than when they attempted to operate by "resolute purpose" and "determined will." This is true of other peoples, too, although Umesao believes that what he calls "an esthetics of drift" is distinctively Japanese and one of the major differences between Japanese and Western cultures. Had he been looking at Europe and America in the past rather than in the present, he would have seen, I think, that "an esthetics of drift" was distinctively Western, too, and worked better for Western cultures than "resolute purpose" and "determined will."

In its very nature, successful economic development has to be open-ended rather than goal-oriented, and has to make itself up expediently and empirically as it goes along. For one thing, unforeseeable problems arise. The people who developed agriculture couldn't foresee soil depletion. The people who developed the automobile couldn't foresee acid rain. Earlier I defined economic development as a process of continually improvising in a context that makes injecting improvisations into everyday life feasible. We might amplify this by calling development an improvisational drift into unprecedented kinds of work that carry unprecedented problems, then drifting into improvised solutions, which carry further unprecedented work carrying unprecedented problems ...

"Industrial strategies" to meet "targets" using "resolute purpose," "long-range planning" and "determined will" express a military kind of thinking. Behind that thinking lies a conscious or unconscious assumption that economic life can be conquered, mobilized, bullied, as indeed it can be when it is directed toward warfare, but not when it directs itself to development and expansion.

An emeritus professor of the Massachusetts Institute of Technology, Cyril Stanley Smith, points out that historically, necessity has not been the mother of invention; rather, necessity opportunistically picks up invention and improvises improvements on it and new uses for it, but the roots of invention are to be found elsewhere, in motives like curiosity and especially, Smith noted, "esthetic curiosity." Metallurgy itself, he reminds us, began with hammering copper into necklace beads and other ornaments "long before 'useful' knives and weapons" were made of copper or bronze. Alloying and heat treatment of metals started in jewelry making and sculpture, as did casting in complicated molds. Pigments (which, incidentally, were the first known uses of iron ore), porcelain and many other ceramics, glass and the practice of welding all started with luxury or decorative goods. Possibly even wheels were at first frivolities; the most ancient known to us are parts of toys. Hydraulics and many mechanical ingenuities and tricks were first developed for toys or other amusements. The lathe was being used to make snuffboxes "a century before heavy industry used it." Malleable cast iron was developed as a cheap substitute for showy wrought-iron gates. "The chemical industry grew from the need for quantities of mordants, bleaches, and alkalies for use in the finer textiles and glass." Blocks for reproducing pictures predated blocks of movable type for printing. Electroplating was first used to give dazzle to statuettes made of base metals, and sparkle to tableware of people who couldn't afford sterling. "Rockets for fun came before their military use or space travel," and, one might add, before they propelled communications satellites into space.

The first successful railroad in the world was an amusement ride in London. Many of us can remember when plastics were used for little except toys and kitchen gadgets, and for piano keys as a lower-cost replacement for ivory. Tennis rackets, golf clubs and fishing rods afforded the first uses of strong, lightweight composites of plastics reinforced with fibers of glass, boron and carbon; now those composites are starting to replace metals in some construction products, some types of springs, pipelines, and aircraft and automobile body parts. Computer games preceded personal computers for workaday use. For years before artificial voices were being incorporated into computerized work tools to call out the temperatures of equipment or to sound explanatory warnings, they were being used in computerized toys and gimmickry for children (e.g., "Speak & Spell") and were being prematurely written off by "serious" developers and users of computers as cute but useless. In my own city today I notice that solar heating is largely a passion of hobbyists, as is drip irrigation, which conserves labor, fertilizer, water and space in home vegetable growing.

"All big things grow from little things," Smith comments, with this cautionary addition, "but new little things are destroyed by their environments unless they are cherished for reasons more like esthetic appreciation than practical utility." One is reminded of Umesao's "esthetics of drift."

Scientists are used to the fact that discoveries are often the unanticipated by-products of other intentions. It is the same in economic drift. The first oil wells were drilled to get lamp fuel only a few decades before electricity was to begin making oil lamps obsolete; but other uses kept turning up for petroleum, once oil wells existed. The glue with which sand is stuck to paper has turned out to have far more ramifications and much more economic utility than sandpaper itself. The early freight rail lines were conceived as being useful only to get cargo to canals; early radios were thought of as only supplements for wire communications lines, to be used where telegraph and telephone connections were impractical, as on ships. Edison, an inventor of the phonograph, thought the chief use of the device would be for business dictation.

There is an order in the open-ended drift by which economic life develops and expands, but it is not the order of "challenge" and "response" to be found in military thinking or in Toynbee's idea that civilizations die because they fail to respond to challenge. Rather, the order at work is more like biological evolution whose purpose, if any, we cannot see unless we are satisfied to think its purpose is us.

Many of the root processes at work in natural ecologies and our economies are amazingly similar, and we can learn much about success and failure in our own arrangements by noticing, for example, that the more niches that are filled in a given natural ecology, other things being equal, the more efficiently it uses the energy it has at its disposal, and the richer it is in life and means of supporting life. Just so with our own economies: the more fully their various niches are filled, the richer they are in means for supporting life. That is another way of saying that economies producing diversely and amply for their own people and producers, as well as for others, are better off than specialized economies like those of supply, clearance and transplant regions. In a natural ecology, the more diversity there is, the more flexibility, too, because of what ecologists call its greater numbers of "homeostatic feedback loops," meaning that it includes greater numbers of feedback controls for automatic self-correction. It is the same with our economies. I have labored the point that too few homeostatic feedback loops is precisely the failing that renders nations so disastrously unstable economically and their cities so poor at economic self-correction.

The other animals don't add new kinds of activities to their older kinds in an open-ended way. But we aren't the other animals. It is natural for human beings to build new kinds of work and skills on earlier kinds because the capacity to do this is naturally built right into us, like the related capacity to understand and use a language in an open-ended way. Without the capacity to add new work to our earlier work, new skills to our earlier skills—as all normal human beings do individually starting in infancy, and as we do collectively in developing human economic life—we might be something else, but we wouldn't be human beings.

Cities are the open-ended types of economies in which our open-ended capacities for economic creation are not only able to establish "new little things" but also to inject them into everyday life. Unfortunately, given the deadly interplay between nations and their cities, we human beings are doomed to spurts of economic development only—sporadic and relatively brief episodes, now here, now there, followed by stagnation and deterioration. This must continue unless and until we drift into means of overcoming that deadly interplay itself. In this sense, we human beings are still in a primitive stage indeed of using our capacities for open-ended creation and development.

Nevertheless, though we may now be faced with economic deterioration, any use we can make of beneficial drift can keep us afloat a little longer by keeping city economies creative a little longer than they otherwise would be, and thus can buy a little more time for nations as well. Even as the deadly interplay proceeds, there are expedient opportunities for slowing down the ruin; many little things that can be done.

Consider, in this light, the value added tax, a measure much favored by European technocrats. VAT, as it is known, is mandatory for members of the European Economic Community, but varies from country to country. The highest rate currently is 35 percent in Ireland, applying to most goods manufactured there. Like all taxes, VAT is ultimately paid by consumers, but in form it is a sales tax on producers, reaching the consumer only as a component of production costs.

The way VAT works is that when any producer in the chain of production sells his goods or services, he adds the VAT sales tax to his sales price, but first subtracts from it what he himself has already paid in VAT on his purchases from other producers. The difference is thus a tax on the value added during his own operation, hence the tax's name. No matter how many or few producers are involved, the total tax at the end of the line is therefore a tax on aggregate added value throughout the production process. Governments like VAT because instead of waiting until wealth is produced, they can get their cut while the wealth is in process of being produced.

The tax works out differently, depending upon whether a product is being produced in a large, integrated enterprise supplying many of its own needs internally or whether it is being produced by many symbiotic independent producers selling multitudinous everyday needs to each other. In the first case, the tax does not figure in the enterprise's many internal transactions. In the second case, it comes into play constantly throughout the production process and must be financed as a cost during the process. A small thing perhaps (until it reaches rates like 35 percent) but no neater little tax contrivance could be imagined for favoring large, relatively self-sufficient enterprises such as multinational corporations with their many subsidiaries and many internal transactions, while penalizing symbiotic production. VAT heedlessly twists the knife in the very vitals of city economies. Any other form of sales tax on producers' goods or services does the same.

When the EEC was being formed, the aim of eliminating trade barriers among member nations was to create a single huge integrated market, particularly and especially to confer economies of scale upon huge integrated enterprises. In that context, of course, VAT makes perfect sense. For that matter, so does a Euroloaf of standardized bread ingredients, one of many standardizations proposed by the EEC secretariat in Brussels. Fortunately, the Euroloaf was rejected by member nations.

As a rule, nationwide or international product standards, other than the relatively few strictly required for health and safety, recklessly harm cities as well as hampering economic development and expansion generally. How can city producers undertake differentiations for their local markets, and then perhaps for exports from the city as well, if deviations from standards are discouraged or forbidden? And who knows what further ramifications in methods of production, materials or purposes are also being doomed?

Similarly, nationally or internationally mandated kinds of solutions to practical problems are at heedless cross-purposes to development, whether in transportation, energy production, pollution prevention or almost anything else. For example, performance standards for polluters are important and necessary both nationally and internationally, since pollution flows into air and water. But such controls are quite different from mandating products and methods to meet the performance standards. As far as those are concerned, the more experimentation and diversification, the better. Incidentally, by the time a new practical problem becomes national or international, it is a symptom that the cities are growing uncreative and feeble. For example, the fact that toxic wastes have become a very widespread problem—a national problem—in the United States means that the problems these wastes involve, problems of prevention and problems of disposal both, were neglected in the cities of the country as they showed up. If American cities in the past had done no better than that with the problems of protecting tap water from contamination by sewage, tap water contaminated by human wastes would be a huge national problem. Cities solve pressing practical problems, then export their solutions to one another and the rural world; if they don't, the problems merely pile up unsolved.

Monopolies gratuitously harm cities and suppress what their economies are capable of achieving. The usual objection to monopolies is that they charge extortionate prices and make unconscionable profits by cornering a market. From this it follows that monopolies can be rendered harmless if their prices or profits are regulated. If, at the same time, a case can be made for economies of scale by protecting monopolies from competition, then they can be thought of as being beneficial. But extortionate prices, harmful though they most certainly are, are the least of the disadvantages of monopolies, for monopolies forestall alternate methods, products, services. This often becomes obvious when monopolies are broken. When the U.S. Congress forced electric utility monopolies to buy independently produced power offered them for distribution and pay for it at the rate of their own most expensive generating costs at the time, a host of small new power producers began springing up. Some of these, especially in the Boston and San Francisco city regions, are using experimental methods of energy production. Others have put back to work small hydro-electric dams which had been abandoned but which, in the aggregate, are now producing appreciable power, do much less environmental damage than an equivalent huge installation, and tend to produce at lower cost as well. When the U.S. courts broke the Bell Telephone System's monopoly over production of equipment used for its communications services, new products promptly appeared, as well as new services made possible by some of the new, unmonopolized production. These are instances in which a nation, without damage to itself as a political unit, has made a little more room in itself for open-ended economic drift.

Even though economic life is sliding into decline, cities themselves can find expedient opportunities for open-ended drift. Historically, Boston had been a creative city for two centuries, but at the beginning of the twentieth century it was stagnating. The old textile, shoe and railroad fortunes were tied up in routinely invested trusts, the city as a whole had become an exporter of capital, not a place in which capital was being put to work productively and diversely. Of course, it kept losing its older export work, as cities do, and was neither generating new export work to compensate for the losses nor replacing wide ranges of its current imports. As Boston's economy thinned and declined, so did that of its region. The popular explanation for the plight of the city and of New England generally was that difficulties beyond the region's control were responsible: cheaper labor in places like Henry Grady's north Georgia, foreign competition and industries whose prime was past.

One man, however, had a different insight and was fortunately in a position to act upon it. Ralph Flanders (who later became a U.S. senator from Vermont) reasoned that Boston's trouble was what he called its low birth rate of enterprises. He persuaded a handful of moneyed colleagues to accept his point of view, and in 1946 they formed a small venture capital firm to do what used to be called merchant banking. The object was specifically to invest in small new enterprises, and specifically in Boston. For this purpose they had a capital of almost $4 million, which, owing to inflation in the meantime, would be the equivalent of about $28 million today.

Apart from the aim of improving Boston's business birth rate, Flanders and his colleagues had no preconceived ideas whatever of what they were doing. The last thing that entered their heads was what we now call a high-tech city economy, for the good reason that no such thing existed. Indeed, if that vision had smitten them, they might well have ridiculed it. Although local universities produced quantities of technologists and scientists, the region's own industry was by this time pathetically obsolete, antiquated, backward. Furthermore, at the time, scientists typically either taught in universities or were employed by large corporations like Du Pont and Eastman Kodak. Scientist-entrepreneurs were extremely rare, and the conventional view of bankers and other financiers and investors was that highly educated scientists or technologists dwelt in ivory towers and "couldn't meet a payroll."

However, it so happened that the first applicants for capital were three young scientists who had started a tiny high-technology enterprise, using their own and their families' savings. They couldn't continue without additional investment and were about to close up because investors in Boston and New York wouldn't advance them capital. The new Flanders group, their last hope, agreed to invest in the fledgling business, and then rapidly in several other small innovative technological enterprises that became the next applicants. Flanders and his colleagues weren't scientists or technologists themselves but why should they be—they weren't trying to control or mastermind or second-guess the people they were financing but were merely giving them a chance to create their work, whatever it might be and whither it might lead.

The enterprises they financed—because these were what offered themselves, and their proprietors seemed realistic in their devotion to what they were trying—began to multiply by division: employees broke away and started new enterprises of their own, many of which Flanders and his colleagues also financed. Upon this base, upon its many subsequent ramifications and breakaways, and upon the multiplying suppliers of materials, instruments, tools and services that served the new enterprises and thus were supported by them and by one another, the Boston regional economy was stunningly rejuvenated. Today Boston has one of the few vigorously extending and intensifying city regional economies in the United States. What happened tells us a number of things useful to know.

First, cities are capable of bouncing back if their faltered economies are indeed corrected. Historically, stagnant cities seldom have recovered, and they seldom do so today; but that is because their economies seldom are corrected, either automatically by appropriate feedback or by germane assistance, as occurred in Boston.

Second, city economies that aren't self-correcting can be helped to correct themselves if what is done is indeed germane.

Third, germane correction depends on fostering creativity in whatever forms it happens to appear in a given city at a given time. It is impossible to know in advance what may turn up, except that—especially if it is to prove important—it is apt to be unexpected. Another city, attempting to duplicate what Flanders and his group accomplished, paradoxically could not duplicate it today because the events in Boston happened almost forty years ago. All that could be successfully repeated would be the process of open-ended drift, taking up opportunities whatever they might be and whither they might lead. That drift is diametrically the opposite of placing faith in the ready-made, as people do when their idea of helping city economies is to woo transplants from other places, lobby for military contracts or work up projects because grants for them are available. The style or form in which Flanders and his group operated was part and parcel of the substantive result, as form and substance always are. Umesao's phrase "an esthetics of drift" is thus precisely to the point, implying, as it does, form or style.

Boston's recovery was good as far as it went, but it is also limited in what it can achieve within a generally declining economy. From time to time, engineers and scientists hold conferences, often enough in Boston, where they trot out ideas they have developed, frequently ideas germane to solving practical problems. But most of these ideas are never even tried, let alone injected into everyday economic life. The same is true even of many advances which have already been proved out and put into production but which barely work their way into the economy. In the United States, new types of equipment that protect firefighters from injury and death, or that put out fires faster, are available, yet little used. Few American cities can afford them. America is no longer a country that puts new products like these to use as fast as they come on the market. Even when new products pay for themselves by reducing the numbers of firefighters needed to handle cumbersome hoses, for example, or by revealing live cinders quickly in concealed places, the equipment is little adopted because there is no alternate work for the firemen who would be displaced.

Facts like these tell us of the limitations of exceptional cases of city economic rejuvenation. Unless many, many cities in a trading network keep their economies going, the creativity of any given city is inhibited. To the extent that the process of import-replacement is diminished, the market for innovations declines and new and needed kinds of everyday work are foregone. In place of those markets, even creative cities such as Boston must depend on trade-offs from transactions of decline, at least in part. Boston, for example, now depends partly on trade-offs from military production.

Historically, in nations where city economies are dying and where, as well, cities are drained in service to transactions of decline, one city remains vivacious longest: the capital city. This is because capital cities thrive on transactions of decline. When a city's principal function is being a capital—like the city of Washington in the United States or Ottawa in Canada—it is obvious that the more transfer payments, subsidies, grants, military contracts and promotion of international advanced-backward trade, the greater the work and prosperity in the capital city. However, the connection is not so obvious when the capital city happens to be, or had once been, a major industrial and commercial city as well, like London, say, or Paris, Lisbon, Madrid, Stockholm . . .

In that case, increasing prosperity associated with presiding over transactions of decline can cloak simultaneous shrinkage, obsolescence and impoverishment of the city's other functions. For example, while Washington's economy has been growing over the last forty years. New York's once outstandingly diverse and creative manufacturing economy has grown obsolete and very thin and the city's growth of service and financial activities has not compensated for those losses of older exports and former employment, much less for its loss of the very capacity to solve pressing practical problems. But suppose the capital of the United States had happened to be in New York (as in fact it briefly was in the country's early history): suppose New York, in effect, were both New York and Washington. In that case, New York's economic decline would have been well veiled indeed by its concurrently booming government work in service to transactions of decline.

Thus, although a capital city would seem, typically, to be the last place in its nation whose economy requires rejuvenation and correction, appearances are deceptive. Behind its busyness at ruling, a capital city of a nation or an empire, vivacious to the last, at length reveals itself as being a surprisingly inert, backward and pitiable place. So it was with Lisbon, Madrid, Istanbul. So it is gradually becoming, one suspects, with London, Paris, Stockholm . . .

Let us fantasize a Big Experimental System in which we are all included. Information feeds back into the system, and from time to time the burden of the feedback is that such-and-such a society has allowed its cities to languish, or that in such-and-such a civilization the cities are already well down the drain. The feedback seems to operate on the premise that people who relinquish the civilized art of maintaining creative cities are not to be entrusted with the risks of developing further. This fantasy is not *entirely* metaphor. If we strip it of the judgmental word "entrusted," we are left with a hard, plain truth. Societies and civilizations in which the cities stagnate don't develop and flourish further. They deteriorate.

ACKNOWLEDGMENTS

Jason Epstein, my editor and publisher, to whom this book is dedicated, has helped me enormously at every stage: with faith and cheerful encouragement when I had nothing to show him, with criticisms, questions and suggestions that sharpened my wits when I did, and with his wonderfully deft and perspicuitous editing when the book took shape.

For their generosity of time and thought as critical readers and discoverers of errors and ambiguities, I am indebted to Patricia Adams, Toshiko Adilman, Decker Butzner, John D. Butzner, Nicholas Graham, James K. Jacobs, Robert H. Jacobs, Denise Machee, Sue Parilla, Lawrence Solomon and Grant Ujifusa. Errors and ambiguities that may remain, although I hope they don't, are my fault, not theirs. I am grateful to Barbara Willson of Random House for her careful copy editing, to Beverly Haviland, for her help in shepherding the book through editing and production, to Howard Bentley for constructing a meticulous and thoughtful index, to Mary Malfara for her aid in stretching my working time, and to Caitlin Broms-Jacobs for effectively imposing a final-draft deadline. My husband, Robert H. Jacobs, has not only saved me from errors, but his interest, good spirits and support have been my mainstay.

Whenever possible (as in taking note, for example, of economic patterns that evolve in city regions or observing the cargo that enters a military base), I have used my eyes and ears, but have also drawn heavily on many other observers, living and dead. The items listed in the Notes by chapter acknowledge debts to reporters, researchers, writers and their publishers, whose work I have drawn on directly for illustrative or elucidating material, as well as to some individuals who have personally helped on specific points. But for indirect help I am indebted to many, many others of the past and present who go unmentioned. Their bits and pieces of observations, verifications and insights, accumulating in my mind over the years, are the drops of water and grains of sand that have gradually built up my underlying mental landscape of economic life. Not least, I am indebted to librarians and reference works in the public libraries of Toronto, New York and Richmond, Virginia.

NOTES

1 Fool's Paradise

For the quotation from Cantillon, I am indebted to a paper by Richard G. Lipsey, "The Place of the Phillips Curve in Macro-economic Models" in *Stability and Inflation*, edited by Bergstrom, Catt, Peston and Silverstone; (New York, John Wiley, 1978).

Adam Smith's views are set forth in *An Inquiry into the Nature and Causes of the Wealth of Nations* (1776). John Stuart Mill expounded his views on credit for producers in *Essays on Some Unsettled Questions in Political Economy* (1844) and *Principles of Political Economy with Some of Their Applications to Social Philosophy* (1848).

In summarizing Marx's reasoning on the relationship between prices and unemployment, I have used the convenient reference work *Marx on Economics*, compiled and edited by Robert Freedman (New York, Harcourt Brace, 1961), drawn from *Capital; The Critique of Political Economy; Theories of Surplus Value; Critique of the Gotha Program; German Ideology; Communist Manifesto*; and a miscellany of Marx's other writings.

Keynes set forth his theory of government fiscal intervention in *The General Theory of Employment, Interest and Money* (London, Macmillan, 1936).

Irving Fisher presented his monetarist theory in *100% Money: Designed to keep checking banks 100% liquid; to prevent inflation and deflation; largely to cure or prevent depressions; and to wipe out much of the National Debt* (New York, Adelphi Company, 1935).

The biographical material on A. W. H. Phillips and information on the genesis of the Phillips curve is from Bergstrom, *op. cit.*, primarily Lipsey's paper.

Report and comment on disillusionment with Keynesianism is now ubiquitous; I am indebted in particular to "Stagflation Reminds Economics Professors How Little They Know," by Laird Hart, *Wall Street Journal*, September 6, 1974; and "Economists at Meeting Voice Self-Doubt, Criticism After a Year of Bad Forecasts," by James P. Gannon, *ibid.*, December 30, 1974. Comment expressing disappointment with results of monetarism and supply-side prescriptions is equally ubiquitous, although more recent. I am indebted in particular to "Milton Friedman's Protégés in Chile See Influence Declining Because of Recession," by Everett G. Martin, *ibid.*, July 27, 1982; "Rumors of Stockman's Departure Persist as Other Reagan Aides Rise in Influence," by Kenneth H. Bacon, *ibid.*, September 15, 1982; and "The Outlook," by Bacon, *ibid.*, October 10, 1983.

For a concise exposition of the differences between M-1 (transaction money), M-2 (savings readily converted to transaction money), M-3 (M-2 plus less liquid savings), and L (a U.S. Federal Reserve measurement of liquid assets), I am grateful for "Confused by All the Money-Supply Talk? Here's a Guide to What the Figures Mean," by Christopher Conte, *ibid.*, June 17, 1982.

The modern monetarist quoted ("When money and output grow at the same pace . . .") is David I. Meiselman, professor of economics at Virginia Polytechnic Institute and State University, in an essay, "Deficits, Money and the Causes of Inflation," *ibid.*, July 21, 1981.

The Okun "discomfort index" is discussed in "The Outlook," by Richard F. Janssen, *ibid.*, January 29, 1979, and in an obituary tribute by Janssen, "Art Okun: The Economist as Philosopher," *ibid.*, March 26, 1980.

The English writer and translator in the Netherlands is James Brockway. His quoted comment appeared in "Undervalued," *New Statesman*, July 23, 1976.

Reports indicating stagflation in Marxist economies are numerous; I am indebted in particular to "Sharply Rising Prices, Other Economic Woes Plague Eastern Europe" by Jonathan Spivak, *Wall Street Journal*, November 29, 1979; "Czechoslovakia, a Showpiece of the Eastern Bloc, Shows First Signs of Going the Way of Poland," by Spivak, *ibid.*, May 4, 1982; and for information on debts of Communist governments to Western banks to "Add the Soviet Union to the List of Those with Cash Problems," by David Brand, *ibid.*, March 18, 1982.

The drastic change in the relationship of U.S. incomes to prices of dwellings was noted in "Rate of Home Ownership Falls, Possibly Signaling Big Change," by Robert Guenther, *ibid.*, August 11, 1982.

The theoretically expedient concept that there is a "natural unemployment rate" has swiftly become accepted by many monetarists and others; the earliest mention of it that has come to my attention is in an essay by Walter Eltis, Fellow of Exeter College, Oxford University, in "The Tory Government's Budget," *ibid.*, June 14, 1979 ("The government could therefore cut both inflation . . . and unemployment . . . if it could get the 'natural' rate of unemployment down from the present 1.4 million or so to around 900,000.")

Continuing befuddlement about effects of the Marshall Plan: as recently as 1983 the plan was still being invoked as a remedy for stagnation and backwardness. E.g., "Mrs. Kirkpatrick Urges U.S. to Adopt Latin Marshall Plan," by Bernard Weinraub, New York *Times*, March 6, 1983, beginning "Jeane J. Kirkpatrick, the United States delegate to the United Nations, said today that Washington should initiate a major economic aid program for Central America similar to the Marshall Plan in Europe after World War II."

2 Back to Reality

The description of Bardou is drawn from "Life of Escape in Private Village," by Alan Bayless, Toronto *Globe and Mail*, March 5, 1976.

Henry Grady's description of the Pickens County funeral comes from *The New South, Writings and Speeches of Henry Grady* (Savannah, Ga., Beehive Press, 1971); it was originally published in the third of a series of five articles by Grady for the New York *Ledger* in November and December 1889, which in turn were based upon his Boston and New York speeches of that year.

For information on how Tokyo developed a bicycle industry, and the significance of the method in Japan's general economic development, I am indebted to *A Short Economic History of Modern Japan*, by G. C. Allen (1867–1937), posthumously published in London by Allen & Unwin, 1946.

Sabel's description of symbiotic enterprises comes from his essay "Italy's High Technology Cottage Industry," in the journal *Transatlantic Perspectives* (Washington, The German Marshall Fund of the United States, December 1982), which Sabel adapted from his book *Work and Politics* (London, Cambridge University Press, 1982).

For those interested in more information and evidence concerning city import-replacing, including the reasons why it operates as a chain reaction, and its relationship to economic support of innovations, I have discussed the process more fully in *The Economy of Cities* (New York, Random House, 1969; paperback edition, Vintage Books, 1970).

3 Cities' Own Regions

All information on Shinohata and its vicinity is drawn from *Shinohata: A Portrait of a Japanese Village*, by Ronald P. Dore (London, Allen Lane, and New York, Pantheon Books, both 1978). The book also contains a wealth of other first-hand, acute observation, along with thoughtful comment by the author.

4 Supply Regions

The historic background of Uruguay's economy, immigration and social policies is to be found in encyclopedias and other standard reference works. For information on the country's recent economic and social history, I am indebted in particular to "A Country Dying on Its Feet," an essay by V. S. Naipaul, *New York Review of Books*, April 4, 1974; "The Decline and Fall of Uruguay," by Everett G. Martin, *Wall Street Journal*, July 18, 1975; "The Former Switzerland," by Phillip Berryman, *Commonweal*, November 21, 1975; "Now It's Official: Uruguay Is Brutal," New York *Times*, "The Week in Review" section, July 2, 1978; and "Bitter Pills Help Uruguay's Economy," by Martin, *Wall Street Journal*, July 3, 1980.

Various medieval and Renaissance supply regions are beautifully described and others alluded to in Vol. I of *The Mediterranean and the Mediterranean World in the Age of Philip II*, by Fernand Braudel, English-language edition translated by Siân Reynolds (London, Collins, and New York, Harper & Row, both 1972). I have drawn on Braudel for much of my historical comment on supply regions.

Hong Kong's ginseng imports and their effects in the U.S. Appalachians are reported in "Hong Kong Will Get Its Ginseng If Snakes Don't Get the Digger," by Chester Goolrick, *Wall Street Journal*, March 3, 1983.

The Canary Islands farmer quoted is the late David Leacock of Galdar, Grand Canary.

For reasons why Tanzania, Bangladesh and the Philippines have lost fiber export markets, I am indebted to "There Are No Islands Left in the World's Economy," by Leonard Silk, New York *Times*, December 12, 1976.

New Zealand's plight is succinctly described in "New Zealand Staggers from Two Hard Blows to Its Economic Base," by Barry Newman, *Wall Street Journal*, January 22, 1979.

The quotations regarding vegetable-oil competition are from "Ivory Coast's Palm-Oil Output Gains; U.S. Gives Aid, Irking Soybean Growers," by Robert Prinsky, *ibid.*, April 7, 1976.

Quotations on colonial shaping of Vietnam are from *Fire in the Lake*, by Frances Fitzgerald (Boston, Little, Brown, 1972; paperback edition, Random House, Vintage Books, 1973).

Quotation from Ibn Khaldun is from *The Muquddimah: An Introduction to History*, translated from the Arabic by Franz Rosenthal, edited and abridged by N. J. Dawood (Princeton University Press, 1967; paperback edition, Bollingen Series, 1969). I am indebted to Carol M. Bier for drawing my attention to this work of 1381, which according to Dawood "can be regarded as the earliest attempt made by any historian to discover a pattern in the changes that occur in man's political and social organization."

5 Regions Workers Abandon

"The old looking after the old" is a characterization of deserted rural settlements by Elizabeth Cape, professor of behavioral science at the University of Toronto, reported in "Ontario Villages Become Homes for Aged," by Geoffrey York, Toronto *Globe and Mail*, April 7, 1983.

All information on Napizaro and its people is drawn from "Mexican Men Illegally Working in U.S. Leave a Void in Their Homes," by George Getschow, *Wall Street Journal*, October 7, 1980.

The Egyptian social worker in Rotterdam is Ahmed el Haddad; his observations were reported in "Foreign Workers Still Flock to West Europe Despite Current Slump," by Bowen Northrup, *ibid.*, February 26, 1975.

The film *Bread and Chocolate* was written by Franco Drusati, Aiai Fiastri and Nino Manfredi; directed by Franco Bursati; produced by Turi Vasile, 1973.

6 Technology and Clearances

Information on the Scottish clearances is drawn from *The Highland Clearances*, by John Prebble (London, Secker & Warburg, 1963; paperback edition, Penguin Books, Harmondsworth, England, 1969).

Carter's remark is drawn from his autobiography, *Why Not the Best?* (Nashville, Tenn., Boardman Press, 1975).

A vivid account of agriculturally transformed Georgia, upon which I have drawn, is included, along with much else about the state, in "From Rabun

Gap to Tybee Light," by E. J. Kahn, Jr., "Profiles," *The New Yorker*, February 6, 1978.

For information on effects of the agricultural clearances in the South, I am indebted, in particular, to *Small Cities: How Can the Federal and State Governments Respond to Their Diverse Needs?*, a report by the Subcommittee on the City of the Committee on Banking, Finance and Urban Affairs, House of Representatives, 95th Cong., 2nd Sess., 1978; "The Farmer's Political Clout," an essay by Robert Spaulding, lecturer in economics, San Diego, *Wall Street Journal*, October 8, 1979; and "Black Teenage Unemployment," by Lindley H. Clark, Jr., *ibid.*, March 17, 1981.

For information on the plight of Soviet agriculture or the overmanning of Soviet commercial, industrial and bureaucratic work, or both, I am particularly indebted to "Will Russia Ever Feed Itself?," by Alec Nove, director of the Institute of Soviet and East European Studies at Glasgow University, *New York Times Magazine*, February 1, 1976; *Stabilizing the USSR's Rural Population Through the Development of the Social Infrastructure*, by B. N. Khomelyansky, Soviet economist (Geneva, United Nations' International Labor Office, 1982); "Soviet Food Shortages Persist as Harvest Lags Fourth Year in a Row," by David Brand and David Satter, *Wall Street Journal*, August 23, 1982; and "Andropov's Economic Dilemma," by Leonard Silk, *New York Times Magazine*, October 9, 1983.

For information on untoward effects of the Green Revolution, I have drawn, in particular, upon criticisms by Gunnar Myrdal, reported in "Asia's Green Revolution Not Helping Those in Poor Countries Find Food, Expert Says," by David Van Praagh, Toronto *Globe and Mail*, September 24, 1970; "Green Revolution: A Just Technology Often Unjust in Use" and "Green Revolution: Problems of Adapting a Western Technology," by Nicholas Wade, *Science*, December 20 and 27, 1974; "The 'Greening' of Java Produces More Rice, but Problems Persist," by Barry Newman, *Wall Street Journal*, June 14, 1978; "Landless and Poor, Indonesian Villagers Get By on Ingenuity," by Newman, *ibid.*, June 7, 1979; and "Farm Machinery Reducing the Role of Women in Developing Countries," report of an address by Zena Tadesse, sociologist and rural development worker in Africa, by Kathleen Rex, Toronto *Globe and Mail*, September 28, 1979.

Myrdal's wishful thinking on overcoming agricultural poverty by labor-intensive rural work is to be found in *Asian Drama: An Inquiry Into the Poverty of Nations* (New York, Twentieth Century Fund, 1968).

For information on World Bank policies and programs, I am indebted, in particular, to "World Bank under McNamara," by Clyde H. Farnsworth, New York *Times*, June 10, 1980; and "Recession Prompts World Bank to Review Policies as Fewer Poor Nations Seek Loans," by Art Pine, *Wall Street Journal*, February 8, 1983.

7 Transplant Regions

Henry Grady's remarks are a continuation of those cited under Chapter 2.

For information on the size and scope of the Marietta plant of Lockheed Aircraft, I am indebted to "What Price Lockheed?," by Berkeley Rice, *New*

York Times Magazine, May 9, 1971. The founding of Lockheed Aircraft is described in *Fortune*, Aug. 1940.

News reports on losses of transplants in transplant economies are ubiquitous; I am indebted, in particular, to "U.S. Textile Industry Beset by Imports and Labor Woes," by Wayne King, *New York Times*, May 15, 1977; "Slack Bootstraps," *Newsweek*, November 10, 1975; "In a Lagging Economy, Puerto Rico Is Trying to Chart New Course," by Karen Rothmyer, *Wall Street Journal*, April 6, 1976; and "Puerto Rico Is Hurt by Investment Slump and Reagan Cutbacks," by Chester Goolrick, *ibid.*, February 3, 1982.

The Sicilian official's comment is drawn from "Sicily Where All the Songs Are Sad," by Howard LaFay, *National Geographic*, March 1976.

The plight of Greece was described by Adonis Tritsis at the Great Cities of the World Conference, Boston, September 21–27, 1980; I am indebted to him for a typescript of his paper and for additional personal comment.

The Taiwanese scheme for creating local enterprises and the growth of the Kaohsiung economy were briefly described by John Fraser in "Taiwan Feeling Pains of Industrial Growth" (a strange headline in view of the article's substance), Toronto *Globe and Mail*, June 20, 1979. I am also indebted to "Taiwan: Business Is Booming Despite the Politicking," by M. N. Tsuji, *ibid.*, October 12, 1976; "Taiwan Still Thrives a Year After the Loss of U.S. Recognition" by Barry Kramer, *Wall Street Journal*, February 8, 1980; and "Taiwan Seeks Move to High Technology; Plan Could Pose Threat to U.S. and Japan," by Art Pine, *ibid.*, January 20, 1983.

The various quotes re domestic demand for transplants in the United States comes from "Domestic Feud: War Among the States for Jobs and Business Becomes Ever Fiercer," by Timothy Schellhardt, *Wall Street Journal*, February 14, 1983.

Catherine's note concerning Moscow and the crumbling towns is included in the appendix to *The Memoirs of Catherine the Great*, edited by Dominique Maroger (New York, Collier, 1961).

The heavy reliance of Soviet economic planners on transplants to combat local unemployment is touched on in "Soviet City Planning: Current Issues and Future Perspectives," by Robert J. Osborn and Thomas A. Reiner, *Journal of the American Institute of Planners*, November 1962.

8 Capital for Regions Without Cities

For information on the Volta Dam in Ghana, I am indebted to Patricia Adams, Third World Researcher of Energy Probe, Toronto; to a round-up article on Third World dams entitled "Aswan Dam Is Found to Hurt as Well as Aid Egyptian Agriculture," by Ray Vicker, *Wall Street Journal*, September 24, 1976; and "Once the Showpiece of Black Africa, Ghana Now Is Near Collapse," by Steve Mufson, *ibid.*, March 28, 1983. The American aluminum refinery is Valco, 90 percent owned by Kaiser Aluminum and 10 percent by Reynolds Metals. The U.N. Food and Agricultural official quoted is H. M. Horning, from Vicker's article, *op. cit.*

For material on the Tennessee Valley Authority, I have drawn on numerous news reports of events as they occurred, but am particularly indebted to "This Valley Waits to Die," by the late William O. Douglas, Associate Justice, U.S.

Supreme Court, *True for Today's Man* magazine, May 1969; "Mississippi Whites Found Deprived," by Roy Reed, New York *Times*, July 25, 1971; "TVA Coal Buying Criticized Anew," by George Vecsey, New York *Times*, April 1, 1972; "TVA Swept by a Flood of Criticism" (from which the quotation "I wouldn't say we're doing things that aren't wrong . . ." by Aubrey J. Wagner, chairman, is drawn), by Reginald Stuart, New York *Times*, January 12, 1975; "U.S. Supreme Court sides with fish, halts building of $100 million dam," Reuters, Toronto *Globe and Mail*, June 16, 1978; "TVA May Restrain Its Nuclear Effort," by Howell Raines, New York *Times*, May 8, 1979; "How to Kill a Valley," an essay by Peter Matthiessen, *New York Review of Books*, February 7, 1980; "UAW's Failure to Organize GM Facility Leaves a Residue of Red Faces and Ill Will," by Janet Guyon, *Wall Street Journal*, February 24, 1981; "TVA Is Overbuilding Nuclear Reactors, Staff Report Says," *ibid.*, January 7, 1982; and "TVA, at 50, Drafting New Role in Region's Future," by Wendell Rawls Jr., New York *Times*, May 15, 1983.

For information on aid to southern Italy, I have drawn particularly on *From Caesar to the Mafia*, by Luigi Barzini, (Freeport, N.Y., Library Press, 1971; paperback edition, Bantam Books, 1972); "Italy's South Gaining, but Still Lags Far Behind," by Marvine Howe, New York *Times*, December 29, 1971; "A Port Project Goes Awry in Italy," by Paul Hofmann, *ibid.*, March 11, 1979; and "Italy's Disenchantment with State Industry," by Jonathan Spivak, *Wall Street Journal*, January 24, 1980.

Ahmed Ben Bella's bitter summation was given in an interview to Daniel Junqua in *Le Monde*, Paris, reprinted under the title "North-South Dilemma" in Toronto *Globe and Mail*, January 13, 1981.

9 Bypassed Places

A sample of Hassan Ragab's paper was incorporated in *Ancient Egypt: Discovering Its Splendors*, along with a brief account of its provenance (Washington, The National Geographic Society, 1978); for a slightly fuller account, I am indebted to a book promotion letter sent to society members on the letterhead of the Papyrus Institute in Cairo, signed by Hassan Ragab.

I am indebted to James I. Butzner for checking that the buildings of little and big stones still stand in Henry, and for documentation on the year of Miss Robison's arrival there.

Although the world abounds today, as it has in the past, with deteriorated stagnant economies and cultures, the phenomenon of deterioration is amazingly little acknowledged. For example, in "Early Man in the West Indies," by Jose M. Cruxent and Irving Rouse, *Scientific American*, November 1969, the authors state as a basic premise of their reasoning "the improbability that lower material cultures are derived from higher ones."

10 Why Backward Cities Need One Another

For information on the Bell helicopter factory in Iran I am immensely grateful to "Many U.S. Firms Felt the Shock When Iran Dropped One Contract," by June Kromholz and Steve Frazier, *Wall Street Journal*, March 8, 1979. An earlier account of Iran's illusory development, from which I have also drawn for background, is "Despite Its Oil Money, Iran's Economy Suffers from Many Shortages," by Ray Vicker, *ibid.*, April 11, 1977. The *masachuseti* epithet was reported in *Fall of the Peacock Throne*, by William Forbis (New York, Harper & Row, 1980).

The reporter who interviewed the angry Iranian teacher was Joseph Kraft, "Letter from Iran," *The New Yorker*, December 18, 1978.

For information on Peter's development projects, I have relied on *Peter the Great: His Life and World*, by Robert K. Massie (New York, Knopf, 1980).

Venice's role in the revival of early medieval European economic life and the patterns of ramifying trade that resulted are set forth in *Medieval Cities: Their Origins and the Revival of Trade*, by Henri Pirenne, translated by Frank D. Halsey (Princeton University Press, 1925; paperback editions, Doubleday Anchor Books, 1956, and Princeton University Press, 1969). An excellent companion volume is *Guilds and Companies of London*, by George Unwin (London, Methuen, 1909). The trade from Constantinople's point of view is discussed in *Byzantium: An Introduction to East Roman Civilization*, edited by N. H. Baynes and H. St. L. B. Moss (Oxford, Clarendon Press, 1948; paperback edition, Oxford University Press, London, 1961). The authors consider that the preference of Constantinople's wealthy classes for investing in land "rather than risk the losses of maritime venture" was responsible for the fact that by the eleventh century Venetian shipping dominated the Constantinople-Venice trade.

For the importance of the bicycle to modern technology and the evolution of the bicycle itself, I have drawn on "Bicycle Technology," by S. S. Wilson, *Scientific American*, March 1973.

The anomalous development of the Indian bicycle-powered spinning wheel is taken from an article by an unnamed New Delhi correspondent of the *Economist*, London, reprinted in Toronto *Globe and Mail*, March 2, 1979, under the heading "India Making Work for Village Industry."

The improvisations by the Colombian rural engineering team were described in "Colombian Gadgetry Seeks to Entice Poor to Hot Grasslands," by Everett G. Martin, *Wall Street Journal*, October 26, 1979.

Examples of obstacles to change and development which have accrued in currently advanced economies are constantly reported: e.g., "Windmills, Solar Homes Face Hurdles in Old Building Codes," by John Curley, *ibid.*, September 3, 1980.

11   Faulty Feedback to Cities

For information on the role of feedback in breathing, I am indebted to Decker Butzner, and for guidance on the working of feedback generally, to James K. Jacobs. I have also drawn on "The Organizing Principle of Complex Living Systems," by A. S. Iberall and W. S. McCulloch, *Journal of Basic Engineering*, American Society of Mechanical Engineers, June 1969; and "The Origins of Feedback Control," by Otto Mayr, *Scientific American*, October 1970.

The comment by the chairman of Wedgwood, Sir Arthur Bryant, appeared in "The Fading Fortunes of Wedgwood," by Sandra Salmans, New York *Times*, March 30, 1980.

The Lao-tzu quotation is taken from *Science and Civilization in China,* Vol. II, by Joseph Needham (London, Cambridge University Press, 1956).

The quotations respecting passivity in the southern and northern Japanese islands are from "Japan's Rural Regions Hustle to Attract Foreign Companies," by Eugene Carlson, *Wall Street Journal,* April 26, 1983, and I have also drawn on "Japanese Farmers Fight Proposals to Ease Curbs on Food Imports, Claiming Inability to Compete," by Urban C. Lehner, *ibid.,* June 10, 1982.

12 Transactions of Decline

For information on the rise of European standing armies, I have drawn primarily on *The Seventeenth Century,* by Sir George Clark (Oxford, Clarendon Press, 1929; paperback edition, Oxford University Press, London, 1960); *Peter the Great,* cited under Chapter 10; and "The All-Consuming Monster," a review by Paul Johnson of the biography of a seventeenth-century warlord, Albrecht von Wallenstein, *New Statesman,* September 24, 1976.

For information on the phenomenal size and geographic spread of U.S. Post Exchanges, I am indebted to "Hands in the Till at the 'Big Store,' " by Walter Rugaber, New York *Times,* November 7, 1971.

Reports if competition for U.S. military installations and contracts are ubiquitous, as well as lobbying and arguments for larger appropriations, on the part of localities or enterprises standing to gain economically. In his *Report from Wasteland* (New York, Praeger, 1970), Senator William Proxmire calls the extravagance "a welfare system for weapons producers."

For reports of jockeying between France and Britain in the EEC for subsidies (France insisting on those for agriculture, Britain trying to get them for depressed industrial regions), I have drawn on reports of events as they occurred, but in particular on "The Common Market's Dishevelment," by Robert D. Prinsky, Common Market correspondent of AP-Dow Jones News Service in Brussels, *Wall Street Journal,* February 7, 1974; "The EEC Is Beset by the Blues," by Jeffrey Simpson, Toronto *Globe and Mail,* April 1, 1982; and "New Disputes Glut Europe's Farm Agenda," by Paul Lewis, New York *Times,* April 4, 1982.

Reports of nations' growing difficulties in meeting their established welfare commitments are also ubiquitous; e.g., "States May Force Federal Bailout of Jobless Funds," by Byron Klapper, *Wall Street Journal,* March 28, 1977, reporting the insolvency of unemployment insurance funds in twenty-two states, requiring interest-free federal loans; "In a Deepening Slump, West Germany Droops from Big Welfare Load; Recipients March to Retain Lofty Benefit Programs, Shaking the Kohl Regime," by Roger Thurow, *ibid.,* December 3, 1982; and "In Western Europe Some Countries Owe Big Sums to Foreigners; Unlike Many Poor Nations, Their Borrowing Is Laid to Huge Social Programs," by David Brand, *ibid.,* December 14, 1982.

For information that transplant investments by no means always pay off —which can be inferred in any case from the scrambles for subsidies on the part of many enterprises setting up transplants—I am indebted to "Many U.S. Firms Find Foreign Subsidiaries Are Major Headaches," by William M. Carley, *ibid.,* January 22, 1975.

13 **The Predicament**

Economic passivity in the peripheral regions of Japan is implied by the competitions for transplants cited under Chapter 11, as well as by reports such as the following: "Japan's Tough Restrictions on Imported Oranges Endanger Settlement of U.S. Trade Agreements," by Greg Conderacci, *Wall Street Journal*, November 1, 1978; and "Japanese Town Faces an Economic Crisis as Steel Industry Pushes 'Rationalization,'" by Masoyoshi Kanabayashi, *ibid.*, February 14, 1979; the town threatened by loss or contraction of its major industry is Kamaishi, four hundred miles north of Tokyo.

The Japanese switch to deficit financing, beginning in 1975–76, is discussed by Peter F. Drucker in "Clouds Forming across the Japanese Sun," *ibid.*, July 13, 1982.

The Japanese switch from tax reductions to tax increases, beginning in 1977, is discussed by Kazuo Nukazawa, director of the financial affairs department of Keidanren, the Japan Federation of Economic Organizations, in "Now Japan Frets About Taxes and the Deficit," *ibid.*, May 9, 1983.

For information on pressures to increase Japanese military spending, I am indebted to "Japan's De Facto Rearmament," by Tetsuya Kataoka, professor at the Graduate School for Policy Science, Saitama University, *ibid.*, May 4, 1981; and "Nakasone Stirs Pride of the Japanese as He Firms Up Ties to West" by Urban C. Lehner, *ibid.*, September 1, 1983.

I am indebted to the Systems Analysis Division of the U.S. Department of Transportation for providing the occasion, and to Robert W. Crosby, Arthur S. Iberall and David Kahn for explaining to me principles of bifurcations.

The political scientists who analyzed dissolutions of political units are Karl W. Deutsch, Sidney A. Burrell, Robert A. Kann. Maurice Lee, Jr., Martin Lichterman, Raymond E. Lindgren, Francis L. Loewenheim and Richard W. Van Wagenen; their findings were summarized in *Political Community and the North Atlantic Area* (Princeton University Press, 1957, and reprinted in *International Political Communities*, a paperback anthology, Doubleday Anchor Books, 1966).

The metaphor of the dog comes from *Catastrophe Theory: Selected Papers 1972–1977*, edited by E. C. Zeeman (Reading, Mass., Addison-Wesley, 1977).

In a previous book, *The Question of Separatism: Quebec and the Struggle over Sovereignty* (New York, Random House, 1980; paperback edition, Vintage Books, 1981), I recounted the story of Norway's separation from Sweden, drawing gratefully on the following: *A History of Modern Norway 1814–1972*, by T. K. Derry (Oxford, Clarendon Press, 1973); *A Brief History of Norway*, by John Midgaard (Oslo, Johan Grundt Tanum Förlag, 1969); *A History of Norway*, by Karen Larsen (Princeton University Press, 1948); *One Hundred Norwegians*, edited by Sverre Mortensen and Per Vogt (Oslo, Johan Grundt Tanum Förlag, 1955).

In Canada, recognition that transfer payments and other economic aids hold the country together politically is constantly expressed; the usual clichés are that they are "glue" and "sinews." Their importance for maintaining "national identity" regardless of whether their disbursement represents economically efficient use of resources is stated as obvious fact in *Comparing Provincial*

Revenue Yields: The Tax Indicator Approach, by James H. Lynn (Toronto, Canadian Tax Foundation, 1968).

Anthony Sampson, in a report on the Pacific Rim economies entitled "The Secret of Success: Mutual Action against Danger," *Observer*, reprinted in Toronto *Globe and Mail*, February 24, 1981, quotes an unnamed Indian government economist: "If you could separate Bombay from the rest of India, of course, it could do as well as Singapore. If the Punjab seceded, it could do as well as Korea. But they can't—they're part of India."

14 Drift

Professor Umesao, director of Japan's National Institute of Ethnology, made his remarks about drift in a speech (which contains much else of interest) delivered to the eighth International Industrial Design congress in Kyoto, October 1973; it is published in English translation in *Soul and Material Things*, Vol. I, *Six Speakers*, Congress Report Committee, Japan Organizing Committee for ICSID '73, Kyoto, 1975.

Professor Smith's remarks are from "Aesthetic Curiosity—The Root of Invention," New York *Times*, August 24, 1975. An excellent statement regarding the unexpectedness of invention and discovery and the relationship of surprise to economic development and resource use is "A Historical Approach to Future Economic Growth," by Glenn Hueckel, *Science*, March 14, 1975.

For a precise explanation of the meaning of diversity in natural ecologies, I am grateful to "Man's Efficient Rush toward Deadly Dullness," by Kenneth E. F. Watt, *Natural History*, New York, February 1972.

The reaction to the proposed Euroloaf was mentioned in "Common Market Delay on Oil Decisions Puts Chill on European Unity," by Richard F. Janssen, *Wall Street Journal*, December 17, 1973.

Parts of the story of Boston's economic rejuvenation are told in "Venture Capital," *Fortune*, February 1949; and in "General Doriot's Dream Factory," by Gene Bylinsky, *ibid.*, August 1967.

The equipment being produced but finding little use was reported in "Fire-Fighting Gear Improves, but Cities Can't Afford to Buy It," by Jeffrey A. Tannenbaum, *Wall Street Journal*, January 30, 1975.

INDEX

Aarhus, Denmark 174

Abandonment *See* Regions workers abandon

Acadians 82

Adams, Patricia 239*n*.

Addis Ababa, Ethiopia 130, 134

Advanced-backward trade *See* Trade between advanced and backward economies

Africa 5, 68, 73, 89, 102, 129, 131 *See also* specific countries

Agricultural price supports *See* Loans, grants and subsidies

Agricultural productivity and yields 14, 79, 83, 88, 91, 107

Aid programs *See* Green Revolution; Loans, grants and subsidies; Volta Dam; World Bank; notes under Development programs

Akron, Ohio 179

Alabama 112, 115 *See also* South, United States

Alberta, Canada 70

Algeria 74

Allen, G. C. 236*n*.

Amsterdam 46, 157, 174

Antwerp 46, 143

Appalachia (United States eastern mountain region) 25, 64

Argentina 5 *See also* Buenos Aires

Athens 99

Atlanta, Ga. 37, 46, 94, 146

Atlantic Provinces (Canada) 66, 99

Attracting industries *See* Transplanted city enterprises

Austria 182

Azmara, Ethiopia 130

Azores 74

Backward trade *See* Trade between advanced and backward economies

Bacon, Kenneth H. 235*n*.

Balance of trade 108, 160, 162, 164

Baltimore, Md. 65

Bangladesh 66, 118

Banks, banking 9, 21, 197 *See also* World Bank

Bardou, France 32, 64, 73, 86, 130, 133

Bari, Italy 121

Barzini, Luigi 121, 240n.

Bayless, Alan 236n.

Baynes, N. H. 241n.

Bedouins 71

Belfast, Northern Ireland 46, 173

Bell Operations (company) 136

Bell Telephone System 227

Ben Bella, Ahmed 122, 240n.

Berlin 157, 173

Berryman, Phillip 236n.

Bicycles — cassava-root shredder 152 — development of 150 — Japanese 38, 148, 154, 167 — spinning wheel 151 — water pump 86, 89

Bier, Carol M. 237n.

Bifurcations 207, 208, 211, 214, 220

Birmingham, England 173

Bismarck, Otto von 191

Boeing Aircraft Company 186

Bogotá 151

Bombay 106, 244n.

Booms, wartime 185

Bordeaux, France 173

Borrowing See Loans, foreign

Boston 37, 45, 46, 145, 228

Brain-stem breathing center See Breathing (as example of feedback control)

Brand, David 235n., 238n., 242n.

Bratislava 176

Braudel, Fernand 236n.

Brazil 5, 46, 118, 197

Bread and Chocolate 77, 120

Breathing (as example of feedback control) 158, 161, 169, 172, 180

Brest, France 173

Bretton Woods Agreements 4

Bristol, England 173

Britain, See Great Britain

British Empire See Great Britain — British Empire

British Wool Society 80

Brockway, James 235n.

Bryant, Arthur, Sir 241n.

Buenos Aires 46, 146

Buffalo, N.Y. 179

Burma 133

Burrell, Sidney A. 243n.

Bursati, Franco 237n.

Business cycles 209

Butzner, Decker 241n.

Butzner, James I. 240n.

Bylinsky, Gene 244n.

Byzantine Empire 177, 182

Camden, N. J. 179

Camp Lejeune 187

Canada 4, 12, 65, 69, 107, 168, 213 See also specific cities and provinces

Canary Islands 64, 65

Cantillon, Richard 9, 12, 23, 30

Canton, China 47

Cape, Elizabeth 237n.

Capital See City capital as a major force; Local economies

Capital cities 231

Cardiff, Wales 46, 72, 173

Caribbean 73

Carley, William M. 242n.

Carlson, Eugene 242n.

Carter, Jimmy, President 82, 237n.

Casting up exports or innovations 37, 41, 109, 114, 119, 144, 146, 163, 178, 190, 204, 217 See also City export work

Castro, Fidel 70

Catherine the Great 103, 239n.

Center for Research on World Political Institutions 212

Central America 235n.

Charleston, S.C. 146
Cheerful face of inflation 9, 12
Chicago 37, 145
Chicago school of economic theory
20
China 3, 5, 108, 129, 134, 177,
217 — Chinese Empire 176,
199 See also specific cities
and provinces
Cincinnati, Ohio 37, 145
Cities — necessary to all development and expansion 109, 132,
140, 151, 193, 212 — not
perpetual motion machines
193
City beginnings 71, Chap 10
City capital as a major force 42,
54, 100, Chap 8; 195, 228 See
also City earnings
City currencies See National
currencies (vs. city currencies)
City earnings 187, 191, 193, 195
See also City capital as a major
force
City export work 39, 119, 171,
178, 185, 188, 204 See also
Casting up exports or innovations; Improvised, innovative
and versatile production
City jobs as a major force 42, 50,
58, 83, 84, 88, 100, 107, 122, 196,
205
City processes 39, 41, 43, 47, 119,
132, 171, 189, 209
City regions 41, 43, Chap 3; 86,
97, 100, 106, 109, 114, 153, 183,
204, 229
City technology as a major force
40, 42, 50, Chap 6; 135, 154, 196
City versatility See Improvised,
innovative and versatile production
Clark, George, Sir 217, 219, 242n.
Clark, Lindley H., Jr. 238n.

Clearances, cleared regions 77,
Chap 6; 107, 109, 151, 196 See
also City technology as a
major force
Cleveland, Ohio 179
Colombia 151
Colonial economies 5, Chap 4;
131, 145, 147, 168, 216
Conderacci, Greg 243n.
Constantinople 133, 141, 241n.
Conte, Christopher 235n.
Copenhagen 46, 57, 106, 174
Cost-push theories of inflation
13
Credit See Loans, foreign;
Loans, grants and subsidies
Credit, expansion or contraction
of (in economic theory) 14, 20
Crosby, Robert W. 243n.
Crusades 184
Cruxent, Jose M. 240n.
Cuba 5, 46, 70
Curley, John 241n.
Currencies, international
exchange 4, 158
Currency Chap 11 See also
National currencies (vs. city
currencies)
Currency feedback information
Chap 11 — countries with
heavily rural or resource exports
163 — city-made exports 170
— little foreign trade 176
See also National currencies
(vs. city currencies)
Cycle of a vigorous city 171, 209
Czechoslovakia 176

Dawood, N. J. 237n.
Deadly interplay between nations
and cities Chap 13; 225 See
also Transactions of decline

Debts *See* Loans, foreign

Declining economies *See*
Stagnant economies *See also*
United States economy —
decline

Deficit financing 17, 206

Demand-side economics 5, 10,
14, 16, 193

Denmark 173 *See also* Copenhagen

Depression, Great 11, 16, 20,
128, 185, 211

Depressions, economic 3, 209

Detroit 109, 163, 179

Deutsch, Karl W. 243*n.*

Development and decline con-
trasted 189

Development process of cities,
developing economies, creative
development work 140, 148,
154, 166, 189, 205, 221 *See also*
City processes

Development programs *See*
Aid programs, and notes;
Clearances, cleared regions;
Colombia; Grady, Henry; Iran;
Italy, southern; Loans, grants
and subsidies; Marshall Plan;
Saint Petersburg; Saudi Arabia;
Sicily; Tennessee Valley
Authority; Transplanted city
enterprises; Uruguay; Volta
Dam; etc.

Discomfort index 24

Discontents *See* Loans, grants
and subsidies

Discontinuities 207, 208, 211,
214, 220

Disparities, regional *See* Loans,
grants and subsidies

Distant city markets 35, 42, 49,
Chap 4; 107, 204

Dis-Tran Products (company)
136

Diversified rural work *See* City
regions

Dog (as illustration of discontinuity) 214

Dore, Ronald P. 48, 167, 236*n.*

Douglas, William O. 239*n.*

Drucker, Peter F. 243*n.*

Dublin 46

Eastern Empire *See* Byzantine
Empire; Roman Empire

Ecology 224

Economic discomfort index 24

Economic drift 223

Economic feedback controls
Chap 11; 211

Economic history, patterns of
206

Economic isolation Chap 9

Economic successes 6, 101, 140

Economics, science of Chap 1; 29

Economy of cities 41, 236*n.*

Edinburgh 46, 81, 173

Efficiency, regional 60, 63, 70

Egypt 74, 118, 124, 130

Elba 64

Electric utility monopolies 227

"Elephant" cities 172, 175, 176,
180

Eltis, Walter 235*n.*

Empires 68, 176, Chap 12 —
two types 199, 202

England *See* Great Britain

Esthetic curiosity 222

Esthetics of drift 221, 230

Ethiopia 73, 129

Europe 6, 12, 74, 99, 131, 143,
183 *See also* Medieval
Europe; specific countries

European Economic Community
4, 5, 67, 78, 106, 201, 213, 217,
225

Expansion 42
Exports Chap 4 *See also* City capital as a major force; City export work; Imports

Family of sovereignties *See* Sovereignties
Farnsworth, Clyde H. 238n.
Faulty feedback *See* Economic feedback controls; Currency feedback information
Feedback controls 158, 224
Finland 173
Fire in the Lake 69
Fisher, Irving 20, 234n.
Fitzgerald, Frances 69, 237n.
Flanders, Ralph 228
Foley Company, Howard P. 136
Forbis, William 241n.
Forces of cities used disproportionately Chaps 4, 5, 6, 7, 8
Forces unleashed by cities 34, 42, 47, 49, 74, 108, 109, 128, 211 *See also* City capital as a major force; City jobs as a major force; City technology as a major force; Distant city markets; Transplanted city enterprises
France 8, 67, 69, 173, 182, 184, 198, 201, 213, 217 *See also* specific cities
Fraser, John 239n.
Frazier, Steve 240n.
Freedman, Robert 234n.
Friedman, Milton 20
Funeral in Pickens County 36, 94, 111, 146

Gannon, James P. 234n.
Garrison towns 186

General Electric Company 136
General Theory of Employment, Interest and Money 17
Genoa 143, 157
Georgia 83, 94, 228 *See also* Atlanta; Carter, Jimmy, President; Pickens County; Savannah; South, United States; Tennessee Valley Authority
Germany 157, 173, 182, 191, 213, 217
Germany, West 8, 74, 106 173
Getschow, George 237n.
Ghana 102, 105, 110
Glasgow 46, 81, 173
Goolrick, Chester 237n., 239n.
Gothenberg, Sweden 174, 219
Grady, Henry 36, 43, 93, 146
Grand Cache, Alberta 70
Grants *See* Loans, grants and subsidies
Graybar Electric (company) 136
Great Britain 3, 5, 8, 12, 13, 18, 26, 108, 134, 145, 160, 173, 184, 202, 210, 213, 217, 219 — British Empire 182, 198 *See also* Ireland, Scotland, Wales
Greece 74, 99
Green Revolution 89
Gross national product, origin of the concept 31
Guangdong (Kwantung) province 47
Guenther, Robert 235n.
Guyon, Janet 240n.

Haddad, Ahmed el 237n.
Haiti 73
Hamburg 65
Hamilton, Ontario 57
Hankow 47

Hanseatic League 157
Hanyang 47
Hart, Laird 234n.
Havana 46, 71
Henry, N. C. 125, 209
Highland clearances Chap 6
Hinterlands See City regions
Hofmann, Paul 240n.
Hong Kong 6, 47, 64, 71, 147, 149, 163, 169
Horning, H. M. 239n.
Howe, Marvine 240n.
Hubei province 47
Hueckel, Glenn 244n.

Iberall, Arthur S. 241n., 243n.
Iceland 217, 219
Imperialism See Empires
Import-replacing 35, 37, 43, 47, 58, 61, 63, 66, 70, 74, 92, 100, 102, 109, 114, 118, 143, 163, 166, 171, 186, 189, 192, 196, 204, 209, 212 — explosive episodes 41, 142, 171, 205, 208, 210 — exuberantly and repeatedly 47, 143, 193
Import shifting 42, 143, 204
Import-substitution See Import-replacing
Imports 36, 43, 119, 162, 189
Imports earned and unearned 119, 122, 135, 139, 163, 169, 176, 187, 193, 195
Improvised, innovative and versatile production 39, 43, 100, 101, 106, 119, 139, 144, 148, 154, 171, 193, 204, 221, 229 — as complex form of order 144, 223
India 5, 73, 129, 151, 244n.
Indianapolis, Ind. 179
Indians, North American 82, 132
Indigenous capital, economies, markets, production, etc. See Local economies
Indochina 69
Indonesia 118
Industrialization programs See Transplanted city enterprises
Inflation See Prices
Innovative production See Improvised, innovative and versatile production
Inquiry into the Nature and Causes of the Wealth of Nations 30
Instabilities and stresses 207, 209, 211, 214
Interest rates in supply-side theory 21
International Monetary Fund 6, 198
Invention 222
Investments as transactions of decline 105, 195, 198
Iran 5, 135, 150, 168
Iran Express (company) 137
Ireland 99, 132, 199, 225
Isfahan, Iran 135
Isle of Man 217, 219
Istanbul 232 See also Constantinople
Italy 74, 172 See also specific cities
Italy, northern 8, 39, 78, 174, 213
Italy, southern 5, 8, 78, 99, 120, 213

Jacksonville, N. C. 187
Jacobs, James K. 241n.
Janssen, Richard F. 235n., 244n.
Japan 6, 12, 46, 70, 134, 146, 167, 174, 182, 191, 204, 213, 221 See also specific cities
Java 89, 102

Johnson, Lyndon, President 3, 19, 24, 115
Johnson, Paul 242n.
Jones Construction Company 136
Junqua, Daniel 240n.

Kahn, David 243n.
Kahn, E. J., Jr. 238n.
Kaiser Aluminum (company) 239n.
Kanabayashi, Masoyoshi 243n.
Kann, Robert A. 243n.
Kaohsiung 101, 109, 147
Kataoka, Tetsuya 243n.
Kennedy, J. F., President 3, 19
Kent County, New Brunswick, Canada 66
Keynes, John Maynard (and Keynesianism) 10, 16, 20, 24, 27
Khaldun, Ibn 70, 237n.
Khomelyansky, B. N. 238n.
Khrushchev, Nikita 3
King, Wayne 239n.
Kirkpatrick, Jeane J. 235n.
Kitchener, Ontario 57
Klapper, Byron 242n.
Knoxville, Tenn. 113, 115
Korea 6, 169 See also Seoul
Kraft, Joseph 241n.
Kramer, Barry 239n.
Kromholz, June 240n.
Kuwait 65, 168

Labor-saving equipment See City jobs as a major force; City technology as a major force
Labor theory of value 12
LaFay, Howard 239n.
Laffer curve 22

Land reform 99
Lao-tzu 170
Latin America 4, 73, 118, 129, 170, 235n. See also specific countries, cities, Mexico
Leacock, David 237n.
Lee, Maurice, Jr. 243n.
Lehner, Urban C. 242n., 243n.
Lejeune, Camp 187
Lenin, Nikolai 217
Lewis, Paul 242n.
Lichterman, Martin 243n.
Lilienthal, David 115
Lille, France 173
Lipsey, Richard G. 234n.
Lisbon 46, 65, 231
Liverpool 46, 173
Loans, foreign 9, 106, 137, 161 See also Banks, banking; Interest rates in supply-side theory; World Bank
Loans, grants and subsidies 4, 8, 54, 67, 71, 82, 91, Chap 8; 152, 176, Chap 12; 206, 213, 217, 219
Local economies (includes local capital, markets, production, use, etc.) 37, 39, 43, 94, 96, 114, 119, 138, 139, 142, 143, 148, 154, 187, 196, 204, 217, 224 See also Import-replacing; Import shifting
Lockheed Aircraft (company) 94
London 46, 57, 143, 149, 173, 231
Los Angeles 46, 75, 94
Lost crafts Chap 9
Loughhead, Allen 95
Luxuries 141, 222
Lynn, James H. 244n.
Lyons 65, 173

Macro-economics 6, 9, 27, 29
Madrid 46, 65, 231

Maine 45, 108

Malaysia 68, 169, 219 *See also* Singapore

Manchester, England 173

Manila 47

Mao Tse-tung 3, 217

Marietta, Ga. 94

Maritime Provinces (Canada) 66, 99

Marseilles 46, 173

Marshall Plan 7, 27, 185, 235*n*.

Martin, Everett G. 235*n*., 236*n*., 241*n*.

Marx, Karl and Marxist economics 10, 14, 23, 31, 193, 218

Masachuseti See Iran

Massie, Robert K. 241*n*.

Matthiessen, Peter 240*n*.

Mayr, Otto 241*n*.

McCulloch, W.S. 241*n*.

McNamara, Robert 90

Medieval Europe 131, 149, 157, 183

Meiselman, David I. 235*n*.

Memory, forgotten practices Chap 9

Mercantilist tautology 30, 44

Mercantilists 29

Mexico 5, 197 *See also* Napizaro

Mexico City 76

Middle Ages *See* Medieval Europe

Middle East 64, 65, 73, 129, 150, 168 *See also* Iran

Migrant labor Chap 5; 122

Milan 46, 65, 106, 157, 172

Milch cow cities 106 *See also* City capital as a major force; Taxes (revenues); Wealth redistribution

Military bases, installations 94, 186

Military production 6, 179, Chap 12; 207, 212, 213, 231

Military thinking 104, 216, 218, 222, 224

Mill, John Stuart 14, 20, 23, 234*n*.

Monetarism 20, 27

Money supply 21, 235*n*.

Monopolies 15, 227

Montevideo 46, 60, 71, 146, 164, 219 *See also* Uruguay

Morocco 74, 103

Morosos 75, 129, 134

Moscow 46

Moss, H. St.L. B. 241*n*.

Mufson, Steve 239*n*.

Multiplier effect 185

Mushroom producing, Shinohata 51

Myrdal, Gunnar 90, 238*n*.

Nagoya, Japan 174

Naipaul, V.S. 236*n*.

Nantes, France 173

Napizaro, Mexico 75, 129

Naples 46, 121, 172

National currencies (*vs.* city currencies) Chap 11; 205, 215

National economic statistics 26, 31, 35, 65, 106, Chap 11

National economies (*vs.* city economies) 6, 29, 35, 43, 208, 210

National policies and transactions counterproductive for cities *See* Transactions of decline

National Soybean Processors' Association 67

Nations, or nations dividing *See* Sovereignties

Nearby hinterlands *See* City regions

Needham, Joseph 242n.
Netherlands 8, 26, 131, 143, 174, 182 *See also* specific cities
New Brunswick, Canada 26, 64, 66, 108
New cities 109, 133, 140, 156, 171, 183, 189
New Hampshire 45
New South *See* South, United States
New York (city) 46, 65, 106, 145, 179, 187, 231
New Zealand 64, 67, 71, 107
Newcastle, England 173
Newfoundland 108
Newman, Barry 237n., 238n.
Nissan automotive works 148
Northern Europe *See* Europe
Northrup, Bowen 237n.
Norway 168, 173, 218, 243n.
Nova Scotia, Canada 81
Nove, Alec 238n.
Nuclear threat 134, 191
Nukazawa, Kazuo 243n.

Oak Ridge, Tenn. 113
Odense, Denmark 174
Oil-producing nations 64, 160, 168
Okun, Arthur M. 24, 235n.
Ontario, Canada 72 *See also* Toronto
Open-ended drift 228
Order, biological 144, 223
Osborn, Robert J. 239n.
Ottawa, Canada 231
Own economies *See* Local economies

Pacific Rim 6, 46, 147, 169
Papyrus Institute 124

Paradoxes of rising and declining empires 182, 190
Paris 46, 65, 67, 143, 173, 231
Passive economies 34, Chaps 4, 5, 6, 7, 8, 9; 205
Pattern states 180, 199, 217
Persian Empire 182
Peter the Great 139, 144
Philadelphia 37, 145
Philippines 66, 118
Phillips, A.W.H. 17
Phillips curves 17, 24
Pickens County, Ga. 36, 93, 111, 146
Pine, Art 238n., 239n.
Pirenne, Henri 241n.
Pittsburgh 37, 145, 179
Poland 4, 64
Political disintegration 212, 216
Political units *See* Sovereignties
Portugal 25, 74, 168, 182, 198 *See also* Lisbon
Prague 176
Prebble, John 80, 237n.
Price supports, agricultural *See* Loans, grants and subsidies
Prices 9, 108, 137 *See also* Stagflation
Primitive economies 129, 218
Princeton University Center for Research on World Political Institutions 212
Prinsky, Robert D. 237n., 242n.
Printing press theory of inflation 12, 16
Producers' goods and services 38, 60, 139, 142, 148, 226 *See also* Symbiotic enterprises
Production *See* Improvised, innovative and versatile production; Agricultural productivity and yields
Production, Adam Smith's view 14

Production, ample and diverse
  See Local economies
Profits, Marx's view 14
Proxmire, William, Senator
  242*n.*
Puerto Rico 46, 98, 102
PXs 187

Quebec 213

Ragab, Hassan 124, 240*n.*
Raines, Howell 240*n.*
Rawls, Wendell, Jr. 240*n.*
Recessions, economic 3, 209
Redundant workers 77, Chap 6;
  151, 196
Reed, Roy 240*n.*
Regions workers abandon Chap
  5; 85, 109, 122
Reiner, Thomas A. 239*n.*
Renaissance Europe 64, 157, 183
Revenues *See* Taxes
Reynolds Metals (company)
  239*n.*
Rex, Kathleen 238*n.*
Ricardo, David 14
Rice, Berkeley 238*n.*
Richmond, Va. 146
Ring City (Netherlands) 174
Rio de Janiero 46
Robison, Martha 125
Rochester, N.Y. 179
Roman Empire 32, 124, 131, 133,
  157, 177, 182, 199
Rome 46, 134, 173
Rothmyer, Karen 239*n.*
Rotterdam 77, 174
Rouen, France 173
Rouse, Irving 240*n.*
Rugaber, Walter 242*n.*
Rural economies *See* City
  regions; Passive economies

Russia (pre-Soviet) 103, 139, 150,
  184, 199, 217 *See also* Soviet
  Union

Sabel, Charles F. 39, 95, 236*n.*
Saint Augustine, Fla. 146
Saint Petersburg, Russia 140
Salmans, Sandra 241*n.*
Sampson, Anthony 244*n.*
Samuelson, Paul A. 19
San Francisco 7, 46, 145
San Juan, Puerto Rico 46
Santiago de Cuba 46
São Paulo, Brazil 46
Sapporo, Japan 46
Sardinia 64
Saskatchewan, Canada 64
Satter, David 238*n.*
Saudi Arabia 64, 150
Savannah, Ga. 146
Say, Jean Baptiste 14
Scandinavia 3, 60 *See also*
  specific countries and cities
Schellhardt, Timothy 239*n.*
Scotland 13, 25, 65, 79, 160, 199,
  213, 215 *See also* specific
  cities
Scranton, Pa. 72, 179
Seattle, Wash. 46, 179, 186
Seesaw image, economic theory
  10, 15, 18
Self-correcting cities 57, Chap
  11; 193, 209, 211, 229
Self-generating economies 99,
  110, 136, 176 *See also* Local
  economies; Import-replacing
Self-sufficient enterprises (con-
  strasted to symbiotic enter-
  prises) 95, 98, 102 *See also*
  Transplanted city enterprises
Seoul 47, 71, 109, 147
Shanghai 47
Sheep, Scots 79

Shinohata, Japan 48, 65, 86, 106, 132, 167

Shinohata: A Portrait of a Japanese Village 48

Sicily 66, 72, 78, 99

Silk, Leonard 237n., 238n.

Simpson, Jeffrey 242n.

Sinclair, John, Sir 80, 86

Singapore 6, 47, 71, 109, 147, 163, 169, 180, 219

Smith, Adam 12, 25, 30, 70

Smith, Cyril Stanley 222, 244n.

Solar heating 41, 152

Sönderborg, Denmark 174

South America *See* Latin America

South Korea 6, 169

South, United States 37, 82, 94, 146, 165, 179, 201, 207, 213

Sovereignties 29, 32, Chaps 11, 12, 13

Soviet Union 3, 5, 46, 87, 108, 144, 199, 217, 218 *See also* Russia (pre-Soviet)

Spain 72, 74, 182, 184, 198, 199 *See also* Madrid

Spaulding, Robert 238n.

Specialization, economic 60, 63, 70

Spivak, Jonathan 235n., 240n.

Stagflation 9, 20, 22, 211 *See also* Prices

Stagflation as normal 25

Stagnant economies 8, 25, 57, Chap 5; 84, 102, 104, 109, Chap 9; 142, 174, 179, Chap 12; 218

Standardizations, product 226, 227, 241n.

Stockholm 174, 219, 231

Strasbourg, France 173

Stuart, Reginald 240n.

Subsidies *See* Loans, grants and subsidies. For export subsidies *See* Chap 11

Subsistence economies 33, 75, Chap 9; 142, 153, 189

Sudan 118, 124

Sunbelt *See* South, United States

Supply regions Chap 4; 83, 99, 109, 141, 142, 189

Supply-side economics 5, 12, 14, 20, 23, 70, 196

Sweden 168, 173, 217, 243n. *See also* specific cities

Switzerland 12, 19, 60, 71, 78, 157, 191, 192

Symbiotic enterprises. 39, 97, 100, 119, 226

Tadessa, Zena 238n.

Taipei 47, 100, 109, 120, 147

Taiwan 6, 99, 120, 169

Tannenbaum, Jeffrey A. 244n.

Tanzania 66

Tariffs 149, Chap 11; 204

Taxes (revenues) 8, 69, 106, 140, Chap 12; 206 — sales tax on producers' goods 226 — value added tax 225

Technology *See* City technology

Technology, "appropriate," 86, 92, 151

Tennessee Valley Authority 110

Texas Authomatic Sprinklers (company) 137

Textron (company) 135

Thurow, Roger 242n.

Tokyo 38, 45, 47, 55, 65, 146, 174

Toledo, Ohio 179

Toronto, Ontario 45, 55, 66, 72, 168

Toynbee, Arnold 224

Toys 222

Trade between advanced and backward economies   Chap 10; 183, 196, 206, 213

Trade, intercity   140, 144, 155, 156, 165, 168, 171, 188, 189, 191, 193, 207, 208, 212

Transactions of decline   Chap 12; 206, 211, 215, 218, 231 — as necessary to empires   198

Transfer payments   *See*   Wealth redistribution

Transplanted city enterprises   37, 42, 43, 45, 51, 55, 58, 61, 74, 84, 90, Chap 7; 107, 175, 195, 205

Tritsis, Adonis   239*n*.

Tsuji, M.N.   239*n*.

Turkey   5, 74, 118, 168, 177, 182, 184, 198

Ulster   81

Ulterwyk Corporation   137

Umesao, Tadao   221, 230, 244*n*.

Unemployment in economic theory   Chap 1

Unemployment rates   19, 27

United States   *See also*   specific cities and states

United States aid   *See*   Loans, grants and subsidies

United States as a pattern state   217

United States. Congress. House. Committee on Banking, Finance and Urban Affairs. *Small Cities: How Can the Federal and State Governments Respond to Their Diverse Needs?*   238*n*.

United States, economy   3, 4, 5, 9, 11, 19, 67, 103, 107, 177, 179, 211 — beginnings and development   145, 177 — decline   5, 26, 207, 230

United States, imperialism, English model   199

United States, international trade   107, 165

United States, military production   6, 94, 185

United States Post Exchanges   187

United States tariffs   177, 180

Unwin, George   241*n*.

Uruguay   5, 59, 67, 71, 97, 107, 136, 149, 163, 178, 194   *See also* Montevideo

Utica, N.Y.   179

Van Praagh, David   238*n*.

Van Wagenen, Richard W.   243*n*.

Vecsey, George   240*n*.

Venice   133, 141

Versatile production   *See*   Improvised, innovative and versatile production

Vicker, Ray   239*n*., 241*n*.

Vietnam   65, 69, 199

Volta Dam   105, 110

Wade, Nicholas   238*n*.

Wage theory of inflation   13

Wagner, Aubrey J.   240*n*.

Wales   46, 64, 72, 78, 86, 199

Wallace Company, Sam P.   137

Wallenstein, Albrecht von   242*n*.

War production   *See*   Military production; United States, military production

Washington, D.C.   231

Waterloo, Ontario   57

Watt, Kenneth E.F.   244*n*.

Wealth of Nations   30

Wealth redistribution 60, 75, 106, 122, 191, 213, 217

Weapons *See* Military production

Wedgwood (company) 160

Weinraub, Bernard 235*n*.

Welfare *See* Wealth redistribution

Wellington, New Zealand 71

West Indies 64

Wilkes-Barre, Pa. 72

Williamsburg, Va. 146

Wilmington, Del. 179

Wilson, S.S. 241*n*.

Windmills 152

World Bank 6, 90, 102, 198

World government 134, 180

World War II 7, 84, 185

Wuhan, China 47

Yields *See* Agricultural productivity and yields

York, Geoffrey 237*n*.

Young, Inc., Daniel F. 137

Yugoslavia 5, 74

Zagreb, Yugoslavia 46

Zambia 64

Zeeman, E. C. 243*n*.

MORE ABOUT PENGUINS, PELICANS, PEREGRINES AND PUFFINS

For further information about books available from Penguins please write to Dept EP, Penguin Books Ltd, Harmondsworth, Middlesex UB7 0DA.

In the U.S.A.: For a complete list of books available from Penguins in the United States write to Dept DG, Penguin Books, 299 Murray Hill Parkway, East Rutherford, New Jersey 07073.

In Canada: For a complete list of books available from Penguins in Canada write to Penguin Books Canada Ltd, 2801 John Street, Markham, Ontario L3R 1B4.

In Australia: For a complete list of books available from Penguins in Australia write to the Marketing Department, Penguin Books Australia Ltd, P.O. Box 257, Ringwood, Victoria 3134.

In New Zealand: For a complete list of books available from Penguins in New Zealand write to the Marketing Department, Penguin Books (N.Z.) Ltd, Private Bag, Takapuna, Auckland 9.

In India: For a complete list of books available from Penguins in India write to Penguin Overseas Ltd, 706 Eros Apartments, 56 Nehru Place, New Delhi 110019.

A CHOICE OF
PELICANS AND PEREGRINES

☐ *The Knight, the Lady and the Priest*
Georges Duby £6.95

The acclaimed study of the making of modern marriage in medieval France. 'He has traced this story – sometimes amusing, often horrifying, always startling – in a series of brilliant vignettes' – *Observer*

☐ *The Limits of Soviet Power* **Jonathan Steele** £3.95

The Kremlin's foreign policy – Brezhnev to Chernenko, is discussed in this informed, informative 'wholly invaluable and extraordinarily timely study' – *Guardian*

☐ *Understanding Organizations* **Charles B. Handy** £4.95

Third Edition. Designed as a practical source-book for managers, this Pelican looks at the concepts, key issues and current fashions in tackling organizational problems.

☐ *The Pelican Freud Library: Volume 12* £5.95

Containing the major essays: *Civilization, Society and Religion, Group Psychology* and *Civilization and Its Discontents*, plus other works.

☐ *Windows on the Mind* **Erich Harth** £4.95

Is there a physical explanation for the various phenomena that we call 'mind'? Professor Harth takes in age-old philosophers as well as the latest neuroscientific theories in his masterly study of memory, perception, free will, selfhood, sensation and other richly controversial fields.

☐ *The Pelican History of the World*
J. M. Roberts £5.95

'A stupendous achievement . . . This is the unrivalled World History for our day' – A. J. P. Taylor

A CHOICE OF
PELICANS AND PEREGRINES

A CHOICE OF
PELICANS AND PEREGRINES

☐ *Crowds and Power* **Elias Canetti** £4.95

'Marvellous . . . an immensely interesting, often profound reflection about the nature of society, in particular the nature of violence' – Susan Sontag in *The New York Review of Books*

☐ *The Death and Life of Great American Cities*
Jane Jacobs £5.95

One of the most exciting and wittily written attacks on contemporary city planning to have appeared in recent years – thought-provoking reading and, as one critic noted, 'extremely apposite to conditions in the UK'.

☐ *Computer Power and Human Reason*
Joseph Weizenbaum £3.95

Internationally acclaimed by scientists and humanists alike: 'This is the best book I have read on the impact of computers on society, and on technology and on man's image of himself' – *Psychology Today*

These books should be available at all good bookshops or news-agents, but if you live in the UK or the Republic of Ireland and have difficulty in getting to a bookshop, they can be ordered by post. Please indicate the titles required and fill in the form below.

NAME _____ BLOCK CAPITALS

ADDRESS _____

_____

_____

Enclose a cheque or postal order payable to The Penguin Bookshop to cover the total price of books ordered, plus 50p for postage. Readers in the Republic of Ireland should send £1R equivalent to the sterling prices, plus 67p for postage. Send to: The Penguin Bookshop, 54/56 Bridlesmith Gate, Nottingham, NG1 2GP.

You can also order by phoning (0602) 599295, and quoting your Barclaycard or Access number.

Every effort is made to ensure the accuracy of the price and availability of books at the time of going to press, but it is sometimes necessary to increase prices and in these circumstances retail prices may be shown on the covers of books which may differ from the prices shown in this list or elsewhere. This list is not an offer to supply any book.

This order service is only available to residents in the UK and the Rep. lic of Ireland.